Secondary Cities and Development

The role secondary cities play in the global space economy and national urban hierarchies is increasingly receiving attention from scholars and international agencies, most notably the Cities Alliance.

Secondary Cities and Development considers the role of secondary cities through the lens of South Africa, a middle-income country with characteristics of both the developed and developing worlds. This book brings together a broad overview of international literature on secondary cities in South Africa and mirrors them against global experience. Chapters emphasise the importance of secondary cities as regional services areas, their potential roles in rural development, the vulnerabilities to which they are prone and their significant potential. By means of review, six South African case studies, and an assessment of contemporary policy approaches towards these cities, this unique volume provides insight into a spectrum of globally significant challenges.

This book would be of interest to academics and policy makers working in urban studies or regional development.

Lochner Marais is Professor in Development Studies at the Centre for Development Support, University of the Free State, South Africa.

Etienne Nel is Professor of Geography at the University of Otago in New Zealand and Visiting Professor, Centre for Development Support, University of the Free State, South Africa.

Ronnie Donaldson is Professor of Geography at Stellenbosch University, South Africa.

Regions and Cities
Series Editor in Chief
Susan M. Christopherson, *Cornell University, USA*

Editors
Maryann Feldman, *University of Georgia, USA*
Gernot Grabher, *HafenCity University Hamburg, Germany*
Ron Martin, *University of Cambridge, UK*
Martin Perry, *Massey University, New Zealand*
Kieran P. Donaghy, *Cornell University, USA*

In today's globalised, knowledge-driven and networked world, regions and cities have assumed heightened significance as the interconnected nodes of economic, social and cultural production, and as sites of new modes of economic and territorial governance and policy experimentation. This book series brings together incisive and critically engaged international and interdisciplinary research on this resurgence of regions and cities, and should be of interest to geographers, economists, sociologists, political scientists and cultural scholars, as well as to policy-makers involved in regional and urban development.

For more information on the Regional Studies Association visit www.regional studies.org

There is a **30% discount** available to RSA members on books in the *Regions and Cities* series, and other subject related Taylor and Francis books and e-books including Routledge titles. To order just e-mail alex.robinson@tandf.co.uk, or phone on +44 (0) 20 7017 6924 and declare your RSA membership. You can also visit www.routledge.com and use the discount code: **RSA0901**

For a complete list of titles in this series, please visit www.routledge.com.

100 Secondary Cities and Development
Edited by Lochner Marais, Etienne Nel and Ronnie Donaldson

99 Technology and the City
Systems, applications and implications
Tan Yigitcanlar

98 Smaller Cities in a World of Competitiveness
Peter Karl Kresl and Daniele Ietri

97 Code and the City
Edited by Rob Kitchin and Sung-Yueh Perng

96 **The UK Regional–National Economic Problem**
Geography, globalisation and governance
Philip McCann

95 **Skills and Cities**
Edited by Sako Musterd, Marco Bontje and Jan Rouwendal

94 **Higher Education and the Creative Economy**
Beyond the campus
Edited by Roberta Comunian and Abigail Gilmore

93 **Making Cultural Cities in Asia**
Mobility, assemblage, and the politics of aspirational urbanism
Edited by Jun Wang, Tim Oakes and Yang Yang

92 **Leadership and the City**
Power, strategy and networks in the making of knowledge cities
Markku Sotarauta

91 **Evolutionary Economic Geography**
Theoretical and empirical progress
Edited by Dieter Kogler

90 **Cities in Crisis**
Socio-spatial impacts of the economic crisis in Southern European cities
Edited by Jörg Knieling and Frank Othengrafen

89 **Socio-Economic Segregation in European Capital Cities**
East meets West
Edited by Tiit Tammaru, Szymon Marcińczak, Maarten van Ham, Sako Musterd

88 **People, Places and Policy**
Knowing contemporary Wales through new localities
Edited by Martin Jones, Scott Orford and Victoria Macfarlane

87 **The London Olympics and Urban Development**
The mega-event city
Edited by Gavin Poynter, Valerie Viehoff and Yang Li

86 **Making 21st Century Knowledge Complexes**
Technopoles of the world revisited
Edited by Julie Tian Miao, Paul Benneworth and Nicholas A. Phelps

85 **Soft Spaces in Europe**
Re-negotiating governance, boundaries and borders
Edited by Philip Allmendinger, Graham Haughton, Jörg Knieling and Frank Othengrafen

84 **Regional Worlds: Advancing the Geography of Regions**
Edited by Martin Jones and Anssi Paasi

83 **Place-making and Urban Development**
New challenges for contemporary planning and design
Pier Carlo Palermo and Davide Ponzini

82 **Knowledge, Networks and Policy**
Regional studies in postwar Britain and beyond
James Hopkins

81 **Dynamics of Economic Spaces in the Global Knowledge-based Economy**
Theory and East Asian cases
Sam Ock Park

80 **Urban Competitiveness**
Theory and practice
Daniele Letri and Peter Kresl

79 **Smart Specialisation**
Opportunities and challenges for regional innovation policy
Dominique Foray

78 **The Age of Intelligent Cities**
Smart environments and innovation-for-all strategies
Nicos Komninos

77 **Space and Place in Central and Eastern Europe**
Historical trends and perspectives
Gyula Horváth

76 **Territorial Cohesion in Rural Europe**
The relational turn in rural development
Edited by Andrew Copus and Philomena de Lima

75 **The Global Competitiveness of Regions**
Robert Huggins, Hiro Izushi, Daniel Prokop and Piers Thompson

74 **The Social Dynamics of Innovation Networks**
Edited by Roel Rutten, Paul Benneworth, Dessy Irawati and Frans Boekema

73 **The European Territory**
From historical roots to global challenges
Jacques Robert

72 **Urban Innovation Systems**
What makes them tick?
Willem van Winden, Erik Braun, Alexander Otgaar and Jan-Jelle Witte

71 **Shrinking Cities**
A global perspective
Edited by Harry W. Richardson and Chang Woon Nam

70 **Cities, State and Globalization**
City-regional governance
Tassilo Herrschel

69 **The Creative Class Goes Global**
Edited by Charlotta Mellander, Richard Florida, Bjørn Asheim and Meric Gertler

68 **Entrepreneurial Knowledge, Technology and the Transformation of Regions**
Edited by Charlie Karlsson, Börje Johansson and Roger Stough

67 **The Economic Geography of the IT Industry in the Asia Pacific Region**
Edited by Philip Cooke, Glen Searle and Kevin O'Connor

66 **Working Regions**
Reconnecting innovation and production in the knowledge economy
Jennifer Clark

65 **Europe's Changing Geography**
The impact of inter-regional networks
Edited by Nicola Bellini and Ulrich Hilpert

64 **The Value of Arts and Culture for Regional Development**
A Scandinavian perspective
Edited by Lisbeth Lindeborg and Lars Lindkvist

63 **The University and the City**
John Goddard and Paul Vallance

62 **Re-framing Regional Development**
Evolution, innovation and transition
Edited by Philip Cooke

61 **Networking Regionalised Innovative Labour Markets**
Edited by Ulrich Hilpert and Helen Lawton Smith

60 **Leadership and Change in Sustainable Regional Development**
Edited by Markku Sotarauta, Ina Horlings and Joyce Liddle

59 **Regional Development Agencies: The Next Generation?**
Networking, knowledge and regional policies
Edited by Nicola Bellini, Mike Danson and Henrik Halkier

58 **Community-based Entrepreneurship and Rural Development**
Creating favourable conditions for small businesses in Central Europe
Matthias Fink, Stephan Loidl and Richard Lang

57 **Creative Industries and Innovation in Europe**
Concepts, measures and comparative case studies
Edited by Luciana Lazzeretti

56 **Innovation Governance in an Open Economy**
Shaping regional nodes in a globalized world
Edited by Annika Rickne, Staffan Laestadius and Henry Etzkowitz

55 **Complex Adaptive Innovation Systems**
Relatedness and transversality in the evolving region
Philip Cooke

54 **Creating Knowledge Locations in Cities**
Innovation and integration challenges
Willem van Winden, Luis de Carvalho, Erwin van Tujil, Jeroen van Haaren and Leo van den Berg

53 **Regional Development in Northern Europe**
Peripherality, marginality and border issues
Edited by Mike Danson and Peter De Souza

52 Promoting Silicon Valleys in Latin America
Luciano Ciravegna

51 Industrial Policy Beyond the Crisis
Regional, national and international perspectives
Edited by David Bailey, Helena Lenihan and Josep-Maria Arauzo-Carod

50 Just Growth
Inclusion and prosperity in America's metropolitan regions
Chris Benner and Manuel Pastor

49 Cultural Political Economy of Small Cities
Edited by Anne Lorentzen and Bas van Heur

48 The Recession and Beyond
Local and regional responses to the downturn
Edited by David Bailey and Caroline Chapain

47 Beyond Territory
Edited by Harald Bathelt, Maryann Feldman and Dieter F. Kogler

46 Leadership and Place
Edited by Chris Collinge, John Gibney and Chris Mabey

45 Migration in the 21st Century
Rights, outcomes, and policy
Kim Korinek and Thomas Maloney

44 The Futures of the City Region
Edited by Michael Neuman and Angela Hull

43 The Impacts of Automotive Plant Closures
A tale of two cities
Edited by Andrew Beer and Holli Evans

42 Manufacturing in the New Urban Economy
Willem van Winden, Leo van den Berg, Luis de Carvalho and Erwin van Tuijl

41 Globalizing Regional Development in East Asia
Production networks, clusters, and entrepreneurship
Edited by Henry Wai-chung Yeung

40 China and Europe
The implications of the rise of China as a global economic power for Europe
Edited by Klaus Kunzmann, Willy A. Schmid and Martina Koll-Schretzenmayr

39 Business Networks in Clusters and Industrial Districts
The governance of the global value chain
Edited by Fiorenza Belussi and Alessia Sammarra

38 Whither Regional Studies?
Edited by Andy Pike

37 Intelligent Cities and Globalisation of Innovation Networks
Nicos Komninos

36 **Devolution, Regionalism and Regional Development**
The UK experience
Edited by Jonathan Bradbury

35 **Creative Regions**
Technology, culture and knowledge entrepreneurship
Edited by Philip Cooke and Dafna Schwartz

34 **European Cohesion Policy**
Willem Molle

33 **Geographies of the New Economy**
Critical reflections
Edited by Peter W. Daniels, Andrew Leyshon, Michael J. Bradshaw and Jonathan Beaverstock

32 **The Rise of the English Regions?**
Edited by Irene Hardill, Paul Benneworth, Mark Baker and Leslie Budd

31 **Regional Development in the Knowledge Economy**
Edited by Philip Cooke and Andrea Piccaluga

30 **Regional Competitiveness**
Edited by Ron Martin, Michael Kitson and Peter Tyler

29 **Clusters and Regional Development**
Critical reflections and explorations
Edited by Bjørn Asheim, Philip Cooke and Ron Martin

28 **Regions, Spatial Strategies and Sustainable Development**
David Counsell and Graham Haughton

27 **Sustainable Cities**
Graham Haughton and Colin Hunter

26 **Geographies of Labour Market Inequality**
Edited by Ron Martin and Philip S. Morrison

25 **Regional Innovation Strategies**
The challenge for less-favoured regions
Edited by Kevin Morgan and Claire Nauwelaers

24 **Out of the Ashes?**
The social impact of industrial contraction and regeneration on Britain's mining communities
Chas Critcher, Bella Dicks, David Parry and David Waddington

23 **Restructuring Industry and Territory**
The experience of Europe's regions
Edited by Anna Giunta, Arnoud Lagendijk and Andy Pike

22 **Foreign Direct Investment and the Global Economy**
Corporate and institutional dynamics of global-localisation
Edited by Jeremy Alden and Nicholas F. Phelps

21 **Community Economic Development**
Edited by Graham Haughton

20 **Regional Development Agencies in Europe**
Edited by Charlotte Damborg, Mike Danson and Henrik Halkier

19 **Social Exclusion in European Cities**
Processes, experiences and responses
Edited by Judith Allen, Goran Cars and Ali Madanipour

18 **Metropolitan Planning in Britain**
A comparative study
Edited by Peter Roberts, Kevin Thomas and Gwyndaf Williams

17 **Unemployment and Social Exclusion**
Landscapes of labour inequality and social exclusion
Edited by Sally Hardy, Paul Lawless and Ron Martin

16 **Multinationals and European Integration**
Trade, investment and regional development
Edited by Nicholas A. Phelps

15 **The Coherence of EU Regional Policy**
Contrasting perspectives on the structural funds
Edited by John Bachtler and Ivan Turok

14 **New Institutional Spaces**
TECs and the remaking of economic governance
Martin Jones, Foreword by Jamie Peck

13 **Regional Policy in Europe**
S. S. Artobolevskiy

12 **Innovation Networks and Learning Regions?**
James Simmie

11 **British Regionalism and Devolution**
The challenges of state reform and European integration
Edited by Jonathan Bradbury and John Mawson

10 **Regional Development Strategies**
A European perspective
Edited by Jeremy Alden and Philip Boland

9 **Union Retreat and the Regions**
The shrinking landscape of organised labour
Ron Martin, Peter Sunley and Jane Wills

8 **The Regional Dimension of Transformation in Central Europe**
Grzegorz Gorzelak

7 **The Determinants of Small Firm Growth**
An inter-regional study in the United Kingdom 1986–90
Richard Barkham, Graham Gudgin, Mark Hart and Eric Hanvey

6 **The Regional Imperative**
Regional planning and governance in Britain, Europe and the United States
Urlan A. Wannop

5 **An Enlarged Europe**
Regions in competition?
Edited by Louis Albrechts, Sally Hardy, Mark Hart and Anastasios Katos

4 **Spatial Policy in a Divided Nation**
Edited by Richard T. Harrison and Mark Hart

3 **Regional Development in the 1990s**
The British Isles in transition
Edited by Ron Martin and Peter Townroe

2 **Retreat from the Regions**
Corporate change and the closure of factories
Stephen Fothergill and Nigel Guy

1 **Beyond Green Belts**
Managing urban growth in the 21st century
Edited by John Herington

Secondary Cities and Development

Edited by Lochner Marais,
Etienne Nel and Ronnie Donaldson

Routledge
Taylor & Francis Group

LONDON AND NEW YORK

First published 2016 by Routledge

2 Park Square, Milton Park, Abingdon, Oxfordshire OX14 4RN
52 Vanderbilt Avenue, New York, NY 10017

Routledge is an imprint of the Taylor & Francis Group, an informa business

First issued in paperback 2019

British Library Cataloguing in Publication Data
A catalogue record for this book is available from the British Library

Library of Congress Cataloging in Publication Data
Names: Marais, Lochner, editor. | Nel, E. L., editor. | Donaldson,
    Ronnie, editor.
Title: Secondary cities and development / edited by Lochner Marais,
    Etienne Nel and Ronnie Donaldson.
Description: New York : Routledge, 2016.
Identifiers: LCCN 2015048686| ISBN 9781138952256 (hardback) |
    ISBN 9781315667683 (ebook)
Subjects: LCSH: Cities and towns—South Africa—Case studies. |
    Urbanization—South Africa—Case studies. | City planning—
    South Africa—Case studies.
Classification: LCC HT148.S6 S43 2016 | DDC 307.760968—dc23
LC record available at http://lccn.loc.gov/2015048686

ISBN: 978-1-138-95225-6 (hbk)
ISBN: 978-0-367-87496-4 (pbk)

Typeset in Times New Roman
By Swales & Willis Ltd, Exeter, Devon, UK

Contents

List of figures	xv
List of tables	xvi
List of contributors	xvii
Foreword	xix
Preface	xxi
Acknowledgements	xxii
List of abbreviations	xxiii

1 Secondary cities in South Africa: national settlement patterns and urban research 1
LOCHNER MARAIS, ETIENNE NEL AND RONNIE DONALDSON

2 The international literature and context 27
ETIENNE NEL, LOCHNER MARAIS AND RONNIE DONALDSON

3 The City of Matlosana 49
DEIDRE VAN ROOYEN AND MOLEFI LENKA

4 EMalahleni 63
MALÈNE CAMPBELL, VERNA NEL AND THULISILE MPHAMBUKELI

5 Emfuleni 83
LOCHNER MARAIS, MOLEFI LENKA, JAN CLOETE AND WYNAND GROBLER

6 George 101
DAAN TOERIEN AND RONNIE DONALDSON

7 Polokwane 125
JOHN NTEMA AND ANITA VENTER

8 **UMlathuze** **141**

JOHANNES WESSELS AND KHOLISA RANI

9 **The role of secondary cities in South Africa's development** **159**

LOCHNER MARAIS, ETIENNE NEL AND RONNIE DONALDSON

Index 179

Figures

1.1 Location of the six case study secondary cities, Matlosana,
    Polokwane, Emfuleni, uMhlathuze, George and eMalahleni,
    in relation to the eight metropolitan areas in South Africa   2
3.1 Location of the City of Matlosana   50
4.1 Location of eMalahleni   63
5.1 Location of Emfuleni   84
6.1 Location of George   102
6.2 The Gross Value Added–population relationship of secondary
    cities in South Africa   110
6.3 The Gross Value Added–population relationship of
    metropolitan areas in South Africa   111
6.4 Cluster analysis for GVA contribution per sector in secondary
    cities and metropolitan areas in South Africa   111
6.5 Formal employment contributions per sector   112
6.6 Normalised sector employment profile of George compared to
    those of other secondary and metropolitan cities   113
7.1 Location of Polokwane   125
8.1 Location of uMhlathuze   141
9.1 Percentage distribution of South African population by
    settlement type (1996, 2001, 2011)   162
9.2 Economic structure of the six secondary cities and
    metropolitan areas (2011)   167

Tables

1.1 Populations in South African metropolitan areas, secondary
cities, large towns, small towns and rural areas
(1996, 2001 and 2011)   4

1.2 Hits in Google Scholar for South Africa's eight metropolitan
areas, September 2013   8

1.3 Hits in Google Scholar for the six case study secondary cities,
September 2013   8

1.4 Key attributes of secondary cities as applied to the six case
study cities in this book   13

2.1 Distribution of the world's urban population by size of
urban settlement, 2014   28

2.2 Sources cited to support secondary city attributes   43

3.1 Employment and economic contribution per sector,
City of Matlosana (1996, 2001 and 2011)   54

4.1 Employment per sector in eMalahleni (1996, 2001 and 2011)   69

5.1 Emfuleni's economic growth by sector, and total economic
growth in Gauteng, South African metros and South Africa
(1996, 2001 and 2011)   87

6.1 Business sectors in George whose annual GVA increased
by more than R100 million, 1996–2011   109

7.1 Differential population growth rates in Polokwane, 2001–2011   128

8.1 Comparison of progress made in respect of plans for the
harbour at Richards Bay   148

9.1 Sizes of the six secondary cities compared with the average
for the metropolitan areas (2011)   161

9.2 Locational attributes for the six secondary cities   164

9.3 Annual economic growth and decline in the metropolitan
municipalities and the six secondary cities (1996–2011)   168

Contributors

Malène Campbell, Department of Urban and Regional Planning, University of the Free State, Bloemfontein, South Africa.

Jan Cloete, Centre for Development Support, University of the Free State, Bloemfontein, South Africa.

Ronnie Donaldson, Department of Geography and Environmental Studies, University of Stellenbosch, Stellenbosch, South Africa.

Wynand Grobler, Department of Economics, University of the North West, Vaal Campus, Vanderbijlpark, South Africa.

Molefi Lenka, Centre for Development Support, University of the Free State, Bloemfontein, South Africa.

Lochner Marais, Centre for Development Support, University of the Free State, Bloemfontein, South Africa.

Thulisile Mphambukeli, Department of Urban and Regional Planning, University of the Free State, Bloemfontein, South Africa.

Etienne Nel, Department of Geography, University of Otago, New Zealand, Dunedin and Visiting Professor at the Centre for Development Support, University of the Free State, Bloemfontein, South Africa.

Verna Nel, Department of Urban and Regional Planning, University of the Free State, Bloemfontein, South Africa.

John Ntema, Department of Development Studies, University of South Africa, Pretoria, South Africa.

Kholisa Rani, Centre for Development Support, University of the Free State, Bloemfontein, South Africa.

Daan Toerien, Centre for Environmental Management, University of the Free State, Bloemfontein, South Africa.

Deidre van Rooyen, Centre for Development Support, University of the Free State, Bloemfontein, South Africa.

Anita Venter, Centre for Development Support, University of the Free State, Bloemfontein, South Africa.

Johannes Wessels, Managing Director: RUICON, Bloemfontein, South Africa.

Foreword

South Africa's urban areas are key to the development of the country. Urban areas play important roles in economic development locally, regionally, and also in terms of international connectedness. Indeed, it is increasingly acknowledged that cities fuel economic growth and provide employment to millions of people. However, the existing local knowledge base is largely orientated to the eight metropolitan areas of South Africa – an endeavour that South African Cities Network (SACN) has been a significant contributor to, being a principally metropolitan network. Although an emphasis on the largest cites is important, this book contributes to building a case for the role of intermediary cities (also known as secondary cities) in the development of South Africa. Thus far, these relatively smaller urban centres have been largely ignored in policy development and research. They are, however, emerging as an area of policy and development focus through the efforts of the United Cities and Local Governments (UCLG) association, with their regional body UCLGA, as depicted in their recommendations on 'Recognising the importance of African intermediary cities' towards the new Habitat III urban agenda, as shared at the AfriCities 7th Summit in Johannesburg in December 2015.

One indicator of the neglect of intermediary cities in policy terms has been the somewhat arbitrary drive to have more urban areas declared as metropolitan municipalities. Without a clear articulation of their development roles or trajectories, many intermediary cities envisage a progression whereby they should eventually obtain metropolitan status. The book rightfully challenges this logic, and begins to provide evidence to suggest that a differentiated approach to urban places is required. The authors thus seek to raise a number of associated policy concerns about intermediary cities, including their economic roles and vulnerabilities; their role in managing urbanisation; the significance of their urban–rural linkages; their main infrastructure and investment requirements; and their institutional capacity requirements, particularly in relation to long-term strategic planning. All of these features lead to a clear case and call for appropriate policy responses, including differentiated policy and institutional support mechanisms.

South Africa's flurry of initiatives focused on *differentiation* over recent years has been driven by an underlying and increasingly critical policy rationale for thinking seriously, and in a differentiated way, about different spaces.

This seemingly common-sense approach – i.e. the need to treat different places differently – has only recently gained traction in our policy space and is challenging the entrenched 'one-size-fits-all' approach to public financing, sector policies, institutional support, and programme design. The authors of the various chapters manage to contextualise the emerging category of South African intermediary cities within the broader urban hierarchy. This is important in that understanding the functional role of these cities is essential towards understanding them as a category, for appreciating their significance for national development and policy consideration, and indeed for determining the unique and differentiated attention that they might require.

When the SACN conceptualised and funded the original work for this project, it was our desire that it would contribute to a conversation on intermediary cities in South Africa. With this book, and the contributions of these dedicated scholars, we hope that the conversation will indeed continue in substance, and eventually towards development impacts as we journey towards putting in place the kinds of responsive policies and systems that make it possible to have an effective range of towns and cities that appeal to, enable and sustain the lives of the many people living in them.

Sithole Mbanga
CEO: South African Cities Network
December 2015

www.sacities.net

Preface

This book is about the life, economy, institutional dilemmas and opportunities of urban areas outside the metropolitan areas of South Africa. An extensive knowledge base exists in respect of South Africa's metropolitan areas, one that is supported by the fact that some of South Africa's leading universities are located in the majority of these metropolitan areas. The establishment of the South African Cities Network has further contributed towards improving the knowledge base of the metropolitan areas. The smaller urban areas are however often forgotten. While some individual papers have been written on selected secondary cities in South Africa, no comprehensive body of literature exists in this regard. This book attempts to provide such a comprehensive reflection. We have put together six case studies, sandwiched between a comprehensive literature review and a conclusion, and we reflect on some of the main lessons associated with the six case studies.

The original research was instigated by the South African Cities Network in 2013. Since then, the case studies have been refined by means of an extensive review process. The publishers provided the first assessment of the original book proposal. The editors assessed all the chapters and made extensive comments. Next, the various chapters were reviewed by external reviewers and their comments were used to improve each of the chapters. We should like to express our appreciation to these reviewers for contributing to the quality of the book.

The book represents a first attempt at reflecting on the smaller urban areas of South Africa. We hope that it will serve as a platform for continued research and reflection.

Lochner Marais
Etienne Nel
Ronnie Donaldson

Acknowledgements

We gratefully acknowledge the funding provided by the South African Cities Network for the original work on the six case studies.

The contribution of a number of external reviewers is also recognised.

Abbreviations

BRICS	Brazil, Russia, India, China and South Africa
CBD	Central Business District
CSIR	Council for Scientific and Industrial Research
GDP	Gross Domestic Product
GVA	Gross Value Add
ICT	Information and Communication Technology
IDP	Integrated Development Plan
HIV	Human Immuno-deficiency Virus
KPI	Key Performance Indicator
LED	Local Economic Development
NGO	Non-Governmental Organisation
NSDP	National Spatial Development Perspective
PACA	Participatory Appraisal of Competitive Advantage
RBIDZ	Richards Bay Industrial Development Zone
SACN	South African Cities Network
SDF	Spatial Development Framework
SLP	Social and Labour Plan

1 Secondary cities in South Africa

National settlement patterns and urban research

Lochner Marais, Etienne Nel and
Ronnie Donaldson

International context and background

Although the world's economic activity mostly happens in big cities, most people do not live in them (World Bank, 2009). This prompts questions about the economic future of the billions of people who live in intermediate or small cities (Rodríguez-Pose and Dahl Fitjar, 2013). Perhaps because the main world cities and metros are the centre of global economic activity, urban research has tended to focus on them (Hall, 1966; Friedman, 1986; Zook and Brunn, 2005). The smaller and intermediate cities have been somewhat neglected. It has been suggested that researchers have paid insufficient attention to relations and networks between cities and towns or between cities and peripheries (De Boeck et al., 2009) and that, because city planners do not properly understand the concept of 'intermediate city', they cannot integrate it into their development strategies (Bolay and Rabinovich, 2004).

Intermediate cities (or 'secondary cities' – the term we have chosen for this book) have been insufficiently researched despite attention being drawn to their importance over the past few decades. Rondinelli (1983) observed some 30 years ago that in developing countries they have important economic and social functions that can contribute to national development. Because they serve as centres for trade and for public and private services, these cities play a particularly important role in rural development. Besides their national and regional functions, they also have increasing connections to the global economy, which brings risks but also opportunities (Bolay and Rabinovich, 2004; Rodríguez-Pose and Dahl Fitjar, 2013). Researchers are becoming interested in how these risks and opportunities play out in the developing world, and particularly in South Africa.

The late 1970s to mid-1980s, the golden period of research on secondary cities, particularly those in the developing world, saw the publication of the two most prominent books on the topic (Rondinelli, 1983, and Hardoy and Satterthwaite, 1986). The interest in such cities at this time was partly because of the failure of 1950s and 1960s economic growth policies that had tried to concentrate large export-oriented, capital-intensive industries into a few regional centres (Rondinelli, 1983). Although this research remains relevant today, it must be acknowledged that geopolitics, the world economy and government policy have changed considerably. In the two decades from the end of the Cold War, the fall of the Berlin Wall and the demise of communism and apartheid to the formation of new geopolitical entities such as the European Union and BRICS the political world has been reshaped. The role of government as the central planning and implementation agency has been considerably reduced in many countries. The world's manufacturing and service industries have been transformed as the global economy has increasingly transcended local and national boundaries. And knowledge, information, communication and technology have come to play an increasingly important part in many sectors.

Research is lagging behind these important changes in the political economy, with only a few papers having been written about secondary or intermediate cities in the past two decades. As countries shift from top-down planning approaches to local responses, it is important to understand how cities respond to globalisation (Bolay and Rabinovich, 2004). Urban research in South Africa is largely dominated by work on Cape Town, Johannesburg and Durban, with the problems of the secondary cities and regions of urban systems being largely ignored (Visser, 2013; Visser and Rogerson, 2014).

This book fills this research gap by presenting case studies of six secondary cities in South Africa: the City of Matlosana (Klerksdorp), eMalahleni (Witbank), Emfuleni (Vanderbijlpark and Vereeniging), uMhlathuze (Richards Bay and Empangeni), Polokwane (formerly Pietersburg) and George. Figure 1.1 shows their location in relation to the eight metros. In the following section we explain the overall structure of the South African settlement landscape and then discuss the different ways that municipal legislation, the National Spatial Development Perspective (NSDP), the Council for Scientific and Industrial Research (CSIR) and the National Treasury categorise settlements.

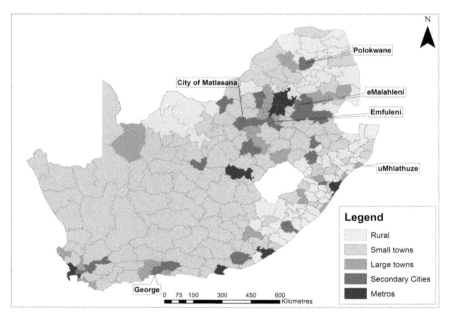

Figure 1.1 Location of the six case study cities, Matlosana, Polokwane, Emfuleni, uMhlathhuze, George and eMalaheni, in relation to the eight metropolitan areas in South Africa

The South African settlement landscape

To understand urban processes and formulate and monitor policy, city planners need a classification of settlement types (Pacione, 2013). The term 'secondary cities' is commonly used in South Africa because these cities are considered to be secondary to metros. 'Secondary' indicates both the *size* of these cities and their *position* in the settlement hierarchy, though with more emphasis on the former; whereas the term 'intermediate' places more emphasis on the latter, and on function. We have used the term 'secondary' in this book, though the two terms may be used interchangeably in other literature. The populations of our case study municipalities varied between 200,000 and 750,000 at the time of the research in 2013, and in some cases these figures included extensive rural populations. Some of these larger secondary city municipalities are similar in population size to the smaller metros, and they are significantly bigger than the average small town in South Africa. Although debates about city hierarchy in South Africa often focus mainly on issues of size, we argue that the key to understanding intermediate cities is the interrelationship between size, function and location (Van der Merwe, 1992).

The complexity of settlement classification in South Africa is evident from, among other policy documents, the *Urban Development Framework* (RSA, 1997) and the *White Paper of Local Government* (RSA, 1998a). Up to 2001, urban and rural areas typically fell under different municipal councils. With the 'wall-to-wall' demarcation of local authorities that came into effect in the early 2000s, urban and adjoining rural areas were integrated into single municipalities. This change had significant implications. For instance, it became more difficult to categorise the urban landscape by means of population numbers. In addition, urban centres had historically been one of the main units used in census data. Since 2001, however, the unit more often used has been the local municipality.

Table 1.1 shows the number of people living in each settlement type in 1996, 2001 and 2011, and the percentages of these populations that were urban. It shows that the number of people living in metros increased significantly from 1996 to 2011, at a rate of 2.5 per cent per annum. The second highest annual growth rate was in secondary cities (2 per cent per annum), followed by 1.8 per cent in small towns and 1.6 per cent in large towns. The growth in rural areas was only 0.24 per cent, much slower than the national growth rate of 1.65 per cent.

Municipal legislation

Government legislation divides municipalities in South Africa into three categories: metropolitan municipalities (A), local municipalities (B) and district municipalities (C). One of the key features of A municipalities is that they are not linked to C municipalities, whereas B municipalities are all linked to C municipalities. Six metros were originally declared in 2001: Johannesburg, Cape Town, eThekwini, Ekurhuleni, Pretoria and Nelson Mandela Bay. In 2011, Mangaung and Buffalo City gained metro status, and Emfuleni (one of our case studies) will follow suit by mid-2016.

Table 1.1 Populations in South African metropolitan areas, secondary cities, large towns, small towns and rural areas (1996, 2001 and 2011)

Settlement types*	1996		2001		2011	
	Total population	Urban population	Total population	Urban population	Total population	Urban population
Metropolitan areas (n = 8)	13,997,887	12,882,514	16,188,421	15,403,941	20,371,095	19,466,887
Secondary cities (n = 21)	5,832,308	3,829,224	6,475,805	4,403,189	7,881,662	5,719,544
Large towns (n = 29)	3,000,682	1,796,074	3,341,625	2,108,021	3,818,514	2,661,854
Small towns (n = 111)	5,370,740	2,617,196	5,979,595	3,222,262	6,983,890	4,291,864
Rural areas (n = 70)	12,294,059	654,309	12,807,760	897,749	12,746,621	1,308,749
Total	40,495,676	21,779,317	44,793,206	26,035,162	51,801,782	33,448,898

Source: Compiled from data provided by Stats SA, 2013

Note: * The National Treasury uses this system of five settlement types – see discussion under the South African settlement landscape

According to the Local Government: Municipal Structures Act No. 117 of 1998 (RSA, 1998b), to be considered for Category A status an area must be:

a   a conurbation featuring –

    i   areas of high population density;
    ii   an intense movement of people, goods and services;
    iii   extensive development; and
    iv   multiple business districts and industrial areas;

b   a centre of economic activity with a complex and diverse economy;
c   a single area for which an IDP is desirable; and
d   having strong interdependent social and economic linkages between its con-stituent units.

The above requirements show that the declaration of metros is not just about size but also about location and function. Yet one of the main shortcomings of the legislation is that it makes secondary cities aspire to metro status, which carries certain benefits such as negotiating intergovernmental financial transfers directly from the National Treasury. The South African Cities Network (SACN) summarises the implications of the decision to 'metropolise' Mangaung and Buffalo City as follows:

> This declaration has led many South African cities, as well as national policy observers, to question what changes must occur in a town for it to be considered an 'aspiring metro'. Are 'secondary cities' the same as aspiring metros – or do these two types of places offer different opportunities, and contribute different things, to the national space economy?
>
> (SACN, 2012, p. 12)

The National Spatial Development Perspective (NSDP)

In an attempt to articulate the policy implications of settlement categorisation, the NSDP arranged South African settlements into six categories according to their development potential and function: innovation and experimentation, the production of high-value goods, the production of labour-intensive mass-produced goods, public services and administration, retail and services, and tourism (The Presidency, 2004). The NSDP required national government departments, provincial governments and local authorities to use these categories to identify the comparative advantage of localities in terms of infrastructure investment and development spending, and to report annually on how their expenditure related to the NSDP.

The NSDP aimed to focus the bulk of the government's fixed investment on those areas with the most potential for sustainable economic development. In areas with limited potential, the government would concentrate on skills development and labour market intelligence to enable people with the required skills living in areas of low potential to migrate to areas of high potential. Although the NSDP was accepted as a guiding document, it never had the policy muscle to ensure compliance.

The Council for Scientific and Industrial Research (CSIR)

The CSIR conducted its first research on the South African spatial economy in 2008 (CSIR, 2008). This body of work points to the existence of a network of settlements with different functional characteristics, which the CSIR categorised as city-regions, cities, regional service centres, service towns, local niche towns and dense rural settlements. The CSIR categorised Polokwane and George (along with Mangaung, Buffalo City and Nelspruit/Mbombela), as cities rather than city-regions, Emfuleni as part of the Gauteng city-region (along with Johannesburg, Ekurhuleni and Pretoria), and Matlosana/Klerksdorp, uMhlathuze/Richards Bay and eMalahleni as regional service centres. The CSIR categorises settlements mainly according to size and function.

The Treasury

Because the category B municipalities differ considerably from one another, the National Treasury segments them into subcategories: secondary cities (B1: n=21), large towns (B2: n=29), small towns (B3: n=111) and rural areas (B4: n=70). These subcategories were created in order to provide differentiated support to municipalities. Initially, 19 cities were considered B1 municipalities, mainly due to their budget size (SACN, 2012). Later, however, the National Treasury's 'Cities Support Programme' listed 22 cities, including all the provincial capitals that were not metro (National Treasury, 2011). This programme also considered aspects such as population size and economic output, but budget size remained the main criterion. The towns or cities identified by the National Treasury as B1 municipalities are: the City of Matlosana (Klerksdorp), Drakenstein (Paarl), eMalahleni (Witbank), Emfuleni (Vanderbijlpark and Vereeniging), George, Govan Mbeki (Secunda), Lephalale (Ellisras), Madibeng (Brits), Mafikeng, Matjhabeng (Welkom), Mbombela (Nelspruit), Mogale City (Krugersdorp), Msunduzi (Pieter-maritzburg), Newcastle, Polokwane, Stellenbosch, Steve Tshwete (Middelburg), Sol Plaatjie (Kimberley), Rustenburg, Tlokwe (Potchefstroom) and uMhlathuze (Richards Bay).

History of South Africa's secondary city research

As a background to the case studies of secondary cities in this book, it is important first to understand the broader context of the post-apartheid South African settle-ment landscape. In the first few hundred years of European settlement, although colonialism and the discovery of minerals were influential factors, South Africa experienced a fairly 'natural' process of urban development. However, this process was interrupted after 1948 by apartheid-era planning policies such as decentrali-sation subsidies and the creation of 'homeland' cities which distorted the naturally evolving urban and space economy. The role of apartheid planning in minimising the urbanisation of black South Africans is well captured in the literature (see for example Mabin, 1991). The 'unbalanced' economic development, together with the apartheid regime's prioritisation of 'homeland' development, led to policies of influx control, growth point development and industrial de-concentration (for example industrial development in Botshabelo and Mdantsane). The basic principle was ruthless yet simple: keep blacks out of white cities (Van der Merwe, 1992). In the process, a number of new towns were developed and the profiles of some existing towns were enhanced. As is well known, these policies were doomed to fail. Dewar et al. (1986) note that after 30 years very few growth points were showing significant success. Today, most of these growth points have collapsed and, with a few exceptions (Marais et al., 2005), the long-term viability of even the more successful ones remains doubtful.

After it was acknowledged in the early 1990s that growth points and decentralisation had failed, the focus shifted to how secondary cities could help to address urbanisation and regional development. Since then, three research projects have been commissioned. First, Izak Van der Merwe (1992) was commissioned to examine the possibility of addressing urbanisation by promoting secondary cities. Using 'self-selection' methodology based on factors such as population size, population growth, ethnic composition, age distribution, literacy and education levels, economic diversity and size of the economically active population, 16 towns were selected as suitable for the project: Bloemfontein, East London, George, Grahamstown Kimberley, Kroonstad, Ladysmith, Newcastle, Pietermaritzburg, Pietersburg, Potchefstroom, Secunda, Umtata, Welkom, Witbank and Worcester. After further analysis, the following were selected as the most suitable: Bloemfontein, East London-Mdantsane, Pietermaritzburg, Pietersburg-Seshego, and Witbank-Middelburg (which was seen at that time as one urban complex). The area known today as Emfuleni was not included as it was considered part of the greater Johannesburg region.

The second research project on secondary cities was by the Urban Foundation (1994). This project identified 23 secondary cities (on the basis of population size) that together contributed one-fifth of South Africa's economic output but had been neglected by policymakers: East London, Ermelo, George, Grahamstown, Kimberley, King Williamstown, Klerksdorp (today City of Matlosana), Kroonstad, Ladysmith, Mmabatho, Nelspruit (today Mbombela), Newcastle, Paarl, Pietersburg (today Polokwane), Potchefstroom, Richards Bay (today uMhlathuze), Rustenburg, Secunda, Stellenbosch, Umtata (today Mtata), Witbank (today eMalahleni), Middelburg and Worcester.

Almost two decades later, the third of these research projects was published by the South African Cities Network (SACN, 2012). It used a quantitative and comparative approach to map South African secondary cities identified by the National Treasury. This book builds on the SACN's project to increase understanding of South Africa's secondary cities and contribute to today's policy debate.

Current research on the six case study cities

The literature dealing with South African cities is heavily concentrated on the main metros, which is not surprising given that most of the top universities in South Africa are located there. Few book-length investigations focus on urban South Africa and the 30 or so contributions are mainly focused on Cape Town, Johannesburg and Durban – none specifically on secondary cities. Tables 1.2 and 1.3, showing the number of 'hits' for each city on Google Scholar, give an idea of the difference in magnitude of research on the metros and the six intermediate cities. The tables make it clear that there is an extensive knowledge base for metros and they suggest that there is an important relationship between universities and places. Further evidence of this is that Ekhuruleni is the only metro municipality without a direct university presence, and its main places (Brakpan, Benoni and Boksburg) received very few hits.

Table 1.2 Hits in Google Scholar for South Africa's eight metropolitan areas, September 2013

Search term	No. of hits	%	Search term	No. of hits	%
'City of Cape Town'	5,780	28.7	'Cape Town'	1,130,000	46.1
'City of Johannesburg'	4,230	21.0	'Johannesburg'	442,000	18.0
'eThekwini'	4,050	20.1	'Durban'	252,000	10.3
'Ekurhuleni'	1,580	7.8	'Brakpan'; 'Benoni'; 'Boksburg'	6,000	0.2
'Buffalo City'	1,350	6.7	'East London'*	24,700	1.0
'City of Tshwane'	1,180	5.9	'Pretoria'	518,000	21.1
'Mangaung'	1,150	5.7	'Bloemfontein'	34,300	1.4
'Nelson Mandela Bay'	809	4.0	'Port Elizabeth'	44,600	1.8
Total	20,129	100.0	**Total**	2,451,600	100.0

Notes: Google rounds numbers above 1,000 to the nearest 10.
Because the figures reflect all papers containing the search terms, authors' addresses could also result in a 'hit' even if the paper does not deal with that particular city.
* 'East London' was narrowed by searching 'East London' + 'South Africa' in order to avoid the 'East London' in London, UK.

Table 1.3 Hits in Google Scholar for the six case study secondary cities, September 2013

Search term	No. of hits	%	Search term	No. of hits	%
'Polokwane'	4,100	76.2	'Pietersburg'	6,030	19.9
'Emfuleni'	517	9.6	'Vanderbijlpark'; 'Vereeniging'	11,900	39.2
'Emalahleni'	347	6.4	'Witbank'	4,330	14.3
'uMhlathuze'	247	4.6	'Richards Bay'	4,810	15.8
'City of Matlosana'	85	1.6	'Klerksdorp'	3,280	10.8
'City of George'	85	1.6	'George'*		0.0
	5,381	100.0		30,350	100.0

Notes: Google rounds numbers above 1,000 to the nearest 10.
Because the figures reflect all papers containing the search terms, authors' addresses could also result in a 'hit' even if the paper does not deal with that particular city.
* The number of places around the world called 'George' makes it virtually impossible to confine search results using this term to the city George in South Africa.

Of the six secondary cities, Polokwane (Pietersburg) and Emfuleni (Vanderbijlpark and Vereeniging) received the most hits. Again, these two cities have a significant university presence: the University of Limpopo is outside Polokwane and the Vaal University of Technology and a campus of the North-West University are in Emfuleni. Of the other four intermediate cities, George hosts a small satellite campus of Nelson Mandela Metropolitan University and eMalhleni a small campus of the Tshwane University of Technology, whereas the other two do not have any university presence. The significant difference in number of hits between the five main metros and the intermediate cities suggests that the knowledge base for the secondary cities remains small.

The amount of research on small towns in South Africa, on the other hand, has grown considerably over the past two decades, following the publication of Etienne Nel's work on Stutterheim and other small towns (Nel, 1994, 2005). The first edited collection of research on small towns in Africa (mainly in South Africa) appeared in 2012 (Donaldson and Marais, 2012). But secondary cities seem to fall into an unfortunate research gap. In the remainder of this section, we examine the nature, scope and scale of existing research on the six case study cities. For many of them there is a small but growing body of postgraduate research, though regrettably only a small percentage of this research has been published in scholarly articles.

City of Matlosana (Chapter 3)

A fair number of academic studies have been done on the City of Matlosana, mostly by postgraduate students and academics at the North-West University and some by other universities such as the University of South Africa and the University of the Witwatersrand. The research output can be grouped into five broad categories. In the first category, education, topics include the Integrated Quality Management System (Makuru, 2006), skills and training (Von Stapelberg, 2006), school governance (Smit and Oosthuizen, 2011) and the quality of teachers (Mahloane, 2011; Liwane-Mazengwe, 2012). The second category is local governance, including participatory governance in ward committees (Thabanchu, 2011), municipal leadership (van der Waldt, 2010), performance appraisal (Bezuidenhout, 2011), by-elections (Dhawraj, 2012), competitive bids (Bolton, 2009) and the delivery of basic services (Krugell et al., 2010) such as sanitation (Mjoli, 2012) and water (De Souza et al., 2006). The third category, health, includes topics such as primary health care (van Deventer et al., 2009), tuberculosis (Shapiro et al., 2012; Hoffmann et al., 2013), HIV and girls at risk (Forbes-Biggs and Maartens, 2012) and the importance of physical fitness (Monyeki et al., 2012; Toriola and Monyeki, 2012). The fourth category is disaster risk management, including the topics of the police service (Brazer, 2011), wildfires (Jansen van Vuuren, 2013) and community development (van Niekerk and Coetzee, 2012; van Riet and van Niekerk, 2012). The fifth category, town planning and business, includes topics such as business dynamics in Klerksdorp (Jeeva, 2010), regional shopping centres (Visser, 2011) and the extension of the Alabama suburb (Pelser, 2012).

EMalahleni (Chapter 4)

One prominent area of research investigates the environmental impact of mining and industry in eMalahleni (Bell et al., 2001; Singer, 2011). Specific topics are underground fires (Pone et al., 2007; Manders et al., 2009), air pollution (Lourens, 2011), water pollution (Blignault, 2011) and acid mine drainage (McCarthy, 2011). Another category of research focuses on international labour (Alexander, 2001), as the Witbank collieries initially relied mostly on Mozambican labour (Van der Walt, 2007), and Mozambican women were deported as far back as 1927 (Alexander, 2001). More recently, a study on migrants and attitudes towards immigrants in Witbank shows that many South Africans think the country is flooded with illegal immigrants, mostly from neighbouring countries (CDE, 2006).

Emfuleni (Chapter 5)

In assessing the knowledge base for Emfuleni, a search for postgraduate research found 56 studies. The topics include development planning (Mphahlele, 2006; Makone, 2007; Skosana, 2007; Myeza, 2009), service delivery (Rademeyer, 2010; Kwaledi, 2011), human resource and performance management (Makhutle, 2005; Sebolao, 2008), poverty (Hatla, 2010) and LED and enterprise development (Van Vuren, 2003; Malan, 2004; Slabbert, 2004; Van der Merwe, 2008; Makhoba, 2011). These topics are closely aligned with the development problems experienced in the area. Approximately 75 per cent of these dissertations were completed at the North-West University, a sign of that institution's important presence in the area. Other dissertations were from the University of the Witwatersrand, the University of Pretoria, the University of Johannesburg and the University of South Africa, which implies that Emfuleni is of national interest.

George (Chapter 6)

George does not have a full-fledged university campus, which explains why the city and its immediate hinterland are the focus of only a handful of university degree studies and very few academic or consultancy research reports. During the major municipal restructurings in 2000, a study compared the spatial transformations of George, Pretoria and Cape Town, painting a positive picture of George's socio-political transformation but noting that the city's apartheid spatial landscape was still intact (Lanegran, 2000). Recently, George's proposed integrated transport strategy has received some attention (Ribbonaar and van den Berg, 2008; Page, 2012). In addition, a handful of papers have focused on LED and tourism development (Ramukumba, 2012), looking specifically at the role of construction (Terblanche, 2007), SMMEs (Mmbengwa et al., 2013) and informal businesses (Smit and Donaldson, 2011). After the drought of the late 2000s, some scholars investigated how the local authorities in the area dealt with the disaster (Raju and Van Niekerk, 2013; Lottering et al., 2015), and others looked at the possibility of the opposite risk – floods (Benjamen, 2008). There has also been increased debate about the impact of climate change (Faling and Tempelhoff, 2012) on the sensitive biodiversity of the Eden District (Pauw, 2009; Vromans et al., 2010). Another study looked at how urban growth and development, particularly the growing number of golf estates, affect the area's physical environment (Van der Merwe, 2006; Van Zyl, 2006). George's good governance has prompted investigations of the municipality's internal communication strategies (Opperman, 2007) and management competencies (Krapohl, 2007). Research into social issues has focused on food security (Modirwa and Oladele, 2012), teenage pregnancies (Sethosa, 2007), crime (Pockpas, 2010) and primary health care (Kapp et al., 2013). The expansion of the Nelson Mandela Metropolitan University campus at Saasveld may result in more research being conducted on the city and surrounding areas in the future.

Polokwane (Chapter 7)

Most of the existing research on Polokwane consists of master's theses from the University of Limpopo (formerly the University of the North), but some journal articles have been published as well. This literature focuses largely on the performance of various public sectors in and around Polokwane city, covering five main themes: municipal capacity and service provision in Polokwane city and the surrounding farms and villages (Ngoatje, 2003; Segooa, 2006; Manamela, 2010; Mojapelo, 2010; Chipu, 2011; Yasmeen, 2011), municipal planning and the implementation and evaluation of poverty alleviation projects (Makamu, 2007; Kganyago, 2009; Mojapelo, 2010; Mmola, 2012), LED and small business development (Mbedzi, 2011; Tauatsoala, 2011; Ramoroka, 2012), migration (Eastwood et al., 2006; Ngomane, 2010), spatial planning and land-use issues (Donaldson and Van der Merwe, 1998a, 1998b; 2000; Donaldson, 1999, 2000; Botha and Donaldson, 2000) and a well-documented account of socio-spatial transformation of the city during an era of transition (Donaldson, 1999, 2001, 2005) backed up by articles on residential desegregation (Donaldson and Kotze, 1996, 2006) (Donaldson and Van der Merwe, 1998b, 1999a, 1999b), the city's links with surrounding settlements (Donaldson and Boschoff, 2000), the status of local governance (Donaldson et al., 1999) and a historical account of colonial Pietersburg (Donaldson and Van der Merwe, 1998a).

UMhlathuze (Chapter 8)

Despite the presence of a campus of the University of Zululand in the city, not many research papers have been published on Richards Bay. Because Richards Bay is a coastal city with a port and a considerable amount of industry, much of the existing research focuses on environmental issues such as coastal and beach management, marine ecology, ground water, water supply and management, and estuaries and wetlands (Grundlingh, 1974; Majer and de Kock, 1992; Van Aarde and Claassens, 1998; Naidoo and Chirkoot, 2004). Interest has also been shown in biodiversity, climate change, ecosystems and air and water quality (Kritzinger and van Aarde, 1998; Vermeulen and Wepener, 1999; Atkins et al., 2004). The significant number of large firms in the area has resulted in some work on the private sector (mining) and community relationships (Kapelus, 2002; Nyahuye, 2013). Economic research has examined LED, tourism, the creation of markets, the informal sector, coal demand and supply (Aniruth and Barnes, 1998; Hall, 2000; Hill and Goodenough, 2005; Hall, 2009; Nel et al., 2009) and the empowerment of women as agents of poverty alleviation (Schreiner, 1999; Nyasani et al., 2009). Social research has looked at religion, crime, education, migration and health (Lurie et al., 2003). Most of the postgraduate research was conducted at the University of Zululand, the North-West University (Potchefstroom campus) and the University of South Africa.

Framework of analysis

Our six case study cities exhibit many differences, but also many similarities. A better understanding of these similarities will help us understand each of these cities better, its place in the settlement hierarchy and its functions. Table 1.4 lists the attributes that they share and Chapter 2 reviews the international literature on secondary cities to provide a more detailed motivation for our choice of these attributes. Each case study chapter deals with some of these attributes in depth. The selected attributes are identified in the introduction to each chapter.

Why do we need a book on secondary cities in South Africa?

A book on secondary cities in South Africa will have value for academic research, policy formulation and practical application. There are five distinct reasons for this.

First, these cities are home to a substantial portion of the South African population and make a sizeable contribution to the country's economy. In 2011 secondary cities were home to approximately 15 per cent of the South African population and 17 per cent of the country's urban population (Stats SA, 2013) and contributed around 20 per cent of the country's GVA (SACN, 2014).

Second, little research has been conducted on these cities in South Africa. The SACN 2012 report *Secondary Cities in South Africa: The Start of a Conversation* has laid the most recent foundation for the discussion, but we still know relatively little about these cities. The SACN report states that the very notion of secondary cities is inadequately understood and poorly developed in this country. The SACN has since acknowledged that the initial conversations focused largely on issues of hierarchy. The report made a start on improving the definition and categorisation of secondary cities. We now need an improved understanding of their attributes, internal workings, economies and social relations.

Table 1.4 Key attributes of secondary cities as applied to the six case study cities in this book

Attributes	City of Matlosana	eMalahleni	Enfuleni	George	Polokwane	uMhlathuze
Size						
Smaller populations than metropolitan areas	•	•	•	•	•	•
Smaller economies than the metropolitan areas	•	•	•	•	•	•
Function						
Likely to have mono-economic rather than multi-economic function	•	•	•			•
A link to mining	•	•				•
Administrative and public sector centres	•			•	•	
Provision of transport and transport technology		•	•	•	•	
A link to the rural hinterland				•	•	
Management of urbanisation	•	•		•	•	•
Location and locational interdependence*	•	•	•	•	•	
Strategy related aspects						
Difficulty in benefiting from institutional decentralisation, as institutional capacity is constrained	•	•	•	•	•	•
Small but significant global linkages	•	•		•	•	•
Global linkage usually by means of one sector	•	•		•	•	•
Higher levels of vulnerability associated with exposure to the international trends	•	•		•	•	•
LED strategy	•	•	•	•	•	•
Knowledge economy plays a role in strategic planning				•		
Usually more directly confronted by environmental concerns than metropolitan areas	•	•	•	•	•	•

Note:
* This relates to the interdependence between secondary cities and other larger urban areas.

A third reason for this book is that current policy for these cities is largely underdeveloped. This book will help to address this issue. In this regard, the SACN (2013) has listed several policy questions specific to secondary cities:

- How should these cities be managed, given their importance in terms of innovation and economic competitiveness?
- How should these cities be viewed against national social and human development objectives?
- Do these cities have alternative trajectories which will allow them to avoid some of the problems associated with South Africa's larger metros?
- What can these cities do differently? How can they harness growth to create greater urban transformation, reform, accountability, and better infrastructure and services?
- Could these cities play a role in overcoming the country's extreme race and class stratifications?
- What role do these cities play in creating a balanced settlement environment?

Fourth, there has been increasing pressure from local governments to expand the number of metros, but in the current unsettled policy environment it is not clear if this is necessarily a positive trend. This pressure can be attributed to local ambitions and the lack of subcategorisation or segmentation within category B municipalities. Three factors complicate this push by local governments to 'metropolise'. Applications are dealt with in an ad hoc manner. The creation of new metros is largely driven by size, with some potential metro areas referring to their population size as a reason to metropolise and others presenting sophisticated arguments about municipal revenue or the size of the municipality's GVA. And aspects such as location, function, municipal performance and an area's role in national development seldom feature in these motivations. Given these three complicating factors, this book asks whether the logical trajectory of a secondary city should end at metro status.

The fifth reason for this book is the importance of understanding secondary cities in the context of debates about the categorisation of settlements and the quest for a differentiated approach to municipal governance in South Africa. Stated differently, if there is a case for secondary cities as a separate category of urban area, what does this mean for national planning and the support provided to these areas?

The structure of the book

The book is structured around the six case studies presented in Chapters 3 to 8. We chose these cities deliberately to reflect the diversity of secondary cities in South Africa. Our initial idea was not to compare these cities with one another but rather to build a better understanding of the drivers of change in each one. The cities we selected closely reflect the mineral-energy complex (Michie and Padayachee, 1998) that has historically been central to the development of South Africa.

We included one provincial capital (Polokwane), one area where mining is booming (eMalahleni), one where mining is in decline (City of Matlosana), a port city (uMhlathuze), a regional service centre (George) and, to allow for discussion of global linkages, three areas with heavy industry (Emfuleni, eMalahleni and uMhlathuze). In Chapter 2 we review the literature relevant to secondary cities and in the concluding chapter (Chapter 9) we summarise and discuss the main lessons that can be learned from the case studies.

We used six main research methods. First, we investigated the historical pathways and factors that shaped each city, to determine whether the cities could modify their pathways. Second, we examined the current knowledge base for these cities. Third, we reviewed media reports for each city, which was helpful for understanding local dynamics and local government. Fourth, we reviewed demographic, population, economic and development data to determine the cities' current development profiles. Fifth, we examined audit reports and other municipal documents to investigate the state of each city's municipal finances. And sixth, we conducted between 15 and 20 interviews in each city with people in local government, business and civil society. There were five reasons for these interviews: to confirm or revise the cities' profiles and details about historical pathways, to gain insight into the cities' strategic planning frameworks, to understand business–local government relations, to learn about the cities' knowledge base, and to determine future risks faced by these cities.

City of Matlosana (Chapter 3)

The City of Matlosana is located in the North-West Province and consists of four main urban areas: Klerksdorp, Orkney, Stilfontein and Hartbeesfontein. This municipality's total population is just under 400,000. Klerksdorp was originally developed as a rural service centre providing trade and social services to the surrounding agricultural communities. Gold mining began in the area in the late 1800s, but it was not until the Second World War that major mining initiatives commenced, giving birth to the towns of Orkney, Stilfontein and Hartbeesfontein. Although some residential development occurred in Klerksdorp as a result of the mining boom, the city has largely retained (and subsequently expanded) its regional service character. By the early 1990s mine downscaling had become a reality. The modern-day story of the City of Matlosana is therefore one of declining gold production and a shrinking economy. But the area's population continues to grow, leading us to ask why the City of Matlosana has fared better than the Free State Goldfields (Marais, 2013).

EMalahleni (Chapter 4)

EMalahleni, lying to the east of Gauteng and including the urban area of Witbank (established in 1903), is the powerhouse of South Africa. Its history has been intertwined with the coal mining industry for more than a hundred years and with the mineral-energy complex that has driven much of South Africa's urban development.

A small but significant steel industry was also established in the area. South Africa's economic growth between the early 1990s and 2008 brought an increased need for energy and the coal mining output in the area therefore increased. The current population is estimated at 395,000, with the population growth between 2001 and 2011 averaging around 3.6 per cent per annum (significantly higher than the national average). This growth has caused informal settlements to spring up, put pressure on land use regulations, increased the need for infrastructure and services, and placed a severe burden on the municipality. EMalahleni faces dire risks in the future. But the critical question about what will happen when the coal resources are depleted does not feature in the municipality's planning, and the long-term environmental risks from acid mine water – particularly for the Olifants River – are likewise largely ignored.

Emfuleni (Chapter 5)

Emfuleni is located in the southern part of Gauteng. Its main urban centres are Vereeniging and Vanderbijlpark. This city's growth is closely related to the mineral-energy complex. The availability of coal led to the establishment of a power station which in turn led to the development of a steel manufacturing industry. With approximately 720,000 people, Emfuleni is scheduled to become a metro by the end of 2016. Its history is closely connected with the South African steel industry. The first South African steel mill was built in Vereeniging in the early 1900s and the state corporation Iscor established its Vanderbijlpark plant there in 1943. Iscor was privatised at the end of the 1980s, resulting in many job losses. By the early 2000s, foreign shares in Iscor had exceeded South African shares and the company became part of a multi-national steel corporation (first Mittal Steel and later ArcelorMittal). In contrast to the privatisation at the end of the 1980s, internationalisation has brought some stability to Emfuleni, but the area continues to face risks associated with the steel industry's dependence on the volatile global market. As with the two mining cities Matlosana and eMalahleni, there is a concern that some of the multinationals in the area may either close down completely or gradually decrease production because of increased global competition or economic decline.

George (Chapter 6)

George is a centre on the south coast of South Africa's Western Cape Province. Before the arrival of European settlers there were already Khoi settlements in the area. The first Europeans arrived around 1710 and referred to the area as 'Houtpos' (place where wood is sourced). George was formally established by the British in 1811. Initially focused on timber and wood products, George soon also became a rural service centre. After the Second World War, George and the surrounding coastal areas experienced increasing growth in tourism and second-home development. The area's tourism function received a boost in 1977 when an airport was built owing to the influence of the then member of parliament

P. W. Botha (later State President). The development of the gas and oil fields near Mossel Bay (to the west of George) in the mid-1980s brought an influx of people from the Eastern Cape. Since the mid-1990s, George has benefited increasingly from the retirement industry and long-distance tourists, including Europeans who want to escape the northern winter. George's population is currently around 200,000, with a growth rate of 2 per cent per annum. The city's future depends on tourism and biodiversity and the municipality's ability to reconcile the conflicts between the two.

Polokwane (Chapter 7)

Polokwane is the country's largest urban area north of the Gauteng conurbation. Once the bastion of Afrikaner nationalism in the north, Polokwane (formerly Pietersburg) is now the provincial capital of Limpopo. It has acquired a striking urban gloss, as a result of the rapidly rising new middle class and their need for luxury goods. Originally established as a rural service centre in 1886, the town of Pietersburg developed along the lines of the racially segregated planning of the day. In the late 1980s, an entrepreneurial town clerk helped to initiate two projects that would set the tone for future development: expanding the N1 road through the centre to a four-lane highway and creating a small but significant industrial base. The municipality currently has around 630,000 people, of whom 166,000 live in what is today known as Polokwane City – the remainder living on communal land in the surrounding areas. The city's importance as a provincial capital can be seen in the large number of provincial government departments headquartered here, many of which used to be in the former 'homeland'. The city has also tried to position itself as a trade destination for countries north of South Africa, with new mall developments that essentially ask 'Why go to Gauteng if you can get it in Polokwane?'

UMhlathuze (Chapter 8)

UMhlathuze is located on the KwaZulu-Natal north coast. It was essentially established as a coal export harbour within the value chain of the mineral-energy complex. UMhlathuze contains two main urban areas: Richards Bay (along with its former R293 township, a once separate 'homeland' town) and Empangeni, but a large percentage of the municipality consists of communal land. The modern history of uMhlathuze is linked to the sugar and forestry industries and the deep-water harbour that was developed in the 1970s and 1980s to export coal mined in the Mpumalanga Highveld (eMalahleni and environs). The town of Richards Bay was established in the 1970s as a result of the port, which was developed by drying out the wetlands in the area (something which would now be virtually impossible under current environmental legislation). The municipality is home to about 330,000 people, of whom 48 per cent are urban dwellers (the remainder live on communal land). Despite significant growth in the 1970s and 1980s, the past 20 years have seen very few new industrial developments in Richards Bay. The country's decision to construct the Coega harbour has directed all port development capital to the Eastern Cape and prevented further expansion of the Richards Bay port. Meanwhile, Durban's harbour is expanding its capacity and depth, and significant private investment is being made in the Maputo harbour. The uMhlathuze chapter considers two main questions: whether Richards Bay will continue to benefit from its harbour or whether, given the world's declining coal needs, the harbour will become a white elephant.

References

Alexander, P., 2001. Oscillating migrants, 'detribalised families' and militancy: Mozambicans on Witbank collieries. *Journal of Southern African Studies*, 27(3), pp. 505–525.

Aniruth, A. and Barnes, J., 1998. Why Richards Bay grew as an industrial centre: lessons for SDIs. *Development Southern Africa*, 15(5), pp. 829–849.

Atkins, S., Pillay, N. and Peddemors, V., 2004. Spatial distribution of Indo-Pacific humpback dolphins (*Sousa chinensis*) at Richards Bay, South Africa: Environmental influences and behavioural patterns. *Aquatic Mammals*, 30(1), pp. 84–93.

Bell, F., Bullock, S., Hälbach, T. and Lindsay, P., 2001. Environmental impacts associated with an abandoned mine in the Witbank Coalfield, South Africa. *International Journal of Coal Geology*, 45, pp. 195–216.

Benjamen, M., 2008. Analysing urban flood risk in low-cost settlements of George, Western Cape, South Africa: investigating physical and social dimensions. Unpublished master's thesis, University of Cape Town, Cape Town.

Bezuidenhout, S., 2011. Guidelines for the implementation of performance appraisal in clinics in the Dr Kenneth Kaunda District. Unpublished master's thesis, North-West University, Potchefstroom.

Blignault, J., 2011. The external cost of coal-fired power generation: the case of Kusile. Pretoria: University of Pretoria and Greenpeace. Available at: http://fractual.co.za/Documents/Full_TrueCostOfCoal.pdf (accessed 17 November 2013).

Bolay, J. and Rabinovich, A., 2004. Intermediate cities in Latin America: risk and opportunities of coherent urban development. *Cities*, 21(5), pp. 407–420.

Bolton, P., 2009. The committee system for competitive bids in local government. *Potchefstroom Electronic Law Journal*, 12(2), pp. 157–168.

Botha, J. and Donaldson, R., 2000. Using a combination of digital aerial photography and satellite remote sensing to assist contemporary restructuring in an urban area of South Africa. *Geocarto International*, 15(3), pp. 53–62.

Brazer, P., 2011. Institutional capacity of the South African Police Service for disaster risk reduction in the Dr Kenneth Kaunda district municipality. Unpublished master's thesis, North-West University, Potchefstroom.

CDE (Centre for Development and Enterprise), 2006. *Immigrants in South Africa: Perceptions and reality in Witbank, a medium-sized industrial town.* Johannesburg: Centre for Development and Enterprise.

Chipu, S., 2011. Institutional capacity of local municipalities in the delivery of services to communities: A case study of the Polokwane municipality in Limpopo Province. Unpublished master's thesis, University of Limpopo, Polokwane.

CSIR (Council for Science and Industrial Research), 2008. A national overview of spatial trends and settlement characteristics, Pretoria: Council for Science and Industrial Research. Available at: http://www.sacities.net/what-we-do/programmes-areas/inclusive/spatial/projects/overview-of-spatial-trends-and-settlement-characteristics (accessed 12 October 2013).

De Boeck, F., Cassiman, A. and Van Wolputte, S., 2009. Recentering the City: An anthropology of secondary cities in Africa. In: K. Bakker, eds. *African Perspectives 2009: The African City: (Re)sourced.* Pretoria (South Africa): University of Pretoria, Department of Architecture, pp. 33–41.

De Souza, P., Ramba, M., Wensley, A. and Delport, J., 2006. Implementation of an internet accessible quality water management system for ensuring the quality of water services in South Africa. Paper presented at Water Institute of South Africa Conference 12–16 June in Durban, South Africa.

Dewar, D., Todes, A. and Watson, V., 1986. Industrial decentralization policy in South Africa: rhetoric and practice. *Urban Studies*, 23, pp. 363–376.

Dhawraj, R., 2012. The predictive power of by-elections. In: S. Booysen, ed. *Local Elections in South Africa. Parties, People and Politics.* Bloemfontein: Sun Media, pp. 315–329.

Donaldson, R., 1999. Restructuring in a South African city during transition: urban development and transformation in Pietersburg during the 1990s. Unpublished doctoral thesis, Department of Geography, Stellenbosch University, Stellenbosch.

Donaldson, R., 2000. Urban restructuring through land development objectives in Pietersburg: an assessment. *Journal of Public Administration*, 35(1), pp. 22–39.

Donaldson, R., 2001. An overview of urban integration and restructuring of Seshego during transition. *South African Geographical Journal*, 83(3), pp. 208–213.

Donaldson, R., 2005. Intro/retrospection on a provincial capital: Polokwane/Pietersburg revisited. *Urban Forum*, 16(4), pp. 351–367.

Donaldson, R. and Boschoff, E., 2000. Household linkages in a dispersed settlement around Pietersburg and implications for household resource management. *Journal of Family Ecology and Consumer Sciences*, 25, pp. 20–27.

Donaldson, R. and Kotze, N., 1996. Residential desegregation dynamics in the South African city of Polokwane. *Journal of Social and Economic Geography*, 97(5), pp. 567–582.

Donaldson, R. and Kotze, N., 2006. Residential desegregation dynamics in the South African city of Polokwane. *Journal of Social and Economic Geography*, 97(5), pp. 567–582.

Donaldson, R. and Marais, L., 2012. *Small Town Geographies in Africa: Experiences from South Africa and Elsewhere.* New York: Nova Publishers.

Donaldson, R. and Van der Merwe, I., 1998a. Social space and racial identity in colonial Pietersburg. *Historia*, 43(1), pp. 29–40.

Donaldson, R. and Van der Merwe, I., 1998b. Residential desegregation and the property market in Pietersburg. *Urban Forum*, 2, pp. 235–258.

Donaldson, R. and Van der Merwe, I., 1999a. Urban transformation and social change in Pietersburg during transition. *Society in Transition*, 30(1), pp. 69–83.

Donaldson, R. and Van der Merwe, I., 1999b. Deracialisation of urban business space: the case of street traders in Pietersburg. *Acta Academica*, 31(1), pp. 140–166.

Donaldson, R. and Van der Merwe, I., 2000. Apartheid urban development and transitional restructuring in Pietersburg and environs. *Historia*, 45, pp. 118–134.

Donaldson, R., Kwaw, I., Mahapha, S. and Ramudzuli, R., 1999. A reality check of four local government authorities in the Northern Province. *Politea*, 18(2), pp. 93–112.

Eastwood, R., Kistern, J. and Lipton, M., 2006. Premature deagriculturalisation? Land inequality and rural dependency in Limpopo Province, South Africa. *Journal of Development Studies*, 42(8), pp. 1325–1349.

Faling, W. and Tempelhoff, J., 2012. Rhetoric or action: are South African municipalities planning for climate change? *Development Southern Africa*, 29(2), pp. 241–257.

Forbes-Biggs, K. and Maartens, Y., 2012. Adolescent girls at risk: The GIRRL Program as a capacity-building initiative in South Africa. *Children, Youth and Environments*, 22(2), pp. 234–248.

Friedman, J., 1986. The world city hypothesis. *Development and Change*, 4, pp. 12–50.

Grundlingh, M., 1974. A description of inshore current reversals off Richards Bay based on airborne radiation thermometry. *Deep Sea Research and Oceanographic Abstracts*, 21(1), pp. 47–55.

Hall, P., 1966. *The World Cities*. London: Weidenfelt and Nicholson.

Hall, P., 2000. Regional development and institutional lock-in: a case study of Richards Bay. *Critical Planning*, Spring, pp. 87–102.

Hall, P., 2009. Regional institutional structure and industrial strategy: Richards Bay and the spatial development initiatives. Unpublished report from the Development Policy Unit, University of Cape Town, Cape Town.

Hardoy, J. and Satterthwaite, D., 1986. *Small and Intermediate Urban centres: Their Role in National and Regional Development in the Third World.* London: Hodder and Stoughton.

Hatla, B., 2010. The impact of government grants on poverty in Sharpeville. Unpublished master's thesis, North-West University, Vanderbijlpark.

Hill, T. and Goodenough, C., 2005. A case study of local economic development in Richards Bay. Unpublished Report conducted for pro-poor LED project funded by the World Bank, Pietermaritzburg.

Hoffmann, C., Variava, E., Rakgokong, M., Masonoke, K., van der Watt, M., Chaisson, R. and Martinson, N., 2013. High prevalence of pulmonary tuberculosis but low sensitivity of symptom screening among HIV-infected pregnant women in South Africa. *PLOS One*, 8(4), p. 1.

Jansen van Vuuren, I., 2013. A framework for rapid impact assessment with special reference to wildfires. *Jamba: Journal of Disaster Risk Studies*, 5(2), pp. 72–80.

Jeeva, Z., 2010. Business dynamics in Klerksdorp and its influence on the spatial landscape 1995–2008. Unpublished master's thesis, North-West University, Potchefstroom.

Kapelus, P., 2002. Mining, corporate social responsibility and the 'community': The case of Rio Tinto, Richards Bay minerals and the Mbonambi. *Journal of Business Ethics*, 39, pp. 275–296.

Kapp, P., Klop, A. and Jenkins, L., 2013. Drug interactions in primary health care in the George subdistrict, South Africa: a cross-sectional study. *South African Family Practice*, 55(1), pp. 78–84.

Kganyago, T., 2009. The evaluation study of Mashashane breeder farms and hatchery project, Polokwane: Unpublished master's thesis, University of Limpopo, Polokwane.

Krapohl, J., 2007. Assessing management competencies in selected southern Cape municipalities, Port Elizabeth: Unpublished master's thesis, Nelson Mandela Metropolitan University, Port Elizabeth.

Kritzinger, J. V. and Van Aarde, R. J., 1998. The bird communities of rehabilitating coastal dunes at Richards Bay, KwaZulu-Natal. *South African Journal of Science*, 94, pp. 71–78.

Krugell, W., Otto, H. and van der Merwe, J., 2010. Local municipalities and progress with the delivery of basic services in South Africa. *South African Journal of Economics*, 7(3), pp. 307–323.

Kwaledi, E., 2011. Implementation of e-administration for enhanced service delivery at Sedibeng District Municipality. Unpublished master's thesis, North-West University, Vanderbijlpark.

Lanegran, D., 2000. The post-apartheid city and the globalization of eroding the landscape of apartheid. *Macalester International*, 9(9), p. 269–278.

Liwane-Mazengwe, N., 2012. Teacher unions and educator professionalism: an education law perspective. Unpublished master's degree, North-West University, Potchefstroom.

Lottering, N., Du Plessis, D. and Donaldson, R., 2015. Coping with drought: the experience of water sensitive urban design (WSUD) in the George Municipality. *Water SA*, 41(1), pp. 1–6.

Lourens, A., 2011. Spatial and temporal assessment of gaseous pollutants in the Highveld of South Africa. *South African Journal of Science*, 107(1–2), pp. 1–8.

Lurie, M., Williams, B., Zuma, K., Mkaya-Mwamburi, D., Garnett, G., Sturm, A., Seat, M., Gittelsohn, J., Abdool Karim, S., 2003. The impact of migration on HIV-1 transmission in South Africa: a study of migrant and nonmigrant men and their partners. *Sexually Transmitted Diseases*, 30(2), pp. 149–156.

Mabin, A., 1991. The dynamics of urbanisation since 1960. In: M. Swilling, R. Humphries and K. Shubane, eds. *Apartheid City in Transition*. Cape Town: Oxford University Press, pp. 33–47.

Mahloane, K., 2011. Nature of in service training to capacitate public secondary school teachers in the Matlosana area: a public management perspective. Unpublished master's degree, North-West University, Potchefstroom.

Majer, J. D. and de Kock, A., 1992. Ant recolonization of sand mines near Richards Bay, South Africa: an evaluation of progress with rehabilitation. *South African Journal of Science*, 88(1), pp. 31–66.

Makamu, R., 2007. An analysis of housing programme challenges faced by the provincial Department of Local Government and Housing and the beneficiaries of Nobody Mothapo Housing project in Polokwane local municipality. Unpublished master's thesis, University of Limpopo, Polokwane.

Makhoba, 2011. A study of informal sector entrepreneurial activity within the townships in Emfuleni Local Municipality. Unpublished master's thesis, North-West University, Vanderbijlpark.

Makhutle, M., 2005. An investigation into the utilisation of voluntary counselling and testing of employees of Mital Steel in Vanderbijlpark: a case study. Unpublished master's thesis, University of South Africa, Pretoria.

Makone, M., 2007. Integrated development planning (IDP) as a tool for promoting sustainable development: the case of Emfuleni Local Municipality. Unpublished master's thesis, North-West University, Vanderbijlpark.

Makuru, E., 2006. Management issues and challenges in the implementation of Integrated Quality Management System (IQMS) in the Matlosana Area Project Office. Unpublished master's degree, North-West University, Mafikeng.

Malan, P., 2004. An investigation of the support systems of small, medium and micro enterprises through local service centres in the Vaal Triangle region. Unpublished master's thesis, North-West University, Vanderbijlpark.

Manamela, K., 2010. An investigation of water delivery constraints at Mabokelele Village, Unpublished master's thesis, University of Limpopo, Polokwane.

Manders, P., Godfrey, L. and Hobbs, P., 2009. *Acid Mine Drainage in South Africa*, Pretoria: CSIR Briefing Note 2009/02.

Marais, L., 2013. The impact of mine downscaling on the Free State Goldfields. *Urban Forum*, 24, pp. 503–521.

Marais, L., 2015. LED outside the centre: reflections from South Africa's secondary cities. *Local Economy*, doi:10.1177/0269094215614265.

Marais, L., Nel, E. and Rogerson, C., 2005. Manufacturing in the former homeland areas of South Africa: The example of the Free State Province. *Africa Insight*, 35(4), pp. 39–44.

Mbedzi, K., 2011. The role of government agencies in promoting SMMEs in Limpopo: A critical assessment. Unpublished master's thesis, Stellenbosch University, Stellenbosch.

McCarthy, T., 2011. The impact of acid mine drainage in South Africa. *South African Journal of Science*, 107(5/6), pp. 1–7.

Michie, J. and Padayachee, V., 1998. Three years after apartheid: growth, employment and redistribution. *Cambridge Journal of Economics*, 22, pp. 623–635.

Mjoli, N., 2012. *Evaluation of sanitation upgrading programmes – the case of the bucket eradication programme*. Gezina: Water Research Commission.

Mmbengwa, V., Groenewald, J. and van Schalkwyk, H., 2013. Evaluation of the entre-preneurial success factors of small, micro and medium farming enterprises (SMMEs) in the peri-urban poor communities of George municipality, Western Cape Province, RSA. *African Journal of Business Management*, 7(25), pp. 2459–2474.

Mmola, D., 2012. An assessment of the role played by Polokwane local municipality in service delivery within Manthorwane community of Limpopo Province. Unpublished master's thesis, University of Limpopo, Polokwane.

Modirwa, S. and Oladele, O., 2012. Food security among male and female-headed house-holds in Eden District Municipality of the Western Cape, South Africa. *Journal of Human Ecology*, 37(1), pp. 29–37.

Mojapelo, H., 2010. Basic infrastructure services provision by Polokwane local munici-pality in Limpopo Province. Unpublished master's thesis, University of Limpopo, Polokwane.

Monyeki, M., Neetens, R., Moss, S. and Twisk, J., 2012. The relationship between body composition and physical fitness in 14 year old adolescents residing within the Tlokwe Local Municipality, South Africa. *BMC Public Health*, 12, pp. 374–387.

Mphahlele, H., 2006. An evaluation of land use and management systems by local municipalities within the Sedibeng District. Unpublished master's thesis, North-West University, Vanderbijlpark.

Myeza, 2009. Beyond compliance: Investigating the strategic function of the integrated development plan (IDP) in Gauteng. Unpublished master's thesis, University of the Witwatersrand, Johannesburg.

Naidoo, G. and Chirkoot, D., 2004. The effects of coal dust on photosynthetic perfor-mance of the mangrove, *Avicennia marina* in Richards Bay, South Africa. *Environment Pollution*, 127(3), pp. 359–366.

National Treasury, 2011. Cities support programme. Framework document – Draft for con-sultation. Pretoria: National Treasury.

Nel, E., 1994. Local economic development initiatives and Stutterheim. *Development Southern Africa*, 11, pp. 363–378.

Nel, E., 2005. Local economic development in small towns. In: E. Nel and C. Rogerson, eds. *Local Economic Development in the Developing World. The Experience of Southern Africa.* London: Transaction, pp. 253–266.

Nel, E., Hill, T. and Goodenough, C., 2009. Multi-stakeholder driven local economic development: reflections on the experience of Richards Bay and the uMhlathuze municipality. *Urban Forum*, 18, pp. 31–47.

Ngoatje, M., 2003. Capacity building and sustainable development with reference to the Pietersburg/Polokwane municipality. Unpublished master's thesis, Rand Afrikaans University, Johannesburg.

Ngomane, T., 2010. The socio-economic impact of migration in South Africa: A case study of illegal Zimbabweans in Polokwane municipality in the Limpopo Province. Unpublished master's thesis, University of Limpopo, Polokwane.

Nyahuye, D., 2013. Corporate social investment: an investigation into communication strategies aimed at curbing unemployment in Richards Bay. Unpublished master's thesis, University of Zululand, Ulundi.

Nyasani, E., Sterberg, E. and Smith, H., 2009. Fostering children affected by AIDS in Richards Bay, South Africa: a qualitative study of grandparents' experiences. *African Journal of AIDS Research*, 8(2), pp. 181–192.

Opperman, Y., 2007. An internal communication assessment of the George municipality Unpublished master's thesis, University of South Africa, Pretoria.

Pacione, M., 2013. *Problems and Planning in Third World Cities*. Abingdon, Oxon.: Routledge.

Page, J., 2012. A comparison of integrated transport and spatial planning instruments: a case study of the Eden District Municipality, Hermanus Local Municipality and Cape Town Metropolitan areas. Unpublished master's thesis, North-West University, Potchefstroom.

Pauw, J., 2009. Challenges to sustainability in the Garden Route: water, land and economy. Unpublished master's thesis, Nelson Mandela Metropolitan University, George.

Pelser, A., 2012. Report on Alabama extension on the remaining extent and townlands near Klerksdorp, Klerksdorp: South African Heritage Resources Agency.

Pockpas, M., 2010. An operational analysis of known rape cases in the greater George area. Unpublished master's thesis, University of South Africa, Pretoria.

Pone, J., Hein, K., Stracher, G., Annegram, H., Finkleman, R., Blake, D., McCormack, J. and Schroeder, J., 2007. The spontaneous combustion of coal and its by-products in the Witbank and Sasolburg coalfields of South Africa. *International Journal of Coal Geology*, 72, pp. 124–140.

Rademeyer, J., 2010. The role of total quality management in enhancing service delivery at Sedibeng District Municipality. Unpublished master's thesis, North-West University, Vanderbijlpark.

Raju, E. and Van Niekerk, D., 2013. Intra-governmental coordination for sustainable disaster recovery: a case-study of the Eden District Municipality, South Africa. *International Journal of Disaster Risk Reduction*, 4, pp. 92–99.

Ramoroka, K., 2012. Participation and utilisation of formal vegetable markets by smallholder farmers in Limpopo: a Tobit II approach. Unpublished master's thesis, University of Limpopo, Polokwane.

Ramukumba, T., 2012. Local economic development in the Eden District Municipality, Western Cape Province, South Africa: a case study of emerging entrepreneurs in the tourism industry. *American Journal of Tourism Research*, 1(1), pp. 9–15.

Ribbonaar, D. and van den Berg, L., 2008. Public transport system transformation within the context of George municipality. Pretoria: SATC.

Rodríguez-Pose, A. and Dahl Fitjar, R., 2013. Buzz, archipelago economies and the future of intermediate and peripheral areas in a spiky world. *European Planning Studies*, 21(3), pp. 355–372.

Rondinelli, D., 1983. *Secondary Cities in Developing Countries. Policies for Diffusing Urbanisation.* Beverly Hills: SAGE.

RSA (Republic of South Africa), 1997. *Urban Development Framework.* Pretoria: Government Printer.

RSA (Republic of South Africa), 1998a. *White Paper of Local Government.* Pretoria: Government Printer.

RSA (Republic of South Africa), 1998b. Local Government: Municipal Structures Act, No. 117 of 1998. *Government Gazette* No. 19614. Pretoria: Government Printer.

SACN (South African Cities Network), 2012. *Secondary Cities in South Africa: The Start of a Conversation.* Johannesburg: SACN.

SACN (South African Cities Network), 2013. *The Differentiated Approach to Local Government. South Africa's Secondary Cities.* Johannesburg: SACN.

SACN (South African Cities Network), 2014. *Outside the Core: Towards Understanding of Intermediate Cities in South Africa.* Johannesburg: SACN.

Schreiner, H., 1999. Rural women, development, and telecommunications: a pilot programme in South Africa. *Gender and Development*, 7(2), pp. 64–70.

Sebolao, L., 2008. Promoting sustainable development through capacity building at Sebideng District Municipality. Unpublished master's thesis, North-West University, Vanderbijlpark.

Segooa, R., 2006. The impact of service delivery in Mankweng township by Polokwane municipality as a third sphere of government. Unpublished master's thesis, University of Limpopo, Polokwane.

Sethosa, G., 2007. Teenage pregnancies as a management issue in townships in George. Unpublished master's thesis, Nelson Mandela Metropolitan University, Port Elizabeth.

Shapiro, A., Variava, E., Rakgokong, M., Moodley, E., Luke, B., Salimi, S., Chaisson, R., Golub, E. and Martinson, N., 2012. Community-based targeted case finding for tuberculosis and HIV in household contacts of patients with tuberculosis in South Africa. *American Journal of Respiratory Critical Care Medicine*, 185(10), pp. 1110–1116.

Singer, M., 2011. Towards 'a different kind of beauty': Responses to coal-based pollution in the Witbank Coalfield between 1903 and 1948. *Journal of Southern African Studies*, 37(2), pp. 281–296.

Skosana, V., 2007. A critical evaluation of the link between integrated development planning and the budget at Emfuleni local municipality/VRP Skosana. Unpublished master's thesis, North-West University, Vanderbijlpark.

Slabbert, T., 2004. An investigation into the state of affairs and sustainability of the Emfuleni economy. Unpublished doctoral thesis, University of Pretoria, Pretoria.

Smit, E. and Donaldson, R., 2011. The home as informal business location: home-based business (HBB) dynamics in the medium-sized city of George. *Town and Regional Planning*, 59, pp. 26–35.

Smit, M. and Oosthuizen, I., 2011. Improving school governance through participative democracy and law. *South African Journal of Education*, 31, pp. 55–73.

Stats SA (Statistics South Africa), 2013. *Census Data for 1996, 2001 and 2011.* Pretoria: Stats SA.

Tauatsoala, M., 2011. The economic impact of agricultural co-operatives on women in the rural areas of Polokwane municipality. Unpublished master's thesis, University of Limpopo, Polokwane.

Terblanche, J., 2007. Construction and infrastructure development in local economic development: a Southern Cape perspective. Unpublished master's thesis, Stellenbosch University, Stellenbosch.

Thabanchu, O., 2011. Enhancing participatory democracy through the ward committee system in Matlosana Local Municipality. Unpublished master's thesis, North-West University, Potchefstroom.

The Presidency, 2004. *National Spatial Development Perspective*. Pretoria: The Presidency.

Toriola, O. and Monyeki, M., 2012. Health-related fitness, body composition and physical activity status among adolescent learners: The PAHL study. *African Journal for Physical Health Education, Recreation and Dance*, 4(1), pp. 795–811.

Urban Foundation, 1994. *Outside the Metropolis: The Future of South Africa's Secondary Cities*. Johannesburg: Urban Foundation.

Van Aarde, A. and Claassens, R., 1998. Soil characteristics of rehabilitating and unmined coastal dunes at Richards Bay, KwaZulu-Natal, South Africa. *Restoration Ecology*, 6(1), pp. 102–110.

Van der Merwe, I., 1992. In search of an urbanization policy for South Africa: towards a secondary city strategy. *Geography Research Forum*, 12, pp. 102–127.

Van der Merwe, S., 2006. Local and sub-regional socio-economic and environmental impact of large-scale resort development. Unpublished master's thesis, Stellenbosch University, Stellenbosch.

Van der Merwe, S., 2008. Small business owner-managers' perceptions of entrepreneurship in the Emfuleni district. *South African Journal of Economic and Management Sciences*, 11(4), pp. 449–464.

Van der Waldt, G., 2010. Project Governance: A Municipal Leadership Challenge. *Politikon*, 37(2–3), pp. 251–268.

Van der Walt, L., 2007. The first globalisation and transnational labour activism in Southern Africa: white labourism, the IWW, and the ICU, 1904–1934. *African Studies*, 66(2/3), pp. 223–251.

van Deventer, C., Couper, I. and Sondzaba, N., 2009. Chronic patient care at North-West Province clinics. *African Journal of Primary Health Care and Family Medicine*, 1(1), pp. 1–5.

van Niekerk, D. and Coetzee, C., 2012. African experiences in community-based disaster risk reduction. In: R. Shaw, ed. *Community-based Disaster Risk Reduction*. London: Emerald Group Publishing Limited, pp. 333–349.

van Riet, G. and van Niekerk, D., 2012. Capacity development for participatory disaster risk assessment. *Environmental Hazards*, 11(3), pp. 213–225.

Van Vuren, L., 2003. Local economic development in the Emfuleni municipal area: a critical analysis. Unpublished master's thesis, North-West University, Vanderbijlpark.

Van Zyl, L., 2006. The Garden Route golfscape: a golfing destination in the rough. Unpublished master's thesis, Stellenbosch University, Stellenbosch.

Vermeulen, L. and Wepener, V., 1999. Spatial and temporal variations of metals in Richards Bay Harbour (RBH), South Africa. *Marine Pollution Bulletin*, 39, p. 304–307.

Visser, G., 2013. Looking beyond the urban poor in South Africa: the new terra incognita for urban geography? *Canadian Journal of African Studies*, 47(1), pp. 75–93.

Visser, G. and Rogerson, C., 2014. Reflections on 25 years of Urban Forum. *Urban Forum*, 25, pp. 1–11.

Visser, H., 2011. Shopping centres: investigating the need for a regional shopping centre in Klerksdorp, City of Matlosana. Unpublished master's degree, North-West University, Potchefstroom.

Von Stapelberg, C., 2006. Skills, skills development and training within the Matlosana Municipality in the North-West Province. Unpublished master's degree, North-West University, Potchefstroom.

Vromans, D., Maree, K., Holness, S., Job, N., Brown, A., 2010. *The Garden Route Biodiversity Sector Plan for the George, Knysna and Bitou Municipalities*, Pretoria: SANParks.

World Bank, 2009. *World Development Report 2009: Reshaping Economic Geography*, Washington, DC: World Bank.

Yasmeen, K., 2011. The impact of HIV/AIDS on service delivery in Polokwane municipality as an organization. Unpublished master's thesis, University of Limpopo, Polokwane.

Zook, M. and Brunn, S., 2005. Hierarchies, regions and legacies: European cities and global commercial passenger air travel. *Journal of Contemporary European Studies*, 13(20), pp. 203–220.

2 The international literature and context

Etienne Nel, Lochner Marais and Ronnie Donaldson

Introduction

Urban research today focuses mainly on 'world' or 'global' cities (Hall, 1966; Dicken, 2015) and the larger metros (Friedman, 1986; Bell and Jayne, 2009). As a result, the smaller members of the urban hierarchy, referred to as 'secondary cities', 'small cities', 'small urban centres', intermediate cities' and so on, have been somewhat overlooked (Norman, 2013; Roberts, 2014), even 'woefully neglected' (Bell and Jayne, 2006, p. 14), and their role poorly understood. De Boeck et al. (2009) note that little attention is paid to 'the relations and networks which develop between diverse cities and towns, or between the city and its various peripheries'. This research gap has been recognised since the 1980s, when Rondinelli (1983a, p. 85) drew attention to the fact that secondary cities in developing countries perform important economic and social functions and contribute substantially to national development, but do not receive the attention they deserve in urban studies. Chen and Kanna (2012) argue that the focus on world cities has led to an over-emphasis on economic development and that secondary city research should embrace wider social aspects, and Bell and Jayne (2009, p. 684) advise that, although 'all cities are important centres of globalization', it is important to look at 'local practices, processes, identities and autonomies'. Neglecting the secondary cities has political implications; Bolay and Rabinovich (2004, p. 407) note that 'urban players still lack an understanding of intermediate cities, and are thus incapable of effectively integrating the concept in their political development strategies'.

Much of the research on secondary cities in the developing world was done in the 1970s and early 1980s (Rondinelli, 1983b) and the two most prominent books on the topic originate from this period (Rondinelli, 1983a; Hardoy and Satterthwaite, 1986). The research emphasis on secondary cities during this period was at least partly a response to 'the failure of economic-growth policies during the 1950s and 1960s that sought to transplant modern, large-scale, export-oriented, capital-intensive industries in a few regional centers' (Rondinelli, 1983b, p. 381).

Although this earlier research is still of value, and its implications still relevant, it must be viewed in the light of changes that have taken place in the world economy and in policy for urban development over the past three decades. The role of government as the central planning and implementation agency has been considerably reduced. As the global economy has transcended local and national boundaries, the world's manufacturing and service industries have been transformed and managers of global production networks now have their eye on valuable urban nodes. Democratic free enterprise is replacing profit-centred big business, and technology is enabling businesses to become decentralised and dispersed. These developments are taking place mainly, but not solely, in the advanced cities of the world. Fashionable conceptualisations of the city – the entrepreneurial city, the postmodern city, the transactional city, the informational city, the post-industrial city, and so on – indicate its changing form and composition under the influence of global change. The expansion of the roles played by knowledge and ICT across various sectors has tended to favour the larger centres (Coe and Yeung, 2015; Dicken, 2015); nevertheless, large numbers of the world's urban population continue to live in small cities. According to the Cities Alliance (Roberts, 2014), 75 per cent of the world's population still live in rural areas or urban settlements of fewer than 500,000 people, and 2,400 of the 4,000 cities in the world have populations of between 100,000 and 750,000 people. Table 2.1 indicates the real significance of the numbers of urban dwellers living in the smaller cities. It shows that in 2014 just below 50 per cent lived in urban areas with a population of under 500,000 and just below 60 per cent in urban areas with a population under 1 million.

In the developing world from 1990 to 2000, according to Swilling (2010, p. 17), 694 new cities were established in areas where previously the population was under 100,000. Of these, 510 became small cities (a population of 100,000 to 500,000), 132 became medium-sized cities (500,000 to 1 million), and 52 grew rapidly into big cities (1 million to 5 million). Since most urban dwellers live in centres with fewer than 500,000 people, the need for a more detailed understanding of these smaller cities is clear (United Nations, 2002). However, Brenner and Schmid (2015, p. 165) advise researchers to steer clear of settlement typologies, which they say have 'outlived their usefulness', and rather to foreground 'processes of sociospatial transformation, which crisscross and constantly rework diverse places, territories and scales'. This, they say, would

Table 2.1 Distribution of the world's urban population by size of urban settlement, 2014 (%)

Area	Urban areas with 10 million people or more	Urban areas with 5–10 million people	Urban areas with 1–5 million people	Urban areas with 500,000–1 million people	Urban areas with fewer than 500,000 people
World total	11.7	7.8	21.3	9.4	49.8
More developed regions	12.5	6.9	20.0	9.1	51.5
Less developed regions	11.4	8.0	21.7	9.5	49.3

Source: Compiled from United Nations (2015).

mean conceptualising urban configurations 'not as discrete settlement types, but as dynamic, relationally evolving force fields of sociospatial restructuring' (Brenner and Schmid, 2015, p. 165).

Attributes of secondary cities

Attributes associated with secondary cities were identified and used to create the framework that guides the discussion in this book (see Chapter 1).

How do we define a secondary city?

As early as the mid-1980s it was noted that there was no agreed-upon definition of 'secondary city' (Hardoy and Satterthwaite, 1986, p. 13), and little progress has been made since then in finding common ground. Further complicating the matter, the literature uses a variety of terms, such as 'metro towns', 'satellite cities' and 'middle cities' and, more commonly, 'secondary cities', 'ordinary cities', 'small cities' and 'medium-sized cities' (Van der Merwe, 1992; Robinson, 2006; Roberts, 2014). The terms 'secondary' and 'intermediate' are generally viewed as being broader in scope, implying a city positioned somewhere around the middle level of the urban hierarchy and playing a supplementary role in respect of functions (Van der Merwe, 1992). Where a city is located is an additional important consideration in identifying secondary cities (Van der Merwe, 1992). The earlier literature suggests that a definition of secondary or intermediate cities should take into account four aspects – population, size, function and location (Hardoy and Satterthwaite, 1986) – and more recent literature confirms this (Roberts, 2014). To sharpen the definition, various thresholds (usually related to size and function) have been used (Hardoy and Satterthwaite, 1986), but despite some attempts it has not proven possible to identify generalised, globally applicable thresholds for secondary cities' population growth or economic structure (Satterthwaite, 2006).

In a recent, fresh look at secondary cities, Roberts and Hohmann (2014, p. 3) divide them into three broad spatial categories: sub-national cities, which are centres of local government, industry, agriculture, tourism and mining; city clusters, consisting of expanded, satellite and new cities surrounding large metros; and economic trade corridors, which are urban growth centres (sometimes called 'growth poles') planned or developing along major transport routes. These authors claim, however, that secondary cities differ considerably as regards their functions and the way they are integrated into a system of cities. They distinguish three broad types: 'lead-secondary cities' that have 'a strong growth path and a dynamic local economy' and are 'well connected nationally and internationally in a system of competitive trade, development, and investment'; secondary cities that represent 'the moderate and boomtown economies, driven by migration and a diverse range of economic activities servicing local and national markets'; and 'highly depressed cities' with large numbers of urban poor. They divide this third type, which they call 'laggards', into two sub-types: those 'experiencing increasing urbanisation, rising poverty, little investment, and scant formal-sector job creation' (like most secondary cities in Africa), and those in economic decline (Roberts and Hohmann, 2014, pp. 4, 5).

What size is a secondary city?

The term 'secondary' implies that, in an urban size hierarchy, such a city will be smaller than a primary city. It will generally be bigger than the typical small town. Indicators commonly used to distinguish a secondary city from a small town are population size, population density and the extent of the built-up area (Van der Merwe, 1992). UN-Habitat defines a secondary city as one with a population of between 100,000 and 500,000 (UNCHS, 2014). Population size is still the determining factor in defining a 'secondary city', but Roberts and Hohmann, (2014) note that, in an age of growing competition, trade, and exchanges between cities globally, the meaning of the term has changed and other indicators are also needed to define it. They say a secondary city will probably have a population or economy that is between 10 per cent and 65 per cent of the size of those of the nation's largest city (Roberts and Hohmann, 2014, p. 11). In many cases, the term 'secondary' is used to indicate that the city is big enough to generate its own growth but small enough to avoid some of the negative effects of massive urban agglomeration, such as environmental and social costs (Van der Merwe, 1992).

How do secondary cities grow?

If we want to investigate a secondary city's economic and population growth, we need to look at the historical and current reasons why this particular area expanded and also examine the relationship between its size and its economic functions (Hardoy and Satterthwaite, 1986). The literature suggests a range of historical and functional reasons for the growth of secondary cities.

In the developing world, colonisation played a crucial role in the creation of an urban hierarchy and the growth in the number of secondary cities (Rondinelli, 1983a), particularly coastal cities, whose function was largely to export raw products. A significant number of these cities grew as a result of the sometimes arbitrary way in which administrative, political and educational centres are selected and develop over time (Rondinelli, 1983a; Hardoy and Satterthwaite, 1986). The literature provides examples of this in South America (Manzanal and Vapnarsky, 1986), Africa (Miracle and Miracle, 1979) and India (Saxena, 1981). The employment of government officials is an important factor in the development of urban areas (Hjort, 1979). Hardoy and Satterthwaite (1986) observe, however, that the relationship between administrative functions and the development of urban centres is not always well understood.

An interesting topic for investigation is the way the presence of a university can foster the growth of secondary cities and peripheral areas and transform urban society (Brennan et al., 2004).

What are the functions of a secondary city?

Today, increasingly, function or role rather than size is used to position a secondary city in the global system of cities, so in assessing what constitutes a 'secondary city' we need to consider its functions as well as its size (Bell and Jayne, 2009; Roberts and Hohmann, 2014, p. 11). Rondinelli (1983a, p. 127) argues that the term 'secondary city' 'connotes functional intermediacy in the flows of power, innovation, people and resources among places' (but points out that it is difficult to determine functional intermediacy), and also notes that '[e]mpirical evidence from both developed and developing countries shows a positive correlation between city size and functional complexity'.

It is difficult to quantify urban function. Two related issues are multi-functionality (as opposed to mono-functionality) and the degree of dependence on an economic sector (Van der Merwe, 1992). Secondary cities have important functions as centres for markets, education, retirement, tourism, agricultural processing, mining and the armed forces, and also as border posts (Satterthwaite, 2006). Bolay and Rabinovich (2004) identify 10 types of secondary city (despite earlier warning to be careful not to categorise too simplistically) according to their functions as regional markets, service centres, regional capitals, economic locations, tourist centres, communication hubs, metro periphery, cities at the national or international interface (such as ports), urban regions (with more than one small urban areas forming such an urban region), and conurban areas or groups of towns. Some of these types are discussed in more detail below.

Worldwide we find many examples where the existence and growth (and often the subsequent decline) of a secondary city are related to its proximity to natural resources (Rondinelli, 1983a; Bryceson and MacKinnon, 2012; Bryceson et al., 2012). Consequently, many of these cities are subject to the 'boom-bust' cycles of specific resources (Collier, 2007; Goodman and Worth, 2011; Steel, 2013). The term 'resource curse' is often used at a national level to explain the negative implications of mining, but Obeng-Odoom (2014) notes that this 'curse' thesis is less often investigated at city level.

Using the examples of two resource-based secondary cities in Indonesia, Wood (1986) shows how a boom period makes it difficult for local governments to provide public infrastructure quickly enough. Another common problem for resource-based secondary cities is that local governments have very little influence over resource extraction activities, as this is usually a national prerogative, and these activities have a direct effect on the area's urban development (Kabamba, 2012; Obeng-Odoom, 2014). For example, local governments have no control over land-use decisions or the increase in urban in-migrants but they must still deal with the effects (Wood, 1986). The close links between resources and international markets also make these cities more vulnerable to price shocks (Wood, 1986; Lawrie et al., 2012). At the same time, mining development in some of these secondary cities could increasingly exclude those who do not benefit from the mining activities (Steel, 2013). Steel (2013) therefore argues that secondary cities can no longer avoid the social problems of segregation and economic exploitation prevalent in many metros. The future of these cities depends on their ability to diversify their economies, obtain long-term commitment from national governments and ensure that planning for mine closure starts as soon as mine activities are initiated (Warhurst and Naronha, 2000). The literature also acknowledges that government policy is often developed and played out in secondary cities. Secondary cities also tend to be used for introducing and testing government programmes (Hardoy and Satterthwaite, 1986), in essence becoming 'laboratories' for policy experimentation

Transport technology plays an important role in the development of secondary cities (Rondinelli, 1983a). The presence of an airport or a harbour or proximity to a national road will boost a city's economy (Bolay and Rabinovich, 2004). A number of studies, mainly in the Global North, have considered the distribution of air passenger transport amongst different city types (Zook and Brunn, 2005; Rozenblat et al., 2005), and the considerable impact of high-speed rail systems on secondary cities has received research attention in Europe (Urena et al., 2009).

Summarising the role of secondary cities, Bolay and Rabinovich (2004, p. 419) say:

> the cities we studied, and by extension a number of urban agglomerations, have a double affiliation: their intermediate function on the one hand, their position of medium-sized town within the hierarchy on the other. Owing to their social and territorial specificities, intermediate cities are a privileged environment for regional planning linking urban growth and regional equilibrium in a positive dynamic between the urban and the rural. They supply goods and public and private services, and often function as administrative centres, representing the provincial and national authorities.

Secondary cities are key to the provision of secondary and tertiary services to society. They function as an important link between the rural hinterlands and the larger national and international centres (Madani and Diafat, 2002; Bolay and Rabinovich, 2004, p. 419), providing services and commerce and trade opportunities to this hinterland (Rondinelli, 1983a; Hardoy and Satterthwaite, 1986; Madani and Diafat, 2002), and 'enabling the territorial dissemination of development' (Caravaca, et al., 2007). They make it possible to achieve rural development goals more easily and cheaply (Berdeque, et al., 2015). Rondinelli (1983b, p. 379) says the rationale for developing small urban centres is that 'widespread economic growth is facilitated by the emergence of an articulated and integrated settlement system of towns and cities of different sizes and functions that are large enough and diversified enough to serve not only their own residents but also those in surrounding rural areas', and he also mentions the important role of these centres in the diffusion of social and technical knowledge from metros to rural areas.

Essentially, secondary cities provide benefits not only to their own populations but also to the rural and regional populations:

As medium-sized cities that are well integrated within a rural region, they are – unlike the great metros – seen as playing a crucial role in rural-urban inter-actions given the usually strong link and complementary relationship with their rural hinterland. They offer rural populations better living conditions, jobs, a less polluted environment, and act as local markets for their products.

(Bolay and Rabinovich, 2004, p. 408)

It is no wonder then that some countries have historically included secondary cities in their rural development strategies (Meissner, 1981). Another important function of secondary cities, closely related to rural development, is the creation of regional markets and trade, and of commerce spaces for more diversified and higher-order goods and services than those generally available in smaller urban or rural areas (Rondinelli, 1983b; Berdeque et al., 2015). Many scholars consider a well-structured system of central places to be a prerequisite for a country's economic growth and development (Akar, 1991), but the validity of this notion is being challenged by the growth of the knowledge economy, which may have far-reaching implications.

Without a doubt, more recent views on the role of secondary cities in addressing urbanisation differ widely from those held in the mid-1980s. The earlier views were premised on the assumption that larger cities would not cope with continued growth and that they are in general not good for the economic development of countries in Africa (Rondinelli, 1985). Generally, the litera-ture suggested that secondary cities help to de-concentrate urbanisation (away from primary cities), alleviate the problems of larger cities, reduce regional inequalities, stimulate rural economies, increase administrative capacity for rural development and reduce urban poverty while increasing productivity (Rondinelli, 1983a; Hardoy and Satterthwaite, 1986). The role that secondary cities play in helping to divert some of the mass migration to primary urban set-tlements is frequently mentioned in the literature (Adepoju, 1983; Otiso, 2005; Klaufus, 2010; UNCHS, 2014), mainly because it was feared that primary urban centres might grow too big (Caroll, 1988). Policy proposals in this respect have often been phrased negatively, the following being a prime example: 'The goal of controlling urbanization was to be achieved by slowing down rural-urban migration to major cities, making intermediate-sized cities more attractive to migrants, and by improving the living standards of rural areas so as to reduce rural-urban migration' (Otiso, 2005). The literature distinguishes two very dif-ferent approaches. Many governments have tried (though few have succeeded) to use secondary centres to reduce movement to the primary cities (also known as 'primate cities', the leading cities in a country or region, disproportionately larger than the others). The World Bank is critical of these attempts, stating that '[N]either the magnitude of urbanization nor the size of mega-cities should motivate policymakers to implement restrictive policies' (World Bank, 2010, p. 43). But a laissez-faire approach prevails in other countries, where there is little or no planning for, or interference with, urbanisation.

Many policy proposals for secondary cities say that better-balanced national development profiles are needed (Richardson, 1981), largely because the urban settlement patterns of many developing countries are deeply entrenched in colonial history. The development of many urban systems has been closely connected with colonial interests – for example, some cities were created largely to ensure the effective exploitation and export of resources. In many cases, therefore, policy for secondary cities focuses on economic de-concentration in order to redress regional imbalances, as does much current research (Otiso, 2005). More recently, the aim of creating a balanced system of urban settlements (of which secondary cities are but one category) has shifted to creating effective links between them, discovering how they complement one another, and understanding their different roles (World Bank, 2010).

Van der Merwe (1992) suggests a middle-of-the-road approach in which a process of self-selection (based on size and function) would identify secondary cities and be used to *manage* (as opposed to restrict or control) urbanisation. This approach is more in line with the recent World Bank (2010) emphasis on small and medium cities helping to address urbanisation, and is premised on two realities. First, over 50 per cent of the world's urban dwellers live in cities with a population of under 500,000 (World Bank, 2010). Second, it is a commonly held assumption that well-managed urbanisation can help to alleviate poverty and promote development and economic growth. The World Bank therefore proposes that, if countries are to 'reap the benefits of poverty reduction through increased urbanization', they will need 'national urban strategies supported by new diagnostic frameworks' (World Bank, 2010, p. 37). At the same time, it is important to guard against the negative impacts of urbanisation. The World Bank (2010, p. viii) notes that:

> Urbanization in the developing world was once considered too fast and unmanageable, something to be resisted and controlled. For many today, the question is not one of how to contain urbanization, but rather how to prepare for it – reaping the benefits of economic growth associated with urbanization while proactively managing and reducing the negative externalities of congestion, crime, informal settlements and slums.

The World Bank (2010, p. 12) further notes that the high proportion of urban dwellers living in urban areas of under 500,000 people 'raises important questions about the process of managing urbanization and delivery mechanisms for urban development assistance in the decade ahead'. It is important, however, to note that different levels of urbanisation require different policy:

> As different parts of a country urbanize at different rates and the binding constraints to promote concentration differ by the stage of urbanization, policies should be formulated according to the stage of urbanization permitting both rural-urban and inter-urban links. At each stage, however, the objective of urbanization policies should be to facilitate economic density by improving the options available to people and to firms. (World Bank, 2010, p. 5)

Two essential points arising from the above quotation are the importance of secondary cities for creating urban–rural links and for facilitating urbanisation, as opposed to deliberate policies for urbanisation.

Policy in favour of secondary cities commonly argues that they avoid social and environmental ills to which larger cities are prone (Otiso, 2005). Some scholars argue that secondary cities can minimise some of the disadvantages of large cities, such as high energy use and greenhouse gas emission. As secondary cities are smaller and not as highly populated, they present (at least in theory) opportunities for creative solutions. The World Bank (2010, p. viii) suggests that urbanisation 'if properly managed, can help advance the climate change agenda through the design of denser, more compact cities that would also benefit from energy efficiency gains and reduced travel time and costs for urban residents and businesses'. Otiso (2005, p. 121) similarly suggests that secondary cities are 'critical in national urban and environmental management because they provide grounds for alternative management approaches' and De Boeck et al., (2009) argue that, because secondary cities are smaller and their problems are of a smaller scale, they present opportunities to improve on current practices and be more innovative.

Internationally, only very poor data and information are available on the economy, land, finance, infrastructure and governance of secondary cities. And according to Roberts and Hohmann (2014, p. 11) this lack of information 'is severely affecting cities' capacity to plan and manage urban development and promote employment and economic growth'. The World Bank (2010, p. 12) stresses the importance of knowledge when it comes to managing urbanisation and points out that urbanisation 'increases the complexity of city management and those cities that are succeeding have generally relied on robust data collection and analysis to underpin policy making'. Secondary cities, with their smaller scale of urbanisation, are more suitable subjects than large cities for researchers who wish to collect and analyse data.

How are secondary cities strategically located?

Besides size, growth and function, the international literature also considers locational aspects and locational interdependence of secondary cities (Airriess, 2008). It is suggested that such a city should be strategically located as regards large metros, infrastructure and resources (agriculture, mining and the environment) (Van der Merwe, 1992). The city's interactions and communication networks with its rural hinterlands and other larger urban areas are essential components of its functioning. The proximity of secondary cities to larger cities is mentioned in the literature as a positive factor in urban growth through the facilitating of networking and agglomeration (Min, 1990; Van der Merwe, 1992). Proximity to a primary city is in some cases the main reason for a secondary city's development and growth (Hardoy and Satterthwaite, 1986). In the 1970s and 1980s it was assumed that a small city near a large metropolis would gain 'most of the benefits of agglomeration without the pains of large size' (Bolay and Rabinovich, 2004, p. 410). However, improvements in transport and communication technology might change the importance of location in future.

Duranton (2008, p. 43) suggests we need a broader understanding of the overall system of cities and how they complement one another:

> First, there is a fundamental asymmetry between primate cities and secondary cities. No secondary city can alone have an effect on the entire urban system whereas primate cities do. There is also considerable heterogeneity in the capabilities of secondary cities to design and implement local policies that would be consistent with a national growth agenda.

The importance of the role of secondary cities within the urban system was also noted by Borsdorf et al. (2012), while Fahmi et al. (2014) emphasised the importance of secondary cities in building networks with smaller cities.

Reflections on strategies for secondary cities

National policies for secondary cities have had mixed success (Bos, 1989). Hardoy and Satterthwaite (1981, p. 213) suggest the reason for this is that 'despite ambitious aims and objectives these secondary city policies seldom supported the towns or the development of the regions they were supposed to benefit'. Yet valuable lessons may be learned from the first generation of policies supporting secondary cities. This section first discusses these and then considers more recent developments. Otiso (2005) says many national policies for secondary cities failed for the following reasons: during the planning phase, status quo analyses were inadequate, resource estimates were unrealistic and objective criteria for determining what a secondary city is were lacking; the policies were top down, selected unviable locations and were not taken seriously; and coordination was poor and the supply of infrastructure insufficient.

The literature frequently refers to the importance of strong political will and administrative capacity in ensuring the implementation of appropriate secondary city strategies. Rondinelli (1983a) cites South Korea as an example of a country that implemented an effective secondary city strategy. The country's success is attributed to political will and significant national government investment in infrastructure and social services in order to create an attractive investment environment. Four distinct aspects related to the failure of secondary city strategies in other countries require more attention. First, other countries seem hesitant to pursue political decentralisation (Otiso, 2005). Second, developing countries seldom actively decentre the administration by transferring administrative functions to various regions (Van der Merwe, 1992). Third, the limited amount of decentralisation should be understood within the limitations of existing funding models. The World Bank (2010, p. 11) uses the term 'decentralised paradox' to make the point that, despite significant lip-service being paid to political and administrative decentralisation, centrally controlled funding allocation systems still dominate local government functions: 'National governments have increasingly devolved service delivery and expenditure responsibilities to the local level but have retained control over significant revenue sources.' One of the most prominent examples of national government control is the way that national governments usually determine which taxes can be levied at the local level. The result is that most local governments have narrow fiscal bases (World Bank, 2010). And fourth, according to some observers, the increasing significance of inter-governmental transfers between national and local governments has simultaneously increased dependency on national coffers (World Bank, 2010). Of course, the other side of the decentralisation debate focuses on the lack of local capacity to perform decentralised functions effectively. Linn (1983, p. 47) notes that 'the quality of management by the urban authorities may have an important effect on whether and how a city grows'. Accordingly, capacity building in secondary cities is a central theme in World Bank policies (World Bank, 2009).

Few developing countries have a clear settlement hierarchy, a situation which results in an inadequate distribution of services and functions and limited urban–rural links (Rondinelli, 1983b). A well-established settlement hierarchy, on the other hand, should help to clarify how different settlement types complement one another and shift the focus away from how they compete (World Bank, 2009).

Secondary city policies have often gone hand in hand with government efforts to deconcentrate the spatial economy, but these attempts have had mixed outcomes. Mohan (1983) warns against simplistic strategies (usually involving some form of subsidy) of infrastructure provision aimed at creating new industrial spaces outside core urban areas. In general, such attempts have been unsuccessful, largely due to poor understanding of the growth pole concept and inability to operationalise policy proposals (Satterthwaite, 2006; Duranton, 2008). According to Satterthwaite (2006, p. 5), governments' records of decentralising industry successfully are very poor, as they 'often push investment into unsuitable locations, or the choice of where public investment is concentrated is determined by political considerations not economic potential'. Arguably the best example is the apartheid South African state's interference in the settlement system in terms of the industrial decentralisation policy in the 1980s which aimed to manipulate the middle level of settlement (Todes and Watson, 1984). The literature also warns against trying to steer industry away from the main urban centres and towards secondary centres. Hardoy and Satterthwaite (1986, p. 352) state that 'premature attempts to steer industry away from primate cities or large cities are likely either to be very expensive for what they achieve, or very expensive for national production because the industries pushed to small or intermediate centres produce high cost goods and/or work far below capacity'. However, other researchers argue that this strategy has shown some success, particularly where secondary urban areas are close to a larger metros (Bolay and Rabinovich, 2004), and case studies from Brazil (World Bank, 2010) and Korea (Henderson, 2002), for instance, have described some success in deconcentrating economic activity. The Israeli new town programme is also often cited as an example of a successful secondary city development programme. However, the political motive for creating settlements outside Tel Aviv and Jerusalem, coupled with the high per capita income and the fact that Israel benefits from significant amounts of foreign aid, helps to explain the relative success of the Israeli programme (Hardoy and Satterthwaite, 1981, 1986).

The dominant theme in much of the growth-point research involving secondary cities has been the way the development of these cities is hampered by poor processes of place selection and inadequate assessment of places (Hardoy and Satterthwaite, 1986; Mushuku and Takuva, 2013). The UNCHS (1984) picks up on criticism that many secondary cities were defined using an imprecise evaluation of their existing circumstances and region of influence, a simplistic understanding of their development, an inadequate interpretation of factors specific to the various centres and an unrealistic understanding of the required investments. As a result, such analyses overlooked the fact that cities generally move up and down the national urban hierarchy (World Bank, 2009) and that any selection or settlement differentiation process should account for the dynamic nature of settlements within the settlement hierarchy. However, Van der Merwe (1992) makes the point that a form of self-selection based on market forces has become far more common since the late 1980s.

Otiso (2005) argues that the continued dominance of primary cities in terms of population size and economic growth has been a principal reason for the failure of policies and programmes for secondary cities. It is claimed that government policies and private sector actions have an inherent bias in favour of large cities. According to Otiso (2005), the reason for this bias is that the economic elites are mainly concentrated in large cities and are therefore unintentionally preoccupied with their host cities.

Many secondary city strategies do not have long-term visions. This focus on short-term benefits has hindered the development of effective policies and programmes for secondary cities. Van der Merwe (1992) suggested that policies and programmes should be designed to cover a minimum period of 20 years, but even 20 years might be too short.

The UNCHS (1984) points out that secondary city strategies are rarely integrated with macro-development and sectoral policies. This prompts three questions. First, do governments use secondary cities (or for that matter the overall settlement hierarchy) to guide their investment in economic and non-economic infrastructure, and if so, how? (Hardoy and Satterthwaite, 1986). Second, do governments understand how their non-spatial policy directions influence the spatial economy? In this regard, Hardoy and Satterthwaithe (1986, p. 387) suggest that understanding 'the social and spatial biases within governments' policies, revenue raising and expenditure is crucial to any special policy on small and intermediate urban centres'. Third, how thoroughly is the envisaged spatial economy considered in macro-development policies? The inclusion of the settlement hierarchy in national development goals has also been mentioned as an important policy imperative. Hardoy and Satterthwaite (1986, p. 399) say that 'the identification of specific developmental roles for selected small and intermediate urban centres within broader social and economic development plans should be the first step towards formulating a special programme for such centres', and they argue further that secondary cities play an important role in providing the infrastructure for development.

The State of the African Cities Report (UNCHS, 2014) emphasises the dominant role of secondary cities in the management of urbanisation in West Africa.

With reference to Africa specifically, the report says that a number of north-African countries, such as Tunisia, Algeria and Egypt, all have specific strategies to support smaller urban areas, although it is unclear how effective these strategies are in terms of national development goals. The report emphasises the importance of helping secondary cities to develop resilience against local and global shocks – this needs to be taken into consideration in future policy development and debates.

Today's challenges

The above section, reflecting on strategies, in the main (but not exclusively) reviewed the 'seminal period' of secondary city research in the 1970s and early 1980s. This section turns to more recent issues and debates.

Secondary cities and globalisation

With globalisation increasingly shaping economic flows, investment patterns and local development opportunities, cities serve as vital gateways to international markets (Coe and Yeung, 2015; Dicken, 2015). Secondary cities have important global links (Borsdorf et al., 2012), but emphasis on global links could decrease regional connectedness (Madani and Diafat, 2002). In China, for instance, secondary cities have benefited from the opening-up of the economy and from the considerable economic growth of the past two decades (Yu and Padua, 2007), but exposure to international markets also carries threats. Bolay and Rabinovich (2004, p. 411) say that:

> unstable markets are not without their dangers. Competition is fierce; one must adapt rapidly to changes in the international markets, and supply high quality 'products' to a very volatile market. These products include both manufactured goods and raw materials, but also the men and women who sell their labour under extremely precarious conditions.

Increasing globalisation has had a noticeable effect on secondary cities The growing influence of global markets and the subsequent erosion of state economic sovereignty over the past two decades have made long-term secondary city planning difficult, while at the same time these cities, especially those linked to a single industry, are facing new opportunities and risks (Bolay and Rabinovich, 2004). Secondary city responses to globalisation differ broadly from those of larger cities, for three reasons. First, secondary cities usually have less capacity for planning within the global context. Second, many are newcomers to the international context – Bolay and Rabinovich (2004, p. 419) observe that the cities they studied struggled to adapt to the pressures of globalisation. Third, in many cases secondary city economies are linked to the international economy only by a single industry. This dependence on a single sector exposes these cities to the volatility of international markets – something which may be new to them and for which they have minimal capacity.

The literature makes it clear that increasing globalisation requires an appropriate response from secondary cities and argues that ignoring this factor is most likely to result in economic degeneration. The combination of increasing globalisation and decentralised planning has shifted the emphasis from national plans for secondary cities to encouraging them to develop appropriate local plans. The evidence of success in this respect is mixed. Some success in creating new enterprises or clusters has been reported (Ferguson, 1992; Wilson, 1992), but Rodríguez-Pose and Fitjar (2013) note many failures in the creation and planning of clusters. Overall, secondary cities have had limited success in competing with the larger urban areas and have found it difficult to overcome the disadvantages associated with their peripheral location (Lessoff, 2008; Weck and Beißwenger, 2014).

The basic assumption of Rodriquez-Pose and Fitjar (2013) is that the world is becoming 'spikier', with increasing agglomerations of economic activity in a few concentrated areas. This, they say (2013, p. 356), means that secondary and peripheral areas 'are left in a precarious position'. They suggest that secondary cities should consider two possible approaches: inward-looking or outward-looking.

The first (more dominant) approach involves local responses and local agglomeration through industrial parks, clusters or even learning regions or regional innovation within the knowledge economy. The important question here is what secondary cities can do internally to attract new investment. Rodríguez-Pose and Fitjar (2013, p. 358) criticise this approach, arguing that 'too much local interaction in small and relatively isolated environments will in all likelihood throttle the diffusion of new knowledge, lead to institutional lock-in and smother productivity and growth'. This first approach, then, is unlikely to reverse the increasing trend towards concentration.

The second, less popular, approach is what Rodríguez-Pose and Fitjar (2013, p. 358) call the 'pipeline' approach. It emphasises interaction beyond boundaries, 'promoting interaction outside the comfort zone of geographical, cognitive, social and institutional proximity', and is 'more likely to succeed in generating interactive learning and in facilitating the generation, diffusion and absorption of innovation'. The idea is to generate links ('pipelines') to economies outside the area. New ones could be developed, but most will already exist in the location. The 'pipeline' approach is, however, expensive. It involves a great deal of uncertainty, is prone to create conflict, and is more difficult to put into practice than the inward-looking approach (Rodríguez-Pose and Fitjar (2013, p. 362).

The sources reviewed above provide the background against which to consider the question of how far South African secondary cities are taking their rural hinterlands into consideration and how they should respond to the pressures of the international economy and the vulnerabilities and opportunities associated with globalisation.

Secondary cities and the knowledge economy

Many of the reasons provided earlier for the rise of secondary cities are related to production and administrative systems in the 1970s and 1980s. The recent rise of the 'knowledge economy' or 'knowledge capitalism' (Powell and Snellman, 2004; Van Winden et al., 2007), however, also has implications for secondary cities. Not much research has been done in this regard, and the studies that have been done have been mainly in the Global North. Carlso and Chakrabarti (2007), for example, examine the relationship between venture capital and secondary cities in the US and note that: i) secondary cities that attract the most venture capital seem to benefit from the presence of a high concentration of enterprises in a particular cluster; ii) smaller cities that attract venture capital benefit from the strong connections among individuals within industries (or a cluster of industries); iii) the presence of institutions of higher education plays a major role in attracting investment; iv) there is a strong correlation between the ability of communities to successfully attract venture capital and the quality of life in these areas; and v) it appears that this correlation can be attributed to both the ease of recruiting high-level technical and management expertise to attractive communities and the propensity for such highly mobile talent to have already migrated to such places.

A study in Europe (Winden et al., 2007) shows that secondary cities with the following prerequisites will benefit from the growing knowledge economy: i) an economic and institutional regime that provides incentives for entrepreneurship, the efficient use of existing knowledge and the creation of new knowledge; ii) an educated and skilled population that can create and effectively use knowledge; iii) a dynamic information infrastructure that can facilitate the effective communication, dissemination and processing of information; and iv) a system of research centres, universities, think-tanks, consultants, firms and other organisations that can tap into the growing stock of global knowledge, and assimilate and adapt it to local needs and create new local knowledge

In Canada, research has shown that the call-centre industry is closely related to the growth of secondary cities (Arledge, 2002). In some of these cities, ICT and the low technology service industry have replaced traditional economic activities such as manufacturing. Two factors seem to play a role here: the quantity, quality and relative low cost of labour; and the Canada–US exchange rate, which for a time made it financially advantageous for companies to locate in Canada (Arledge, 2002). And in France, Levy and Jegou (2013) argue, there is evidence of increasing knowledge being created in small cities (not only by university staff) and also evidence of the internationalisation of science in these cities. This section has emphasised not only the need for secondary cities to respond effectively to global economic shifts and new economic activity, but also their vulnerability to processes beyond their control.

Secondary cities and urban sustainability and the environment

Cities must be able to respond to environmental concerns such as global warming (UNCHS, 2014). Yet environmental issues have received rather scant attention in research on secondary cities (Véron, 2010). The World Bank (2010) suggests that, because of their smaller size, secondary cities are better positioned than large cities to explore more creative possibilities (World Bank, 2010). Despite having the opportunity to plan differently, many secondary cities find it more problematic and difficult to implement climate change adaptation because of their lower capacity and consequently larger degree of resistance (Hamin et al., 2014). As is the case with increased globalisation, secondary cities are unlikely to escape the pressures associated with the need to ensure higher levels of urban sustainability. Furthermore, as the histories of many secondary cities associated with mining would suggest, secondary cities are often also plagued by long-term environmental concerns.

Conclusion

In this chapter we reviewed some of the important literature on secondary cities. We started off by discussing the difficulty of finding a definition for secondary cities and followed this with a more detailed discussion of the attributes that are used to describe or define secondary cities in the literature. The chapter also considered functions of secondary cities and some concerns about national secondary city strategies. These strategies have generally been criticised and have seldom generated long-term dividends. Despite this, secondary cities, as we have seen, play an important role in national urban and economic systems, not least because a significant proportion of the global urban population live there. If secondary cities are to grow and develop sustainably, more research will be needed to investigate, measure and understand what drives their development, and citizens and local governments will have to find ways to develop these cities despite not benefiting from the economies of scale that larger cities enjoy. How secondary cities engage in these processes will determine how they succeed in the future and with what degree of success they are able to take on the challenges of the future.

Chapter 1 provided an assessment framework for the different chapters, with Table 1.1 setting out how the different cities in the book relate to some of the main attributes. Table 2.2 justifies the inclusion of these attributes by referring to sources reviewed in this chapter. The chapter and Table 2.2 emphasise not only the importance of economic and population size in defining secondary cities but also the increasing importance of urban function and its link with indicators of size. Finally, Table 2.2 lists a number of strategic realities that secondary cities need to deal with. Secondary cities are frequently linked to global markets. Yet, these links are often in single economic sectors. Furthermore, decentralisation efforts have seldom benefited secondary cities. Capacity constraints and the volatility associated with global markets seem to be the main hindrances in this respect. Across the world, secondary cities have found it difficult to benefit from the knowledge economy and have tended to foster inward-looking economic development strategies instead of building networks to other areas and economies. Finally, considering the emphasis on sustainability, it is also noteworthy that many secondary cities (largely because of the mining link) are more directly affected by their effect on the environment.

Table 2.2 Sources cited to support secondary city attributes

Attributes	Sources
Size	
Smaller populations than metropolitan areas	Van der Merwe, 1992
Smaller economies than the metropolitan areas	Van der Merwe, 1992
Function	
Likely to have mono-economic rather than multi-economic function	Van der Merwe, 1992
A link to mining	Rondinelli, 1983a; Wood, 1986; Goodman and Worth, 2011; Bryceson and MacKinnon, 2012; Kabamba, 2012; Lawrie et al., 2012; Obeng-Odoom, 2014; Steel, 2013
Administrative and public sector centres	Hjort, 1979; Miracle and Miracle, 1979; Saxena, 1981; Rondinelli, 1983a; Hardoy and Satterthwaite, 1986; Manzanal and Vapnarsky, 1986; Fongwa and Wangenge-Ouma, 2015
Provision of transport and transport technology	Rondinelli, 1983a; Urena et al., 2009; Bolay and Rabinovich, 2004; Rozenblat et al., 2005; Zook and Brunn, 2005
A link to the rural hinterland	Meissner, 1981; Rondinelli, 1983a; 1983b; Harday and Satterthwaite, 1986; Akar, 1991; Madani and Diafat, 2002; Bolay and Rabonovich, 2004; Caravaca et al., 2007
Management of urbanisation	Richardson, 1981; Adepoju, 1983; Rondinelli, 1983a; 1985; Hardoy and Satterthwaite, 1986; Caroll, 1988;; Otiso, 2005; Klaufus, 2010; World Bank 2010; UNCHS, 2014
Location and locational interdependence	Richardson, 1981; Van der Merwe, 1992; Bolay and Rabinovich, 2004; Airriess, 2008; Duranton, 2008; World Bank, 2010; Borsdorf, 2012
Strategy related aspects	
Difficulty to benefiting from institutional decentralisation, as institutional capacity is constrained	Bolay and Rabinovich, 2004
Small but significant global linkages	Bolay and Rabinovich, 2004; Yu and Padua, 2007; Borsdorf et al., 2012
Global linkage usually by means of one sector	Bolay and Rabinovich, 2004
Higher levels of vulnerability associated with exposure to the international trends	Lessoff, 2008; Weck and Beißwenger, 2014; Bolay and Rabinovich, 2004
LED strategy – limitation of clusters but finding external networks suggested	Ferguson, 1992; Wilson, 1992; Rodríguez-Pose and Fitjar, 2013
Role of the knowledge economy in strategy development	Arledge, 2002; Carlso and Chakrabarti, 2007; Winden, et al., 2007; Levy and Jegou, 2013; Rodríguez-Pose and Fitjar, 2013
Usually more directly confronted by environmental concerns than metropolitan areas	Véron, 2010; World Bank, 2010; Hamin et al., 2014

References

Adepoju, J., 1983. *Selected Studies on the Dynamics, Patterns and Consequences of Migration: Medium Size Towns in Nigeria.* Paris: Unesco.

Airriess, C., 2008. The geographies of secondary city growth in a globalized China: Comparing Dongguan and Suzhou. *Journal of Urban History*, 35(1), pp. 134–149.

Akar, O., 1991. The functions of intermediate-sized cities in innovation diffusion and national socio-economic development in developing countries. *African Urban Quarterly*, 6(3/4), pp. 131–154.

Arledge, S., 2002. *Second Tier Cities, First Tier Service.* Dallas: Arledge and Partners.

Bell, D. and Jayne, M., 2006. *Small Cities: Urban Experience beyond the Metropolis.* New York: Routledge.

Bell, D. and Jayne, M., 2009. Small cities? Towards a research agenda. *International Journal of Urban and Regional Research*, 33(3), pp. 683–699.

Bolay, J. and Rabinovich, A., 2004. Intermediate cities in Latin America: risk and opportunities of coherent urban development. *Cities*, 21(5), pp. 407–421.

Berdeque, J., Carriazo, F., Jara, B. and Modrego, I. and Soloaga, I., 2015. Cities, territories, and inclusive growth: Unraveling urban–rural linkages in Chile, Colombia, and Mexico. *World Development*, 73, pp. 56–71.

Borsdorf, A., Santiago, C. and Sánchez, R., 2012. Changes in urbanization processes: the intermediate cities in the Chilean urban system. In: D. Salazar, ed. *Chile: Environmental, Political and Social Issues*. Chillán: University of Concepción, pp. 159–173.

Bos, D., 1989. Prospects for the development of intermediate size cities as part of a decentralisation programme for Southern Africa. *Development Southern Africa*, 6(1), pp. 58–81.

Brennan, J., King, R. and Lebeau, Y., 2004. The role of universities in the transformation of societies. An international research project synthesis report. London: Association of Commonwealth Universities. Available at: https://www.open.ac.uk/cheri/documents/transf-final-report.pdf (accessed 16 July 2016).

Brenner, N. and Schmid, C., 2015. Towards a new epistemology of the urban? *City: Analysis of Urban Trends, Culture, Theory, Policy, Action*, 19(203), pp. 151–182.

Bryceson, D. and MacKinnon, D., 2012. Eureka and beyond: Mining's impact on African urbanisation. *Journal of Contemporary African Studies*, 30(4), pp. 513–537.

Caravaca, I., González, G. and Mendoza, A., 2007. Indicators of dynamism, innovation and development and their application in Andalusian intermediate cities. *Boletín de la A.G.E*, 43, pp. 383–385.

Carlso, C. and Chakrabarti, P., 2007. Venture capital in New England Secondary Cities. *New England Community Developments*, 1, pp. 1–7.

Caroll, G., 1988. National city size distributions: what do we know after 67 years of research? *Progress in Geography*, 2(1), pp. 23–40.

Chen, X. and Kanna, A., 2012. *Rethinking Global Urbanism: Comparative Insights from Secondary Cities.* New York: Routledge.

Coe, N. and Yeung, H., 2015. *Global Production Networks.* Oxford: Oxford University Press.

Collier, P., 2007. Managing commodity booms: Lessons of international experience. Oxford: Paper prepared for the African Economic Research Consortium Centre for the Study of African Countries.

De Boeck, F., Cassiman, A. and Van Wolputte, S., 2009. Recentering the city: an anthropology of secondary cities in Africa. In: K. Bakker, eds. *African Perspectives 2009:*

The African City: (Re)sourced. Pretoria (South Africa): University of Pretoria, Department of Architecture, pp. 33–41.

Dicken, P., 2015. *Global Shift: Mapping the Changing Contours of the World Economy.* London, Sage.

Duranton, I., 2008. Cities: engines of growth and prosperity for developing countries? Washington DC: Working paper no 12, Commission of Growth and Development, World Bank. Available at: http://siteresources.worldbank.org/EXTPREMNET/Resources/489960-1338997241035/Growth_Commission_Working_Paper_12_Cities_Engines_Growth_Prosperity_Developing_Countries.pdf (accessed 21 August 2014).

Fahmi, F., Hudalah, D., Rahayu, P. and Woltjer, J., 2014. Extended urbanization in small and medium-sized cities: the case of Cirebon, Indonesia. *Habitat International*, 42, pp. 1–10.

Ferguson, B., 1992. Inducing local growth: two intermediate-sized cities in the state of Parana, Brazil. *Third World Planning Review*, 14(3), pp. 245–265.

Fongwa, S. and Wangange-Ouma, G., 2015. University as regional development agent: a counterfactual analysis of an African University. *Africa Education Review*, 12(4), 544–551.

Friedman, J., 1986. The world city hypothesis. *Development and Change*, 12, pp. 12–50.

Goodman, J. and Worth, D., 2011. The minerals boom and Australia's 'resource curse'. *Journal of Australian Political Economy*, 66, pp. 144–165.

Hall, P., 1966. *The World Cities*. London: Weidenfelt and Nicholson.

Hamin, E., Gurran, N. and Emlinger, A., 2014. Barriers to municipal climate adaptation: examples from coastal Massachusetts' smaller cities and towns. *Journal of the American Planning Association*, 80(2), pp. 110–122.

Hardoy, J. and Satterthwaite, D., 1981. *Shelter, Need and Response*. London: John Wiley & Sons.

Hardoy, J. and Satterthwaite, D., 1986. *Small and Intermediate Urban Centres: Their Role in National and Regional Development in the Third World*. London: Hodder and Stoughton.

Henderson, J., 2002. Urbanization in developing countries. *World Bank Research Observer*, 17(1), pp. 89–112.

Hjort, A., 1979. Sedentary pastoralists and peasants. The inhabitants of a small towns. In: A. Southall, ed. *Small Urban Centres in Rural Development in Africa*. Madison: University of Wisconsin, pp. 45–55.

Kabamba, P., 2012. A tale of two cities: urban transformation in gold-centred Butembo and diamond-rich Mbuji-Mayi, Democratic Republic of the Congo. *Journal of Contemporary African Studies*, 30(4), pp. 669–685.

Klaufus, C., 2010. Watching the city grow: remittances and sprawl in intermediate Central American cities. *Environment and Urbanization*, 22(1), pp. 125–137.

Lawrie, M., Tonts, M. and Plummer, P., 2012. Boomtowns, resource dependence and socio-economic well-being. *Australian Geographer*, 42(2), pp. 139–164.

Lessoff, A., 2008. Corpus Christi, 1965–2005: a secondary city's search for a new direction. *Journal of Urban History*, 35, pp. 108–133.

Levy, R. and Jegou, L., 2013. Diversity and location of knowledge production in small cities in France. *City, Culture and Society*, 4(4), pp. 203–216.

Linn, J., 1983. *Cities in the Developing World*. Oxford: Oxford University Press.

Madani, S. and Diafat, A., 2002. Intermediate cities and sustainable development: the case of Setif – Algeria. *Nederlandse Geografische Studies*, 303, pp. 183–193.

Manzanal, M. and Vapnarsky, C., 1986. The development of the Upper Valley of Rio Negro and its periphery within the Comahue region, Argentina. In: J. Hardoy and D. Satterthwaite, eds. *Small and Intermediate Urban Centres: Their Role in National and Regional Development of the Third World*. London: Hodder and Stoughton, pp. 18–79.

Meissner, F., 1981. Growth without migration: towards a model for integrated regional/ rural development planning. *Ekistics*, 48(291), pp. 442–446.

Min, M., 1990. Growth of small and intermediate cities in Korea, 1975–1980. *Korea Journal of Population and Development*, 19(1), pp. 47–70.

Miracle, M. and Miracle, D., 1979. Commercial links between Grand Bassam, Ivory Coast and rural populations in West Africa. In: A. Southall, ed. *Small Urban Centres in Rural Development in Africa*. Madison: University of Wisconsin, pp. 88–107.

Mohan, R., 1983. India: coming to terms with urbanisation. *Cities*, 1(1), pp. 46–58.

Mushuku, A. and Takuva, R., 2013. Growth points or ghost towns? Post-independence experiences of the industrialisation process at Nemamwa growth points in Zimbabwe. *International Journal of Politics and Good Governance*, 4(4), pp. 1–27.

Norman, J., 2013. *Small Cities USA: Growth, Diversity and Inequality*. New Brunswick: Rutgers University Press.

Obeng-Odoom, F., 2014. *Oiling the Urban Economy. Land, Labour, Capital and the State in Sekondi-Takoradi, Ghana*. London: Routledge.

Otiso, K., 2005. Kenya's secondary cities growth strategy at a crossroads: which way forward? *GeoJournal*, 62, pp. 117–128.

Powell, W. and Snellman, K., 2004. The knowledge economy. *Annual Review of Sociology*, 30, pp. 199–220.

Richardson, H., 1981. National urban development strategies in developing countries. *Urban Studies*, 18, pp. 267–283.

Roberts, B., 2014. *Managing Systems of Secondary Cities*. Brussels: Cities Alliance.

Roberts, B. and Hohmann, R., 2014. *The Systems of Secondary Cities: The Neglected Drivers of Urbanising Economies*. Brussels: Cities Alliance.

Robinson, J., 2006. *Ordinary Cities: Between Modernity and Development*. Abingdon: Routledge.

Rodríguez-Pose, A. and Fitjar, R., 2013. Buzz, archipelago economics and the future of intermediate and peripheral areas in a spiky world. *European Planning Studies*, 21(3), pp. 355–372.

Rondinelli, D., 1983a. *Secondary Cities in Developing Countries: Policies for Diffusing Urbanisation*. Beverley Hills: Sage.

Rondinelli, D., 1983b. Towns and small cities in developing countries. *Geographical Review*, 73(4), pp. 379–395.

Rondinelli, D., 1985. Population distribution and economic development in Africa: the need for urbanisation policies. *Population Research and Policy Review*, 4(2), pp. 173–196.

Rozenblat, C. et al., 2005. *Worldwide Multi-Level Networks of Cities Emerging From Air Traffic*. Santiago de Compostela: IGU.

Satterthwaite, D., 2006. Outside the large cities. The demographic importance of small urban centres and large villages in Africa, Asia and Latin America. United Nations Centre for Human Settlements: Human Settlements Discussion Paper – Urban Change 3.

Saxena, K., 1981. Chandigarh City – its influence on regional growth. *Habitat International*, 5(6), pp. 637–651.

Steel, G., 2013. Mining and tourism: urban transformations in the intermediate cities of Cajamarca and Cusco, Peru. *Latin American Perspectives*, 40(2), pp. 237–249.

Swilling, M., 2010. Sustainability and a sense of the city: Ways of seeing Cape Town's futures. In: M. Swilling and L. Thompson-Smeddle, eds. *Sustaining Cape Town: Imagining a Liveable City*. Stellenbosch: SUN Media, pp. 3–22.

Todes, A. and Watson, V., 1984. Growth pole theory and regional development in South Africa: Results of a survey in selected growth areas. Cape Town, Carnegie Conference Paper No. 245, 13–19 April 1984, University of Cape Town.

UNCHS (United Nations Centre for Human Settlements), 1984. *Middle-ranked Human Settlements in Territorial Oganization Strategies in Latin America and the Caribbean*, New York: UNCHS.

UNCHS (United Nations Centre for Human Settlements), 2014. *State of the African Cities: Re-Imagining Sustainable Urban Transitions*. Nairobi: UN Habitat.

United Nations, 2002. *World urbanization prospects*. New York: United Nations.

United Nations, 2015. *World urbanisation prospects. The 2014 revision*. New York: United Nations.

Urena, J., Menerault, P. and Garmendia, M., 2009. The high-speed rail challenge for big intermediate cities: A national, regional and local perspective. *Cities*, 26, 266–279.

Van der Merwe, I., 1992. In search of an urbanization policy for SA: towards a secondary city strategy. *Geographical Research Forum*, 12, pp. 102–127.

Van Winden, W., Van den Berg, L. and Pol, P., 2007. European cities in the knowledge economy: towards a typology. *Urban Studies*, 44(3), pp. 525–549.

Véron, R., 2010. Small cities, neoliberal neoliberal governance and sustainable development in the global south: a conceptual framework and research agenda. *Sustainability*, 2(9), pp. 2833–2848.

Warhurst, A. and Naronha, L., 2000. Corporate strategy and viable future land use: planning for closure from the outset of mining. *Natural Resources Forum*, 24, pp. 153–164.

Weck, S. and Beißwenger, S., 2014. Coping with peripheralization: governance response in two German small cities. *European Planning Studies*, 22(10), pp. 2156–2171.

Wilson, P., 1992. Secondary cities in the global economy: the growth of export-oriented small and medium-sized producers: the case of Mexico. *Investigaciones Geograficas: Boletin del Instituto de Geografía*, Special Issue, pp. 215–218.

Winden, W., Van den Berg, L. and Pol, P., 2007. European cities in the knowledge economy: towards a typology. *Urban Studies*, 44(3), pp. 525–549.

Wood, W., 1986. Intermediate cities on a resource frontier. *The Geographical Review*, 76(2), pp. 149–159.

World Bank, 2009. *Cities in Transition. World Bank Urban and Local Government Strategy*. Washington DC: World Bank.

World Bank, 2010. *Systems of Cities: Harnessing Growth for Urbanisation and Poverty Alleviation*. Washington, DC: World Bank Finance, Economics and Urban Department.

Yu, K. and Padua, M., 2007. China's cosmetic cities: Urban fever and superficiality. *Landscape Research*, 32(2), pp. 255–272.

Zook, M. and Brunn, S., 2005. Hierarchies, regions and legacies: European cities and global commercial passenger air travel. *Journal of Contemporary European Studies*, 13(20), pp. 203–220.

3 The City of Matlosana

Deidre van Rooyen and Molefi Lenka

Introduction

The City of Matlosana Municipality is in the centre of the Dr Kenneth Kaunda District Municipality. Klerksdorp, the City of Matlosana's main urban centre and the economic hub of the greater municipal area, was established in the late 1800s as a service centre for the gold mining areas of the Rand and the diamond mining areas of the Cape. The substantial growth of the mines between 1940 and 1990 contributed to the development of the area, but Klerksdorp never became specifically a mining town. Instead, it has retained its historical role as a regional service centre and this has helped to mitigate the effects of the mine downscaling that began in the early 1990s. Klerksdorp is important for agricultural supplies, retail facilities, schools and medical services. The areas it supplies stretch beyond the boundaries of the Dr Kenneth Kaunda District Municipality, the North-West Province and even into Botswana (Dauskardt and Hart, 1994).

The main urban areas of the City of Matlosana Municipality are Alabama, Hartbeesfontein, Jouberton, Klerksdorp, Kanana, Khuma, Manzilpark, Orkney, Vaal Reefs, Stilfontein and Tigane. Figure 3.1 shows its location, south west of Johannesburg, on the N12 'treasure corridor' that links Matlosana to Gauteng to the east, the Northern Cape to the south-west and the platinum belt of Rustenburg to the north.

This chapter first looks at mining and economic development in South Africa and the influence of mining on Matlosana's development. It then describes three phases of Matlosana's history. This is followed by an overview of internal trends and pressures, particularly those associated with mine downscaling. The reactions of local government actors and businesses to the downscaling are discussed. The chapter then discusses external pressures faced by the city. It concludes with some policy lessons for taking advantage of opportunities and avoiding future risks, and suggests some reasons why the City of Matlosana has not been as badly affected by the gold mining slump as Matjhabeng in the Free State Goldfields (Marais, 2013).

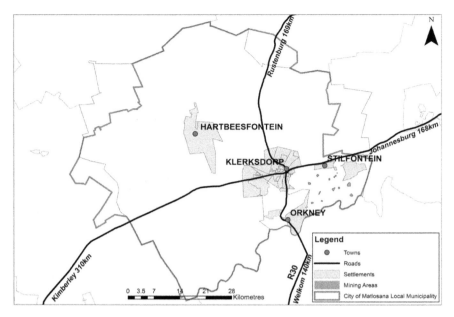

Figure 3.1 Location of the City of Matlosana

Mining and economic development in South Africa

Mining has long played a critical role in the South African economy and the planning of mining towns has been closely linked with the development of the economy (Schoeman, 2008). Gold mining was the most prominent mining sector for more than 100 years, until the early 1990s, when it began to decline because of declining reserves, the increased depth of the mines, which increased costs and labour accidents, and a changing labour regime (Crankshaw, 2002). The industry has lost some 250,000 jobs (Binns and Nel, 2001). Some miners have been able to move to other mining sectors (such as platinum), but overall employment in mining has been in decline since the early 1990s.

The history of the mining industry in South Africa is also associated with migrant labour, low wages and high-density single-sex hostels (Crush, 1989; Crush and James, 1991). Since the start of democracy, policy has been formulated to deal with these socio-economic ills (DME, 1998) and new legislation has been introduced (RSA, 2002). The Mineral and Petroleum Resources Development Act (RSA, 2002) requires mining companies to develop social and labour plans (SLPs) so as to become involved in developing the urban communities in which they are located. The SLPs are in effect a 'social licence' to mine. They also encourage collaboration between mining companies and local authorities in strategic planning at the local level (Donovan and Lukhel, 2013). Applicants for mining or production rights develop and implement comprehensive programmes for human resources and LED (DMR, 2010). These programmes should help to transform the mining sector, save jobs and manage downscaling or closure

(Rogerson, 2012), which is often traumatic for the local community (Strongman, 2000). Overall, the intention of SLPs is 'not simply to assist the municipalities in their everyday functions, but rather to have a positive impact on the everyday life of a community above and beyond what the municipalities provide' (Marais and Van der Walt, 2011, p. 29). This imperative to improve local planning and ensure collaborative planning through SLPs is discussed in more detail below.

History of Matlosana

We describe this history in three phases: the early days (1837 to 1929), the discovery of gold (1930 to 1989), and the downscaling of the mines (1990 to the present day).

The early days (1837–1929)

In 1837 the first white inhabitants of the area, a group of 12 Voortrekker families, settled next to the Schoonspruit river, which flows through the town of Klerksdorp, on the farm Elandsheuwel. This area is known today as the 'Oudorp' (the old town). They established a town which they called 'Clerqsdorp', after the first magistrate north of the Vaal river, Jacob de Clercq (Gaffen, 2012). The recurring theme of the town being a service centre comes across during various stages of the development of the town: the discovery of gold and the development of several shafts, and subsequently the decline in mining in the area. After gold was discovered in 1885, the area developed rapidly and Klerksdorp was declared a town on 12 September 1888 by State President Paul Kruger.

One of the pioneer diggers drawn to the then Western Transvaal region by the gold discoveries of the late 1880s was Simon Fraser, whose claim was on the farm Witkoppies ('white hills'). Fraser hailed from the Orkney Islands off the north coast of Scotland and called his mine Orkney – hence the name of the town (Brown, 1987). Stilfontein also has a Scottish connection in its origins. Jack Scott, from Strathmore in Scotland, acquired a farm in these parts and called it Strathvaal. In 1888 he discovered the outcrop of a gold reef on this farm and named it Strathmore Reef. Upon Scott's death, his son Jack continued the search and acquired an option on the farm Stilfontein ('quiet spring') nearby (Brown, 1987).

Klerksdorp was connected by rail to Krugersdorp (on the outskirts of Johannesburg) to join the Rand gold rush in 1897 and to Kimberley in 1906 to connect to the diamond rush.

During the Second South African War (1899–1902), heavy fighting occurred in the area, which also housed a large concentration camp. In 1903 Klerksdorp achieved municipal status when Johannes Adriaan Neser was elected the first mayor (Marx, 1987).

The discovery of gold (1930–1989)

As mentioned in Chapter 2, many secondary cities are resource towns and depend heavily on these resources. In the 1920s the gold mining industry almost came to a standstill because the quick excavation surface methods were no longer effective and the gold had to be mined at a greater depth, but in the early 1930s a new excavation process using cyanide was developed in Europe and this gave the gold mining industry new life (Brown, 1987). Extensive new gold reserves were discovered in the early 1930s in the Greater Klerksdorp area. The gold mining industry was thus revived in 1932, with large mining companies, such as the old Western Reefs (under the logo of Anglo American), bringing economic revitalisation to the town. After the Second World War some small mines (Afrikander Lease, East and West Bonanza, Dominion Reefs and Ellaton) also helped to accelerate the growth of the area.

In 1949 the Stilfontein Gold Mining Company was registered and a town laid out. Production started in 1952. Four mines, in Stilfontein, Hartbeesfontein, Zandpan and Buffelsfontein, employed many of the inhabitants of the area. It was during this high financial period that various services were established to develop the town: the hospital in 1939, the water scheme in 1940 and electricity in 1944. House building began in Jouberton, the first black township, in 1949 and the P. C. Pelser airport was constructed in 1964. Klerksdorp grew extensively during the 1950s and 1960s and the council often argued that since this was the largest town in the area and the number of wards had increased from nine to eleven, it could apply for city status (Dunn, 1987).

The City of Matlosana benefited extensively from gold mining for more than a century. Although the initial mining activities were on a small scale, gold production dominated the local economy for nearly five decades (1945 to 1990).

Decline (1990 to the present day)

The third phase began with the substantial decline in gold mining that started in the early 1990s. Between 1996 and 2011 there was a large-scale decline in the mining economy and in the employment rates in the Greater Klerksdorp area. The annual growth rate in the mining sector declined by 15 per cent during this period. Employment in the mining sector decreased by 44 per cent between 1996 and 2001 and by another 23 per cent by 2011 (UFS, 2013). Currently only six of the 28 developed shafts remain operational in the area (Jacobs, 2013).

Two factors in particular have contributed to this decline. Continued resource depletion has necessitated mining at deeper levels, which has implications for human resources (more accidents) and costs (shaft sinking and electricity) (Cornish, 2013). At some point mining activities become unviable because the risks and costs outweigh the income. And the mining industry has changed considerably over the past 20 years. What was a South Africa-oriented industry has become an international industry with large international shareholding. This has meant that peripheral mining functions (such as sports clubs) and broader support for local urban areas have lost their importance for the mine managers.

Attempts to diversify the economy by the mid-2000s coincided with the creation of the City of Matlosana's municipality. The City of Matlosana was officially recognised on 1 July 2005. It incorporates the towns of Klerksdorp, Orkney, Stilfontein and Hartbeesfontein, which previously each had their own municipalities and were collectively known as KOSH. The name *Matlosana* means 'People helping each other to move from one area to another' (City of Matlosana, 2013) and the city's defining slogan is 'City of people on the move'. According to the executive mayor, these words originally referred to the forced removals during apartheid but have now been given a positive spin, to encourage the city to 'move' – in the sense of increasing its population and boosting its economy.

Internal trends and pressures

This section discusses internal pressures on the City of Matlosana that have developed over the past 20 years and the responses to these pressures.

Demographic and economic trends

The total population of the City of Matlosana was 398,676 in 2011. Nearly 100 per cent of the population are urbanised (mining villages form part of the urban areas). The population of the municipality makes up 11 per cent of the North-West Province. The largest population concentrations are in the historical black townships of Jouberton (28.5 per cent), Kanana (19.7 per cent) and Khuma (11.5 per cent) which represent 59.7 per cent of the total population. The population and household growth of the City of Matlosana declined between 1995 and 2010: the average annual population growth was 1.45 per cent and the average annual household growth was 3.46 per cent. In 2010 the household growth rate was at 0.0 per cent. Since 2010 the population has grown slowly, at 0.75 per cent per annum – lower than the national population growth rate, which is estimated at between 1 per cent and 1.4 per cent per annum (Stats SA, 2013).

The City of Matlosana's contribution to the economy of the North-West Province is nearly 28 per cent (Maxim Planning Solutions, 2012). Table 3.1 shows the proportions contributed by the main economic sectors of the City of Matlosana for 1996, 2001 and 2011, and also the proportions of employment in these sectors.

As might be expected, the mining sector's economic contribution to the City of Matlosana has decreased, dropping from 58.5 per cent in 1996 to less than 30 per cent in 2011. The contribution that the sector made to the North-West Province also decreased, from 37.8 per cent in 1996 to 28.8 per cent in 2011. The close proximity of the Rustenburg platinum belt can be considered one of the factors that saved Matlosana from total decline. Although several mineworkers moved to Rustenburg, a large proportion of this skilled population have invested in property in the City of Matlosana and therefore commute to Rustenburg for employment during the week and return to their families over weekends. The sectors whose contributions to the economy of the City of Matlosana increased from 1996 to 2011 are trade (from 6.2 to 13.2 per cent), transport and communication (from 7.8 to 11.0 per cent), finance (from 9.3 to 17.7 per cent) and services (from 12.5 to 21.9 per cent) (SACN, 2014). The decline of mining thus appears to have encouraged a more diversified economy, with these sectors increasing their share of the economy. The proportional growth of these sectors is a direct result of the decline in mining (Marais, 2013), and the table clearly indicates the increasing importance of the regional services function of the City of Matlosana.

Table 3.1 Employment and economic contribution per sector, the City of Matlosana
(1996, 2001 and 2011)

Sector	Economic contribution %			Employment contribution %		
	1996	*2001*	*2011*	*1996*	*2001*	*2011*
Agriculture	0.8	0.7	1.0	4.6	6.9	6.1
Manufacturing	2.3	2.4	3.4	3.4	3.1	3.8
Utilities	1.0	0.6	0.4	0.6	0.9	0.8
Construction	1.6	1.2	2.0	2.0	2.2	3.4
Transport and communication	7.8	7.7	11.0	3.3	3.4	4.0
Trade	6.2	7.4	13.2	8.0	10.4	14.6
Finance	9.3	10.5	17.7	3.6	5.0	8.1
Services	12.5	17.2	21.9	11.1	19.8	28.0
Mining*	58.5	52.3	29.4	(73,945) 63.4	(41,488) 48.3	(24,704) 31.2

Source: UFS (2013).

Notes: Employment within households was excluded for this exercise.
* Mining employment numbers included in brackets.

The sectoral composition of the city's economic activity indicates its level of diversification. This can be measured by the Tress Index, in which the closer the figure is to 100, the more dependent the area is on a single sector and the more vulnerable to climate conditions and commodity fluctuations. In 1998 the Tress Index figure for Matlosana was 54.6 and in 2008 it was 39.3, clearly indicating that the area's economy had become more diverse (SACN, 2014).

According to a representative of the Wesvaal Business Chamber, mining employment is predicted to decrease still further in the next few years because the mines in the area have been laying off workers faster than the projected eight to ten years. However, as mentioned above, the scale of the decline in employment in Matlosana's mining sector has not been as drastic as that of the Free State Goldfields, where the number of employees decreased from 180,000 in 1988 to 34,000 in 2011 (Marais, 2013). It has been estimated that at its peak of mining employment (during the late 1980s), the City of Matlosana had approximately 120,000 mine workers (Marais et al., 2015).

The increase in the services sector's contribution to employment is largely due to the drop in mining employment but also represents an increasingly diverse economy. The service economy of the City of Matlosana is fairly equally distributed between the main service subsectors: public administration (27.7 per cent), education (31.8 per cent), health (19.8 per cent) and other services (20.8 per cent) (UFS, 2013).

Poverty and development

Mine downscaling is expected to lead to increased poverty. In Matlosana the number of people living in poverty increased from 118,865 in 1996 to 212,892 in 2011, an increase of nearly 80 per cent (City of Matlosana, 2013). This is partly because of the high unemployment level in the municipal area in 2011 (19.6 per cent), although this is lower than the South African average (25 per cent). It is noteworthy that, despite an initial increase in unemployment between 1996 and 2001 in Matlosana, the percentage of the total population defined as unemployed in fact declined between 2001 and 2011 (Stats SA, 2013).

The Gini coefficient for the entire population of the City of Matlosana hovers around 0.6 (0.55 in 1996 and 0.62 in 2011) (UFS, 2013), which suggests some increase in inequality. This figure is slightly lower than the figure of 0.67 for South Africa in 2011, which indicates a medium level of human development (World Bank, 2013).

The City of Matlosana's Human Development Index (HDI) figures for 1996 and 2011 are the same as those for South Africa: 0.56 in 1996 and 0.63 in 2011. More importantly, it should be noted that, despite the considerable economic decline, there has been an increase in South Africa's overall HDI. This places South Africa in a group of countries with a medium level of human development. According to Prinsloo (2014), the increase in life expectancy indicates that the positive roll-out of antiretroviral treatment for people living with HIV and AIDS has been effective.

Internal responses

Like many other local government structures in South Africa, the City of Matlosana struggles to perform some of its basic municipal functions. In order to improve performance and service delivery, the City adopted a new corporate strategy (Vision 2020) in August 2013 with three core values: integrity, dignity and performance. The Director of Strategic Planning, Monitoring and Control noted that the strategy aimed to improve several aspects: financial recovery; internal motivation; external stakeholder alignment; and leadership; management and supervision (Lourens, 2013). From the interviews it appeared that political and administrative components of Council maintain a sound working relationship by ensuring respect of procedures and protocols.

The City of Matlosana's integrated development plan (IDP) reflects its development priorities. In all the city's communities, these have always been storm-water drainage, road maintenance, community halls, sports facilities, and street and high-mast lighting. Service backlogs have been reported for water, sanitation, roads, refuse removal and electricity. The executive mayor noted, however, that there have been minimal service delivery protests in the City of Matlosana. Despite its slogan 'city on the move', the city appears to be catching up with backlogs and putting most of its budget and effort into alleviating poverty rather than into economic growth and future development. It has become clear that the mining sector in the area has already experienced a sharp decline and therefore the city's economy will have to cope independently of the mining sector.

The Matlosana LED strategy was approved in September 2007 and revised in October 2012. It is aligned with the national and provincial spatial frameworks, and also with the North-West growth and development strategy and the Dr Kenneth Kaunda District Municipality growth and development strategy. However, although these strategies stress the importance of LED and what should be done to promote the potential of the area, they do not sufficiently propose activities for implementing the strategies. Nevertheless, the City of Matlosana does seem to take LED seriously, as it has a staff component of four people working towards building sustainable relationships with private investors and businesses. Three active forums have been established to allow for more communication between public and private entities, including a mining forum, a formal business forum and a trader's forum. Furthermore, the LED projects are aligned with the economic plans of the Dr Kenneth Kaunda District Municipality and the Dr Kenneth Kaunda District Economic Development Agency. These entities liaise regularly with the City of Matlosana and support its plans, projects and investment opportunities. Together, the three economic entities of the area (the agency, and the district and municipality LED departments) are currently investing time and effort in planning several projects as alternative means to mitigate unemployment and improve economic growth in the area. Some of these, referred to as the Big Bank (Mega) projects, are in the advanced stage of planning. Many of these projects are aligned with improvements planned for the east–west development of the N12, such as a meat processing plant and an airport. The N12 development is a diverse combination of land use (retail, sport, leisure, commercial, showroom, residential and community projects). This area is seen as the future focal developmental node of Matlosana. Also among these projects are the Goudkoppie Heritage Hill Project, the Oppenheimer Stadium and the Archbishop Desmond Tutu Heritage Village (IDC, 2013). These plans are a means to diversify the economy and reduce dependence on the mining sector. However, the level of implementation remains low.

The City of Matlosana has made a specific effort to distribute its municipal offices across Matlosana's main towns. This has helped to spread the people associated with different municipal services across the municipal area. The main administrative offices are in the Klerksdorp CBD. The LED function, value chain and procurement offices are in Stilfontein in the old municipal council offices. Lastly, the Dr Kenneth Kaunda District Municipality (of which the City of Matlosana Municipality forms part) has its administrative offices in Orkney. The location of the district municipality offices in Orkney confirms the importance of the City of Matlosana's regional services function.

Despite the good intentions outlined above, the reality on the ground seems somewhat different. The previous council experienced several misfortunes with the municipal manager and tender irregularities (Cilliers, 2010). Filling the vacant posts on the municipality's organogram is still a challenge – the total vacancies stood at 884 or 28 per cent at the end of the 2012/13 financial year. There is often insufficient cooperation and coordination between the municipal directorates. A business interviewee working with the municipality suggested that the directorates are striving to achieve their own goals and not working as a team to improve the City of Matlosana. Problems that the City of Matlosana currently experiences are lack of document management, poor project planning, poor ICT systems and lack of staff training. An interviewee from the municipality's finance department said the municipality's inefficient billing system, which can be traced back to the days when mining companies owned properties in the mining towns and paid the bills in bulk, is hindering debt collection. To deal with this problem, consultants have been employed to administer and maintain the billing system of the municipality and to train municipal staff in the debt collection processes.

A major weakness of the LED and IDP documents is that they do not consider what downscaling in the mining sector means or suggest an appropriate response but confine themselves to outlining grand plans.

The good intentions of the above plans are not always met with enthusiasm from other role players and three problems are making implementation difficult: financial difficulties and disclaimer audits, strained relationships hindering cooperation, and excessive focus on a few big projects to the detriment of other important smaller projects.

Firstly, there are concerns about the municipality's financial status and financial management. The current municipal finance managers are struggling to deal with inherited debts to bulk suppliers of more than R92 million (SA Local Government Research, 2013). The problem has been caused partly by bad credit control of the municipality's clients, but also by mine downscaling and people's inability to pay. The City of Matlosana has received disclaimer audits for six years (2007–2013), meaning that it provided insufficient documentary evidence on which to base an audit (Auditor General, 2012). External support was brought in and although some success has been achieved, a long road lies ahead to ensure adequate financial management (Ranthla, 2013). The largest portion of the municipality's income in 2012 was generated through services charges (47.3 per cent), followed by government grants and subsidies (25.9 per cent) and property rates (13.4 per cent). Other revenues (10.2 per cent) came from reconnection of cut-off electricity and water supply, rentals, and transfer of funds and reserves. Investment revenue made up the last 3.2 per cent. The government's equitable share and the operating grants have been increasing gradually since 2006/7. The proportion of revenue generated by property tax has decreased since 2011/12, suggesting that mine closure is also felt at this level.

A second problem hindering the implementation of plans is constrained relations between the municipality and the business and mining sectors. Often the relationship looks good on paper when participative processes are mentioned but in reality it is not always cordial between all stakeholders. A representative of the Matlosana Taxi Association said businesses in general have relationships only with certain individuals working in the municipality and not with the City of Matlosana as an entity. Several forums have been developed and managed by the LED subdivision. However, stakeholders often claim that the meetings are one-sided and communication and cooperation are lacking. They are often only an information-sharing session from the municipality and not a truly consultative platform.

The Klerksdorp Sakekamer Afrikaanse Handels Instituut and the Wesvaal Chamber of Commerce are trying to build better relationships, working together to find solutions, but there is little agreement between the various organised business groups. As a representative from the Wesvaal Chamber of Commerce noted, often each party has its own agenda it would like to present and as a result the problems affecting all are left unresolved. Interviewees felt that the business sector was not given a real opportunity to participate in the IDP process and that the mining sector was not consulted either.

A similar pattern in the changing ownership of mine shafts and the changes in elected politicians in the municipality has made it difficult to develop collaborative relationships between the mining sector and the municipality. The various mining companies operating in the area do not cooperate or implement projects together – each has its own vision and problems that it has to solve. AngloGold Ashanti often takes the leading role in partnerships when getting projects off the ground because they are the largest company operating at present. To them it is not only about compliance but also about obtaining a 'social licence to mine'. This mine reaches out to the community by hosting a special breakfast or lunch event to give feedback on their projects to NGOs, the municipality and businesses in the area. AngloGold Ashanti aspires to leave communities better off for having the company operate in the area. They therefore leverage partnerships with the municipality to stimulate and support local development in areas where they operate (Moloko, 2012). However, despite these intentions, there seems to be limited integration between the IDPs and the mining companies' SLPs. Mining companies make use of the IDP (and inputs from the LED processes in the municipality) as a guide to determine the projects or programmes that should be included in their SLPs (Moloko, 2012). This was not the intention when the idea of the SLP was proposed – it was supposed to be a means of collaborative planning between local government and the mining sector so that they could work together to develop the area. Currently, the SLP projects are sought from unfunded projects that the City of Matlosana may have. This implies that the IDP is a municipal master plan and not an area-based plan to develop the city. In fact, the mining contributions to the area could rather be seen as a form of corporate social responsibility (Hamann, 2004). This is not a good sign for the future of the area because instead of planning for the long-term in a responsible way the mine is then focusing on the short-term gains.

A third hindrance to the implementation of plans is that the IDP, the growth and development strategy and the LED strategy focus on big projects (such as the N12 development, airport development and meat processing plant) and tend to overlook some of the important smaller developments in the area (such as improving health facilities and clearing service backlogs). An interviewee from the Klerksdorp Sakekamer offered the example of the need to develop the medical sector. The medical infrastructure is already available, with several private hospitals (Wilmed, Sunningdale, Anncron and Duff Scott) as well as a large regional public hospital (Tsepong Complex) and the Klerksdorp District Hospital serving the surrounding areas. The cosmetic surgery and drug dispensary (Matlosana Medical Services) subsector in the medical field has not been hampered by the mine personnel lay-offs and therefore has the potential to be enhanced in a health-based economic growth hub. An official at the Macro City Planning and Development Department said there are plans to set up a training college for nurses, which will be linked to the regional hospital as an academic hospital. This is only briefly mentioned and insufficiently planned for in the IDP.

The planning documents need to zoom in closer to the existing role of Matlosana as a regional service centre, particularly considering that the city has 12 large building material suppliers (Faurie, 2013) and 25 second-hand motor vehicle sales dealerships. These two services provide the surrounding areas with building materials as well as an organised second-hand motor vehicle industry for trade options. This issue was further highlighted by a representative of the Matlosana Tourism Association, who said that accommodation and restaurants are mushrooming and a good tourism base with high occupancy rates is developing. The importance of school and business entities expanding their influence into Botswana has also received limited attention. In this regard, access routes between Gauteng and Botswana play an important role, facilitating trade between South Africa and Botswana with the City of Matlosana as a stopover point.

The above three problems – irregularities in financial systems, unsatisfactory relationships between business (including the mines) and the municipality, and plans that focus on large projects to the neglect of smaller ones that could bring social change to the area – continue to prevent Matlosana's good intentions from being put into practice.

External pressures

The state of Matlosana's environment in a post-mining era is a matter of concern. Mining has left the area with a degraded environment that requires urgent attention. The City of Matlosana adheres to the integrated environmental management standards. Integrated environmental management is an essential tool of South Africa's National Environmental Management Act No. 107 of 1998 (RSA, 1998). The National Environmental Management Act promotes the integrated environmental management of activities that may have a significant impact (positive or negative) on the environment. Integrated environmental management provides the overall structure for the integration of environmental assessment and management principles into environmental decision-making (DEAT, 2004). Because the greater part of the City of Matlosana is being mined, its environment is affected by mine dumps that have not been rehabilitated and by slime dams. Many environmental concerns remain and the mines' ecological footprint continues after downscaling. River systems, water quality, groundwater quality, dust generation and abandonment of land are problems that the municipality needs to deal with and that have not been highlighted as essential aspects in the planning documents (Marais, 2013). There is conflict between mining and agricultural land use. Mines have bought most of the surrounding land for mining purposes and to decrease the chance of farming land being affected by the acid water.

Dolomitic areas are also a major concern, especially for a township near Stilfontein called Khuma. Large parts of this township have been developed on a dolomitic area which is geologically unstable because the mines have created several tunnels beneath the area. Plans are being made to move 5,000 residents.

Synthesis

This chapter has focused on mining decline and the City of Matlosana's response to this loss of its main economic sector. Despite the rapid decline in gold mining activities, the City of Matlosana has been safeguarded by its regional service function, its position on the transport route between Gauteng and both Cape Town and Botswana and the proximity of the area to the platinum belt, the West

Rand and Gauteng (South Africa's economic hub). Economic decline has been directly linked to the decline in gold reserves and the costs of deep mining. However, this decline has not caused the out-migration of large portions of the population of the City of Matlosana.

Four important lessons can be learnt from the City of Matlosana's experience. First, the city was ill prepared for mine downscaling. In fact, the downscaling was quite unexpected and continues to be largely ignored – it is not considered as a key strategic factor in the city's IDP. Second, new mining legislation promulgated at the beginning of the 2000s to ensure more collaborative planning in the area has had limited effect. The potential collaborative planning in terms of SLPs and IDPs has been narrowed down to a project-by-project approach. Within this approach, mining companies are on the whole happy to fund projects identified by the IDP where the municipality lacks funds. The municipality sees this as important, as the right boxes can be ticked in respect of their strategic planning (City of Matlosana, 2011). The result, however, is that no long-term collaborative planning takes place. Admittedly, such planning is far more difficult in a period of downscaling. Downscaling means that mining companies do not want to share their information with outsiders and it also leads to rapid change in ownership which, in turn, does not support local partnership building. A further consequence of all this is that some of the historical racial divide persists between the mining companies (mainly white owned) and the municipality (mainly black), with limited mutual trust and virtually no collaborative planning.

A third lesson is that a national framework for the development of mining towns is urgently required. Developers of such a framework should carefully consider the motivation for settlement near mining, the development of infrastructure, mine downscaling and collaborative planning. The long-term environmental consequences of mining should also be considered in planning initiatives. As mentioned above, the historical role of Klerksdorp as a regional service centre has helped to mitigate the negative consequences of mine downscaling. It is also unlikely that many mining areas (in either decline or growth) would have the local capacity to manage the rapid changes generated by mining activities. Developers of such a national framework should consider the establishment of technical capacity to support local planning related to mining activity. And a fourth lesson is that mine downscaling is not all negative – it also has unintended positive outcomes. In the case of Matlosana, two positive effects have been a reduction in water and energy needs and increasing levels of residential racial desegregation.

There is evidence that a large proportion of the skilled people and thus also a large percentage of the economically active population have left the area. This holds a long-term risk for the area and may undermine its potential for finding alternative economic opportunities. Continued mine downscaling puts the city at risk of losing more people in the long run. The rural service nature of the city and the private and public services related to this function should be considered as important in strategic planning and in thinking about the future of the area. Aging infrastructure and lack of appropriate maintenance and repairs could reduce the city's regional service capabilities. The City of Matlosana has also not escaped the environmental damage associated with mining and will have to deal with more of this in future.

References

Auditor General, 2012. General report on the audit outcomes of local government. Mafikeng: Auditor General of South Africa.

Binns, T. and Nel, E., 2001. Gold loses its shine: decline and response in the South African goldfields. *Geography*, 86(3), pp. 255–260.

Brown, A., 1987. Die geskiedenis van die Klerksdorpse myne. In: R. Marx, ed. *Klerksdorp groeiende reus: 1837–1987*. Klerksdorp: Stadsraad van Klerksdorp, pp. 12–27.

Cilliers, S., 2010. Matlosana se raad skors bestuurder oor tenders. *Beeld*, 15 August, p. 6.

City of Matlosana, 2011. *Integrated Development Plan (IDP) Review*. Klerksdorp: City of Matlosana Local Municipality.

City of Matlosana, 2013. *City of Matlosana Draft Integrated Development Plan (IDP) 2013–2014*. Klerksdorp: City of Matlosana.

Cornish, L., 2013. South Africa's deep level gold mines: Ripe with opportunity in the twilight years: gold. *Inside Mining*, 6(2), pp. 10–12.

Crankshaw, P., 2002. Mining and minerals. In: A. Lemon and C. M. Rogerson, eds. *Geography and Economy in South Africa and its Neighbours*. Aldershot: Ashgate, pp. 63–80.

Crush, J., 1989. Accommodating black miners: Home ownership on the mines. In: *South African Review 5*. Johannesburg: Ravan Press, p. 335–347.

Crush, J. and James, W., 1991. Depopulating the compounds: Migrant labor and mine housing in South Africa. *World Development*, 19(4), pp. 301–316.

Dauskardt, R. and Hart, T., 1994. *Outside the Metropolis: The Future of South Africa's Secondary Cities*. Johannesburg: Urban Foundation Research.

DEAT (Department of Environmental Affairs and Tourism), 2004. Environmental Auditing, Integrated Environmental Management, Information Series 14, DEAT, Pretoria. Available at: https://www.environment.gov.za/sites/default/files/docs/series14_environmental_auditing.pdf (accessed 27 September 2015).

DME (Department of Minerals and Energy), 1998. White Paper on the Energy Policy of the Republic of South Africa, December 1998. Pretoria: Department of Minerals and Energy. Available at: http://www.energy.gov.za/files/policies/whitepaper_energypolicy_1998.pdf (accessed 27 September 2015.

DMR (Department of Mineral Resources), 2010. Guidelines for Review of Social and Labour Plans. Available at: http://www.dmr.gov.za/guidelines-revised-social-and-labour-plans/summary/119-how-to/221-guidelines-revised-social-and-labour-plans-.html (accessed 27 September 2015).

Donovan, D. R. and Lukhel, S., 2013. Fixing mining industry woes is essential for South Africa's domestic stability: Southern Africa – issue in focus. *Africa Conflict Monitor*, August, pp. 69–74.

Dunn, C., 1987. Plaaslike bestuur. In: R. Marx, ed. *Klerksdorp groeiende reus: 1837–1987*. Klerksdorp: Stadsraad van Klerksdorp, pp. 28–45.

Faurie, J., 2013. *Klerksdorp on the Up and Up*. Klerksdorp: RealNet.

Gaffen, B., 2012. *Klerksdorp Museum. Cultural Heritage Information*. Klerksdorp: Klerksdorp Museum.

Hamann, R., 2004. Corporate social responsibility, partnerships, and institutional change: the case for mining companies in South Africa. *Natural Resources Forum*, 28, pp. 278–290.

IDC (Industrial Development Corporation), 2013. The importance of a conducive environment. Dr Kenneth Kaunda Economic Development Agency, Johannesburg: SALGA, LED Network.

Jacobs, D., 2013. Golden era comes to an end. *Klerksdorp Record*, 9 July.

Lourens, M. 2013. Council adopts new corporate strategy. *Klerksdorp Record*, 8 August.

Marais, L., 2013. The impact of mine downscaling in the Free State Goldfields. *Urban Forum*, 24, pp. 503–521.

Marais, L. and Van der Walt, M., 2011. Mining downscaling: The Matjhabeng case study. Sandton: Industrial Development Corporation (IDC).

Marais, L., Nel, E., Van Rooyen, D. and Lenka, M., 2015. Mine closure, the resource curse and Marikana flu: responses to mine downscaling in Matlosana and Matjhabeng. Pretoria: Economies of Regions Learning Network (ERLN) Conference-Economies of Regions: Economic Development at the Sub-National Level 14–16 October 2015.

Marx, R.1987. *Algemene Geskiedenis: 1937–1987. Klerksdorp Groeiende Reus.* Klerksdorp: Perskor.

Maxim Planning Solutions, 2012. Matlosana socio-economic report. Klerksdorp: Maxim.

Moloko, S., 2012. Developing and bettering our communities: Sustainable development projects 2012–2013, Klerksdorp: AngloGold Ashanti.

Prinsloo, D. 2014. The Human Development Index: where South Africa stands. Johannesburg. Available at: http://www.urbanstudies.co.za/the-human-development-index-where-south-africa-stands/ (accessed 27 September 2015).

Ranthla, T., 2013. Local expert appointed to run affairs in the municipalities. *The New Age*, 19 April, p. 11.

Rogerson, C., 2012. Mining dependent localities in South Africa: The state of partnerships for small town local development. *Urban Forum*, 23(1), pp. 107–132.

RSA (Republic of South Africa), 1998. National Environmental Management Act No. 107 of 1998 (NEMSA). Pretoria: Government Printer.

RSA (Republic of South Africa), 2002. Mineral and Petroleum Resources Development Act No. 28 of 2002 (MPRDA). Pretoria: Government Printer.

SACN (South African Cities Network), 2014. *Outside the Core: Towards Understanding of Intermediate Cities in South Africa.* Johannesburg: SACN.

SA Local Government Research, 2013. Klerksdorp municipal manager faces perjury charge over Eskom debt. SA Local Government Briefing, November.

Schoeman, C., 2008. The process of functional change within mining towns and regions. Unpublished reports, North-West University. Potchefstroom.

Stats SA (Statistics South Africa), 2013. *Census Data for 1996, 2001 and 2011*. Pretoria: Stats SA.

Strongman J. 2000. Mine closure: an overview of issues. Presentation to the government of Indonesia, Mine Closure Workshop, Jakarta, Indonesia, 24 October 2000.

UFS (University of the Free State), 2013. City of Matlosana: city on the move. Bloemfontein: UFS.

World Bank, 2013. *World Development Indicators 2013*. Washington, DC: World Bank. Available at: http://data.worldbank.org/data-catalog/world-development-indicators (accessed October 2013).

4   EMalahleni

*Malène Campbell, Verna Nel and
Thulisile Mphambukeli*

Introduction

EMalahleni, a secondary city located in Mpumalanga Province about 40 km east of
the border of Gauteng Province, South Africa's economic heartland (see Figure 4.1),
owes its fortunes and growth to its abundant coal reserves. Its mines provide the
raw material for energy creation and its coal-driven turbines produce the electricity that keeps South Africa's lights on. EMalahleni's economy has been growing
rapidly for the past two decades due to the country's increasing energy demands
and the local steel industry.

This rapid expansion has led to the development of a range of business and
social facilities, greatly reducing dependence on Gauteng for all but the most
specialised goods and services. However, the recent growth in industry and

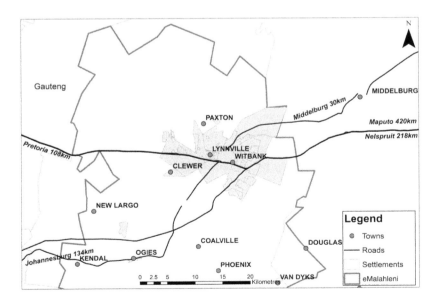

Figure 4.1 Location of eMalahleni

population has outpaced eMalahleni's ability to provide basic services and housing. In addition, the city is struggling with water and air pollution problems, which are compounded by the municipality's governance difficulties: eMalahleni Municipality was placed under government administration in 2013. The case study on which this chapter is based revealed uncontrolled and unplanned growth with very little thought for when the coal reserves run out.

Internationally, mining growth is often associated with the 'resource curse' thesis. This is most often investigated at national level, to the neglect of the local level (Obeng-Odoom, 2014). Some African studies have investigated the relation between mining, development and urbanisation (Bloch and Owusu, 2012; Bryceson and MacKinnon, 2012). International studies have looked at planning for mining decline (Pattison, 2004) and economic revitalisation of former mining areas (Caravelis and Russel, 2001). In South Africa, studies have been done of mining booms (Cloete and Marais, 2009; Cloete et al., 2009; Marais and Cloete, 2013), partnerships in mining towns (Rogerson, 2011, 2012) and the damage caused by mining decline (Binns and Nel, 2001; Nel and Binns, 2002; Nel et al., 2003; Marais, 2013a, 2013b).

EMalahleni provides a good example of the complexities involved in the growth of mining towns and cities. This chapter looks at the pressures that mining growth has placed on eMalahleni and how this secondary city with limited institutional capacity has reacted. We look at the history of the region, current trends in the city today, some pressures it is facing, and its concerns and challenges for the future. Finally we sum up in a brief synthesis.

Historical perspective

This section describes the historical development of eMalahleni. EMalahleni has followed a development path rather similar to that of Emfuleni (Chapter 5) with a similar shared dependence on resource exploitation (which has negative connotations) and value-adding (which has positive connotations). We focus particularly on the coal industry, labour practices and the development of a small but noteworthy steel industry. The section concludes with a discussion of the regional spatial linkages.

Witbank, the main town in eMalahleni, was founded in 1903, declared a town in 1910 and became a city in 1994. The name 'Witbank' referred to a nearby white quartz outcrop. The city was renamed eMalahleni, meaning 'place of coal', in 2006. Initially established because of the area's coal reserves, eMalahleni has been at the heart of the South African coal industry for more than a century. At first, small-scale mining operations transported coal to local markets. But shortly thereafter the completion of the Delagoa Bay railway line connecting Pretoria and the Witwatersrand goldfields with the port of Lourenço Marques (now Maputo) in Mozambique provided the means to transport eMalahleni's coal to a larger market. Along with coal mining, power generation was an important component of the early Witbank economy. By 1920, the Witbank Colliery had acquired a 10-year licence to generate electricity for the town. Eskom, the national power generator, established an office in Witbank in 1923 and started building the Witbank power station in 1925.

As in the gold mining industry, there was a marked racial division of labour on the coal mines. Whites were employed as either 'staff', who received a salary, or 'men', who were paid hourly wages. The latter were either 'miners' (i.e. supervisors of a gang of labourers) or 'mechanics' (skilled workers). Blacks were confined by law to the role of 'labourer' for most of the twentieth century. Workers from Mozambique, recruited by the Witwatersrand Native Labour Association, made up between 45 per cent and 60 per cent of labourers on the region's collieries. Initially, labour conditions were extremely poor, but in 1914, after a strike by migrant Mozambican labourers, the coal industry established minimum conditions of employment. Workers were thereafter permitted to settle near the mines. Women could obtain a permit to live on a colliery: their numbers in 1914 were nearly 25 per cent of the number of black workers living in the Witbank district (Alexander, 2008). Many of the immigrants had families and friends on the Witwatersrand, but Witbank's coal industry provided jobs that were not available in the crowded Transvaal (CDE, 2006). It appears that labourers at Witbank's collieries were more settled and urbanised than those at the gold mines, where migrant labour was the norm. Witbank even set aside land for 'native gardens' (Alexander, 2008).

With the implementation of apartheid legislation in 1948, a strict limit of 3 per cent was set for the percentage of black workers who could be accommodated in 'family housing'. This increased slowly over time, reaching 4.4 per cent in 1984. Others were accommodated in hostels, where male miners shared cramped living quarters. The widespread strike by the National Union of Mineworkers in 1987 calling for the dismantling of the hostel system eventually led to the conversion of former hostels into family housing, which is now firmly entrenched government policy (Lewis, 2003). In practice, however, hostels and migrant labour remain prominent features of South Africa's mining system (Marais and Venter, 2006).

The South African mines' historical dependence on foreign migrant labourers and short-term contracts began to change in the 1980s. By the 1990s, many mineworkers were South Africans who commuted from the 'homelands', the apartheid-created racial reserves within South Africa. More recently the mine workforce has been reverting to its previous composition, with the percentage of Mozambican and Lesotho miners increasing from 25.5 per cent and 8.6 per cent, respectively, in 1991 to 37.4 per cent and 40.4 per cent in 2002 (Lewis, 2003). This may be due to the decline of the gold mining industry, which had historically employed many South Africans (Nel and Binns, 2002).

Marketing by the *Witbank News* in the first half of the twentieth century created awareness of Witbank as a regional industrial centre and helped to attract industries and residents (Singer, 2011). By 1938, in addition to the collieries, the town was also home to several large industries such as the Rand

Carbide Corporation (established in the 1920s), Witbank Engineering, SA Cyanamid and a power station. In addition, several large power stations, constructed as part of the Eskom grid, were operating in the coalfields by 1927 (Singer, 2011).

The development of Highveld Steel began in 1957, when Mineral Engineering of Colorado established a factory to produce vanadium pentoxide. Then, in 1964, Anglo American began construction of an integrated iron and steel mill in Witbank that would be a major catalyst for future development (Witbank News, 2006). According to an interviewee in the private sector, Anglo American's chairman Harry Oppenheimer said in his opening speech in 1968 that building this mill had been 'an act of faith'. The site was chosen because of its proximity to the railway line and the availability of water, coal and power. The development included a railway line from the Mapochs vanadium mine to the steel mill that is still used today. Other industrial developments followed in the 1970s, such as Ferro Metals' ferrosilicon-producing furnace and Afrox's acetylene purification plant (Witbank News, 2006).

From 1895 the Pretoria–Delagoa Bay railway line linked Witbank to the larger South African economy and the international market (Alexander, 2008). The construction of the Delagoa Bay railway line connecting the goldfields and Pretoria with the port of Lourenço Marques (now Maputo) enabled the establishment of the town of eMalahleni, commonly known as Witbank up to 10 years ago, as it provided the means to transport the coal to the market. Much of the area's coal is used locally, but some lower grade thermal coal with low ash and sulphur content is exported to India, China and the European Union.

Witbank's recent history has much to do with its location. It lies on the N4 Maputo Development Corridor, which links South Africa to Mozambique. Following the N4-road that stretches 630 km from Pretoria in Gauteng through Mpumalanga to Maputo in Mozambique, the Corridor is one of the most ambitious development initiatives undertaken in southern Africa. The vision was to rehabilitate the core infrastructure (roads, ports, the electricity network and the border post) in the Corridor through public-private partnerships, thereby re-establishing linkages and opening up under-utilised economic development opportunities. Other policy goals include broadening the ownership base, integrating regional economies and increasing international competitiveness. The governments of South Africa and Mozambique signed protocols to facilitate the implementation of the corridor in July 1996 (Horne, Nelspruit, 2 July 2011).

A study by Campbell et al. (2009) of the Corridor's potential role in wealth creation confirmed that Nelspruit, Witbank, Middelburg and the Highveld Ridge (all on the N4) are major employment centres. These and other towns close to the Corridor have grown at a faster rate than those further away from it, although this pattern is less pronounced in resource-dependent sectors such as agriculture and mining. The Chair of the Afrikaanse Handelsinstituut (Chamber of Commerce for the Afrikaans business community) stated that Witbank did not receive much benefit from the Corridor because the N4 bypasses the Witbank CBD, but both a private and a public sector interviewee said the Corridor has played an important role in Witbank's economic development, as the road and rail networks connecting Witbank to the Maputo and Richards Bay harbours offer export opportunities for coal and steel products. Approximately 20 per cent of coal mined in the area is exported to the global market via Richards Bay.

Current trends and pressures

Although eMalahleni's economy is booming and there is a commensurate increase in employment, the city faces a number of challenges. First, the population has grown rapidly and is currently over 500,000. The city has been unable to provide sufficient bulk water, sewerage or electricity services for the increasing number of residents and as a result these services are fragile, overloaded and unreliable, with frequent water shortages and power outages. Second, although the municipality has provided around 5,300 subsidised housing units, more than 40,000 are still needed. Over 30,000 households live in informal settlements and many others live in backyard shacks, in hostels, on farms and in rental units or rented rooms. As in other mining towns, up to 99 per cent of the rental units are illegal, according to the eMalahleni City Administrator, Theo van Vuuren, who cited one instance of a street with 200 rooms crammed into 16 plots designed for single dwellings. Third, environmental degradation resulting from mining, industry and power generation threatens both the local water supply and that of the entire watershed. Fourth, the roads are in poor condition, a problem exacerbated by the large numbers of heavy vehicles that operate in the area (McCarthy, 2011). Finally, the municipality is under government administration due to its financial problems.

The following sections provide an overview of the municipality's demographics and population change, the economy and employment, social concerns, natural resources and the environment, municipal governance, spatial planning, innovation and skills, and future challenges.

Demographic and population change

Both Mpumalanga and the eMalahleni Municipality have grown over the past two decades. The population of Mpumalanga increased from 3,123,869 in 1996 to 4,039,939 in 2011. This is a 29.3 per cent increase, which is higher than the national population increase of 21.6 per cent over the same period (Stats SA, 2012). Mpumalanga's share of the national population decreased from 7.7 per cent in 1996 to 7.5 per cent in 2001, but then increased to 7.8 per cent in 2011 (CoGTA, 2009; Stats SA, 2012). The net migration of people from other provinces to Mpumalanga between October 2001 and March 2011 was 52,845 (Stats SA, 2012). It is estimated that 2.6 per cent of Mpumalanga residents are not South African citizens (Stats SA, 2012). Much of eMalahleni's population growth is due to South Africa's recent economic growth and the increased demand for coal, which has brought a flood of people seeking jobs in the coal mining industry. In-migrants are also seeking work in the construction of the Kusile power station, the steel manufacturing sector and the growing secondary and tertiary industries. As a result, eMalahleni's population has expanded twofold to threefold in less than two decades.

The economy and employment

The 2006 National Spatial Development Perspective (NSDP) listed Witbank as an area of mass production and specialised economic concentration that should be specifically targeted for public policy interventions to grow the national economy by at least at 6 per cent per annum (RSA, 2006). The National Development Plan also identifies eMalahleni for intervention because of its location on the trans-national Maputo Development Corridor and because it is experiencing rapid growth and has competing interests: mining, water and the environment (RSA, 2012). Meanwhile, the economic importance of eMalahleni has prompted the Mpumalanga provincial government to investigate the possibility of expanding the steel and other metal manufacturing in the area.

The availability of coal, power, water and transport routes has attracted the steel industry. Witbank currently has more than 20 collieries, and several iron and steel plants, including large plants such as Highveld Steel (now Evraz Highveld Steel and Vanadium) and Ferro Metals. Much of the coal mined locally is used by Evraz and by the Duvha and other power stations. These activities have attracted foreign investment. Many international companies have a presence in the area: Anglo American, BHP Billiton, Evraz, Eskom, Exxaro, Joy, Komatsu, the Renova Group, SABMiller, Samancor Chrome, Shanduka Beverages, Xstrata and Zenith (EMalahleni Local Municipality, 2013). Formal employment increased in the Witbank area by about 43 per cent – from 73,437 jobs to more than 105,000 – and informal employment more than tripled from 7,190 to nearly 23,000 jobs over the same period. According to eMalahleni's IDP, the unemployment rate decreased from 38.4 per cent to 27.3 per cent between 1996 and 2011 (Emalahleni Local Municipality, 2013). Table 4.1 shows the changes in employment per standard industrial classification sector between 1996 and 2011 (UFS, 2013). All sectors other than agriculture and energy have grown. Mining and manufacturing (the two largest sectors) have grown rapidly, and employment in the trade and hospitality sector and the finance and real estate sector has almost doubled. Employment in the public services has also increased. A public sector interviewee said that the breakdown of employment growth by sector indicates not only that the economy is growing, but also that the growth appears to be balanced and not solely dependent on mining. However, detailed data on the eMalahleni economy's value chains were not available, hence it was not possible to determine exactly what effect the change in the mining or manufacturing industries could have on other economic sectors.

Table 4.1 Employment per sector in eMalahleni (1996, 2001 and 2011)

Sector	1996		2001		2011	
	N	%	N	%	N	%
Agriculture and forestry	3,390	4.6	3,552	4.8	2,864	2.7
Mining	17,120	23.2	15,985	21.4	25,318	24.1
Manufacturing	14,388	19.6	12,383	16.6	17,591	16.8
Energy	4,336	5.9	4,142	5.5	3,981	3.8
Construction	3,267	4.5	3,381	4.5	5,678	5.4
Trade and hospitality	7,857	10.7	9,725	13.0	14,512	13.8
Transport and communication	3,934	5.4	3,772	5.0	4,844	4.6
Finance and real estate	3,399	4.6	4,566	6.1	7,893	7.5
Public services	7,590	10.3	9,341	12.5	12,810	12.2
Other services and households	8,156	11.2	7,933	10.6	9,528	9.1
Total	73,437	100.0	74,780	100.0	105,019	100.0

Source: UFS (2013).

Agriculture is the largest employer in the province. Since 1996 Mpumalanga has contributed roughly 12 per cent of national employment in the agricultural sector. However, in the eMalahleni municipality, which includes the city formerly known as Witbank and surrounding rural areas, agriculture has shown a persistent decline in terms of both GVA and employment. As far back as the 1920s, the coal mining industry took precedence over agricultural, environmental and other concerns (Singer, 2011), and land that could be used for agriculture was often put to other uses. Although only 2 per cent of the 872,000 hectares of Class II agricultural land in Mpumalanga has been converted to other uses, there are prospecting applications and rights on a further 86 per cent of this land. A similar trend applies to the 2 million hectares of Class III land: only 2 per cent has been removed from agricultural production, but there are prospecting applications and rights on another 68 per cent, implying that up to 70 per cent of this land could be removed from agricultural production. If we apply these provincial figures to eMalahleni, we can see that most of the land in the municipality could be subject to prospecting or mining. Clearly a balance needs to be struck between the needs for energy, exports (to earn foreign reserves) and food security.

The main economic sectors in terms of employment in eMalahleni are coal mining, steel manufacturing, energy generation, retail, wholesale and hospitality. Coal mining is the largest industry in eMalahleni and one of the oldest. Much of the area's coal is mined using open cast methods. Underground 'bord and pillar' and other processes are also used (Mining Weekly, 2010), but the 'bord and pillar' method leaves up to half of the coal seam in place (Eberhard, 2011).[1] The eMalahleni and Highveld coalfields combined produce about 80 per cent of the country's coal, which is almost entirely from large-scale producers (Blignaut et al., 2011; Eberhard, 2011). Among the large international companies operating mines in the area are Anglo American, Exxaro, Sasol, BHP Billiton and Xstrata (EMalahleni Local Municipality, 2013). Several smaller companies are also present in eMalahleni, both black economic empowerment and foreign-owned, operating the smaller and older mines that have been abandoned by the bigger companies as unprofitable (Mining Weekly, 2010).

Social concerns

The social issues faced by the city are best understood in the context of its history. EMalahleni has always been a mining and industrial centre. Apartheid laws shaped its spatial structure and led to the current acute housing shortage. Informal settlements are growing, illegal rental arrangements are rife, affordable housing is urgently needed, and service delivery has not kept pace. In a 2003 survey of mineworkers, housing conditions were found to be correlated with their sense of safety at work: those living in single-sex and family unit hostels were less concerned about safety than those with rental or bond subsidies. Nonetheless, insecurity and violence were major concerns, as were transport difficulties and commuting time for those not living on the mines' premises (Lewis, 2003). The post-1994 national housing policy has focused on family housing, including the conversion of hostels into family units, but the mining industry has not produced a coherent plan for mine housing (Lewis, 2003). Mining corporations and local governments sometimes form partnerships to provide housing, but in many cases it is the municipality's responsibility to provide housing and basic services.

The housing shortage aside, economic growth has had positive consequences. The area's poverty rate decreased from 34.6 per cent in 2007 to 26.2 per cent in 2011, and the unemployment rate from 29.9 per cent to 27.9 per cent over the same period, despite the increase in population (EMalahleni Local Municipality, 2013). Emalahleni's score on the Human Development Index has consistently been higher than the national average, increasing from 0.63 in 1996 to 0.71 in 2011 (UFS, 2013). The area's Gini coefficient increased from 0.52 in 1996 to 0.61 in 2011 and income appears to be increasing across the board (UFS, 2013). Educational attainment has also increased, with a corresponding decrease in the number of people with no schooling (Stats SA, 2012). The percentage of people with a tertiary qualification has also increased, from 1.02 per cent in 1996 to 2.3 per cent in 2011 (Stats SA 2012), but these people may not be in the sectors most needed by the South African economy (RSA, 2012).

Natural resources and the environment

The coal industry has had a severe environmental impact in the region, as have the activities of the region's other major industries, steel and energy. Among the various problems are water pollution from acid mine drainage, air pollution and spontaneous combustion in mines and dumps, which releases dangerous chemicals and causes ground subsidence (Bell et al., 2001). These problems will affect the region for decades to come, influencing the future development of not only eMalahleni but the entire Olifants river watershed.

In 2010, the Mpumalanga coalfields were identified as a priority area for immediate intervention to prevent acid mine drainage from contaminating fresh water sources (DME, 2010). Polluted water can be desalinated by reverse osmosis, but the costs of the process are extremely high (McCarthy, 2011). A panel of experts appointed to advise an inter-ministerial committee warned against a 'one size fits all' approach to dealing with acid mine drainage. They instead provided detailed recommendations on how to prevent mine water from pouring over into fresh water sources and how to manage water quality (DME, 2010). The eMalahleni Water Reclamation Plant, commissioned in 2007, desalinates rising underground water from Anglo American Thermal Coal's collieries using HI recovery precipitating reverse osmosis (HiPro) (Hidalgo et al., 2013). In 2012 the mining industry put further plans on the table to decontaminate acid mine water in Mphumalanga (De Lange, 2011), but an interviewee at a tertiary institution said the extent of the future problem is still being debated.

The air pollution that has affected Witbank for many years has been found to be correlated with detrimental health effects (Blignaut et al., 2011). Various studies have identified high levels of nitrogen dioxide, sulphur dioxide, benzene, toluene, ethylbenzene and ozone over Witbank. These contribute to asthma and bronchitis and also cause damage to vegetation (Lourens, 2011). Other pollutants found in high concentrations are chromium and barium (Sejake, 2013). Action is currently being taken to deal with the air pollution. In 2007 the Minister of Environmental Affairs and Tourism proclaimed the greater eMalahleni region a national air pollution hotspot, the 'Highveld Priority Area', in terms of the National Environmental Management: Air Quality Act (No. 39 of 2004). As a result, by enforcing the use of catalytic converters in vehicles and emission standards for incinerators, the national government has now taken responsibility for monitoring, managing and mitigating air pollution in conjunction with local and provincial governments (Lourens, 2011).

Self-sustaining coal fires – both underground and at mine dumps – have plagued eMalahleni for years. Often caused by the spontaneous combustion of coal as oxygen enters a mine, these fires release toxic chemicals such as arsenic, mercury, toluene, benzene and xylene, some of which are carcinogenic (Pone et al., 2007; De Lange, 2011). Apart from the long-term threat, there is the more immediate threat of ground subsidence in areas where coal fires are burning underground, and several informal settlements are located on top of these areas.

Municipal governance

The eMalahleni municipality is currently under administration as a result of mismanagement, corruption and lack of service delivery. In 2009 the municipality had already been identified as being in financial distress. The following excerpts from a government report reveal the poor state of municipal governance:

The lack of values, principles or ethics in these cases indicates that there are officials and public representatives for whom public service is not a concern, but accruing wealth at the expense of poor communities is their priority . . . [Communities are frustrated] over poor institutionalisation of systems, poor service delivery and poor political governance. A culture of patronage and nepotism is now so widespread in many municipalities that the formal municipal accountability system is ineffective and inaccessible to many citizens.

(CoGTA, 2009, p.10)

Theo van Vuuren was appointed the administrator of eMalahleni in April 2013. Within a month he had prepared a draft turnaround strategy noting the following problems (Van Vuuren, 2013):

- high levels of corruption by councillors and staff alike, '*wat 'n ryk munisi-paliteit bankrot gesteel het*' ('who robbed a rich municipality to the verge of bankruptcy');
- excessive charges and payments for goods and services;
- a militant union, with members reluctant to work, controlling the municipality;
- acute financial problems, including an audit disclaimer;
- an inefficient and ineffective administration that did not plan for population growth or increased development;
- an unresponsive council with poor community engagement;
- the near collapse of service delivery, leading to frequent complaints from residents and businesses;
- lack of capacity to provide bulk services; and
- a number of firms and residents (who could afford to do so) moving to Middelburg (Steve Tshwete Municipality), resulting in the loss of potential revenue for the city.[2]

Spatial planning

The international post-positivist shift of the past three decades has seen a move from rationalist theories and methods in urban planning to an increased emphasis on the role of communication, power and discourse (Allmendinger, 2009; Coetzee, 2012). Urban planning is concerned with the city of the future and the implications for its people (Hiller and Gunder, 2003; Coetzee, 2012) and is supposed to prioritise improving the quality of places for the people who have to live and work in them (Healey, 2007; Nel, 2011). Although neoliberalism is hostile to many aspects of state-led planning and condemns planning as an imperfect product of modernity, the neoliberals do agree that a form of land use control is needed (Allmendinger, 2009; Nel, 2011). Land-use management, or 'development control' as it was called in the past, was associated with control. The current aim is to link spatial planning and development facilitation with development control to create a system of land-use management (Nel, 2011).

Plans must be locally appropriate while also addressing the social context (Harrison, 2006; Todes, 2011) and implementing the plans should ideally be a process of negotiation and trade-offs (Harrison, 2006; Healey, 2007). Planning should be an interactive process that will improve the quality of places, making them socially inclusive and fair to all residents (Mphambukeli, 2012). Planners are supposed to consider how their interventions affect people and to understand the local dynamics and context (Healey, 2007). Diversity is an important aspect of urban life and should not be ignored in governance strategies. The government should focus on the quality of urban areas and consider how their place-shaping interventions might affect people (Healey, 2007). South Africa's spatial development framework (SDF) has long reflected this normative approach (DLA, 2001).

However, the reality is very different. The five-year municipal IDP and accompanying SDF have been described as 'increasingly stale', 'standardised', 'guideline-driven' and 'mechanistic', with a 'user-unfriendly presentation style' and 'voluminous form' (Oranje, 2014) and not very successful in achieving their goals (Du Plessis, 2013; Du Plessis and Boonzaaier, 2015).

These criticisms can be applied to eMalahleni's planning. Although the city's IDP contains a spatial analysis chapter that discusses 'key development projects per node' (Chapter 10), it does not appear to contain an SDF, nor does it say how the municipality plans to accommodate future growth or decline, or mitigate environmental degradation (EMalahleni Local Municipality, 2013). Van Vuuren (2013) was extremely critical of the planning department for not anticipating population or economic growth and thus failing to prepare the city for the problems it now faces.

An official in the planning department said the SDF has been neglected for some time. Whereas the IDP is a five-year plan focusing on short-term goals and should guide councils for their term of office, the SDF is a 10- to 30-year projection of economic growth. Ideally, an IDP focuses on short-term goals that help a municipality reach the long-term vision of an SDF, and projects should help to grow the economy and integrate communities. In eMalahleni, however, this has not been the case. Instead, according to a public sector interviewee, the council has focused on projects that might have immediate payoffs. An interviewee in the municipal planning department said that, since there is no appropriate SDF in place with a long-range vision, many of the municipality's objectives cannot be implemented because the IDP envisages only a five-year period.

A planning department official pointed out that spatial planning could create opportunities for investment, particularly in the townships. According to this official, when one investor enters an area, for instance the Shoprite retail group, others will follow, creating employment opportunities and boosting economic growth. A World Bank Studies publication (Sandeep, 2014) confirms the potential of township economies. When a city has land available, it should be described in the municipality's SDF as a proposed industrial or commercial hub in order to attract investors. An interviewee in the public sector said that in eMalahleni such areas should be in both the eastern (more affluent) and the western (less affluent) suburbs.

Mining determined the initial location of eMalahleni and continues to influence its development, and apartheid planning caused the fragmentation of the residential areas that persists today. The vast Kwa-Guqa area is isolated from the city centre, with limited road access worsened by the multiple streams that separate this area from other residential areas. The nearby industrial area of Ferrobank and the mine dumps also contribute to Kwa-Guqa's spatial isolation. Ackerville, Lynville, Thushanag and the large informal settlement to the north of these settlements are separated from the CBD only by a railway line and thus enjoy better access to the CBD. Lower-income housing is situated largely to the west of the city centre, although there are pockets of informal housing to the south-east as well. To the north is low- to middle-income housing, including informal settlements and the mixed income Klarinet development, and the area around Duvha (which was originally built as artisan housing) also has middle-income housing. The upper-income areas are to the east of the city. This spatial configuration separates the poorer communities from the richer both physically and economically, and limits access to the employment opportunities in the CBD and to the wealthier residential areas (Turok, 2010; Kihato, 2014).

Innovation and skills

Generating new products and processes is important for sustaining regional development, boosting local economies, encouraging competitiveness and making communities more prosperous (Turok, 2010; World Bank, 2010; Hague et al., 2011).

EMalahleni's economy has always been based on coal extraction, power generation and other primary industries. While these sectors have undoubtedly been innovative to some extent in making their processes more efficient, the region's industries as a whole are not particularly innovative. Indeed, one of the main problems identified in the local iron and steel industry is the lack of innovation, research and development, and skills (Van Vuuren, 2013). As proof of this, specialist skills and equipment had to be imported from foreign companies for the construction of the Kusile power station (EMalahleni Local Municipality, 2013). Even the skills needed to maintain and rehabilitate the municipal infrastructure appear to be in short supply. Thus, although the availability of a ready pool of skilled labour is one of the typical characteristics of a secondary city, eMalahleni falls short in this regard. In addition to public and private schools there is a University of Pretoria Campus as well as a campus of the Technical University of Tshwane (TUT), but the lack of innovative industries and limited tertiary education available in the city are holding it back.

EMalahleni's future challenges

Despite South Africa's heavy dependence on coal for energy production, there is no specific national 'coal policy' that addresses greenhouse gas emissions, the declining coal reserves in the Highveld basin or the nation's long-term energy needs (Eberhard, 2011). This makes the area and its residents vulnerable in a range of areas, from environment to employment. Within the industry, however, and particularly within the eMalahleni region, there are growing concerns about the future of coal mining, given that the economically exploitable reserves are dwindling (Mining Weekly, 2010). There are other reserves, but the estimated extent of these is being revised downwards, with some estimates indicating a peak as early as 2020 (Hartnady, 2010).

In eMalahleni as in many parts of Africa and in other regions globally, such as northern Canada (Jackson and Illsley, 2006), the economy is based on exports of primary products. Being dependent on a single activity leaves the economy vulnerable (O'Faircheallaigh, 1992; Caravelis and Russel, 2001). In many parts of South Africa these primary products are minerals and energy, and these are now declining in some areas because of increased production costs or the depletion of the resources. Historically, it was argued that cities grow and become economically diverse through import substitution – replacing goods they formerly imported with goods they manufacture themselves (Jacobs, 1985). Policy responses to the 1960s model of import substitution not only discourage the export of primary products but also encourage a shift towards diversification of manufactured exports (Le Pere and Ikome, 2009; Rodrigues, 2010). An example is Tumbler Ridge in British Columbia, which was forced to diversify its economic base when it lost its commodity markets and has since been referred to as 'the mining town that refuses to die' (Jackson and Illsley, 2006, p. 163).

The probable future decommissioning of old coal-fired power stations as a result of declining coal reserves and commitments to decrease greenhouse gas emissions is another risk for eMalahleni (Eberhard, 2011). Therefore, although the closure of eMalahleni's coal mines is not imminent, the municipality should start planning now for a post-coal-mining future. Planning for closure is critical, as the closing down of mines has detrimental consequences for a whole community, especially when the mines are among the largest employers in the area (Gilbert, 1995; Caravelis and Russel, 2001; Stephenson and Wry, 2005; Cloete and Marais, 2009; Marais and Cloete, 2013). In contexts such as these local role players are often ill-equipped to generate post-mining economies (O'Faircheallaigh, 1992). The magnitude of mine downscaling can be such that it would be unfair to expect local initiatives alone to absorb the impact (World Bank, 2002). Years after the closing down of mines in Romania, Russia and the Ukraine the former employees still struggle to find permanent employment and wages that compare favourably with those previously earned on the mines (Haney and Shkaratan, 2003). Increased unemployment has also decreased the standard of living in the affected areas (Morar, 2011).

The downscaling of mining not only affects local residents but also has direct implications for the local government (Petkova et al., 2009; Marais and Cloete, 2013). During the boom period the demand for housing, basic services such as water and sanitation, and social facilities such as schools grows rapidly; only to wane as the population declines through out-migration. The investment in infrastructure becomes a heavy burden on the municipality as the ability of the residents to contribute to its maintenance diminishes (Marais and Cloete, 2013).

The mining industry's long history of serious environmental impacts such as spontaneous combustion of mines and mine dumps, air and water pollution, and acid mine drainage (Bell et al., 2001), has been discussed above.

The South African steel industry, the largest in Africa, contributed R12.7 billion to the country's GDP (0.6 per cent) and R4 billion to the national fiscus in 2008. This was despite having shed more than 5,500 jobs between 2002 and 2008; in 2008 only 12,800 people were directly employed by the industry, down from 18,400 people in 2002 (Kumba Iron Ore, 2011; Dednam, 2013). Currently, however, there is excess production capacity, partly because of flat demand for steel products internationally and the limited range produced by the South African steel industry (Kumba Iron Ore, 2011). Other problems faced by the steel industry are competition from foreign imports, lack of innovation, research and development, and an acute skills shortage (Dednam, 2013). Most of the steel produced in the eMalahleni area consists of primary and semi-finished products such as slabs (used for manufacturing heavy equipment), hot and cold rolled coils (used for light manufacturing, e.g. 'white appliances') and heavy sections (such as I-beams) (Dednam, 2013).

Steel is currently in a scenario of oversupply globally and South Africa's steel industry is at risk (Van Rensburg, 2015). Evraz Highveld Steel and Vanadium has been eMalahleni's main steel producer since 1957, with production in 2008 being approximately 0.8 MT (Kumba Iron Ore, 2011), which decreased to 0.6 MT in 2011 (Evraz Highveld Steel and Vanadium, 2012). The company's Emalahleni facilities were designed to process iron ore with high vanadium content from the Mapochs mine, which produces both vanadium and steel. A private sector interviewee said that while this company's annual reports paint a glowing picture, some local role players criticise its lack of engagement with the community, weak adherence to pollution control standards and poor quality products, and describe the management as 'a bunch of cowboys'. Currently Evraz Highveld Steel 'seeks bidders for its assets after running out of cash' and is going to retrench about 1,200 of its employees (Van Rensburg, 2015)

Another large steel plant in eMalahleni is Ferro Metals, owned by Samancor Chrome. When established in 1959 it was one of the largest chrome producers in the world, and it still employed over 500 people in 2008 (Samancor Chrome, 2008). Built on coal and sustained by mining and coal-related industries, eMalahleni has developed into a strong regional centre. However, it is the future of the mining industry, the social-ecological impacts of mining, and the manner in which these impacts are managed that will ultimately determine eMalahleni's future.

In order to address the problems – and realise the potential – of the region's steel and iron industries, the Mpumalanga Provincial Government, in partnership with the South African Iron and Steel Institute, is exploring the possibility of establishing a Steel and Metals Fabrication Hub between eMalahleni and Middelburg. The goals of the Hub would be to train entrepreneurs and emerging producers in the industry, to provide newly established and existing small businesses with support services to increase their survival rates and profitability, and to generate a larger return on investment from manufacturing and road infrastructure (Dednam, 2013).

According to Global Insight data, employment in the electricity sector accounted for slightly fewer than 4,000 jobs but 15 per cent of the municipality's GVA in 2011 (UFS, 2013). This employment figure excludes jobs related to the construction of the nearby Kusile power station. More than 70 per cent of South Africa's electricity is derived from coal-burning power stations operated by Eskom (which supplies over 84 per cent of the country's electricity) (Blignaut et al., 2011), and around 53 per cent of the 224 million tons of coal mined annually in South Africa is used for electricity generation (Eskom, 2013). In 2009 roughly 21 per cent of all power generated through coal-fuelled power stations was generated in Duvha (3450 MW) and Kendal (3840 MW) (Eberhard, 2011). Consequently, the electricity and coal industries are inextricably linked, and any assessment of the environmental implications of electricity production should take into account the consequences of both mining and burning coal (Blignaut et al., 2011). Planning for a future with radically reduced dependence on coal must commence now. It requires developing other industries – preferably those with a lower ecological footprint than eMalahleni's current economic drivers. There will have to be a move from the current dependence on primary industries to secondary and tertiary sectors.

Synthesis

Several intertwined themes emerge from this chapter. First, eMalahleni is experiencing economic growth and reduced unemployment because of the current coal mining boom. One role of a secondary city is to create a balanced settlement milieu and contribute to national economic growth, and eMalahleni has managed to do this. Second, because of its economic growth, the city's population is expanding faster than the national average, and the municipality has been unable to provide adequate infrastructure and services. Third, despite this, the future of coal mining is unclear, and any changes in the mining industry will have a serious effect on the local economy. And finally, mining and industry have had negative implications for the physical environment.

While the rapid population growth has certainly contributed to the city's service delivery crisis, the problem has been exacerbated by inept and corrupt municipal governance. Little attention has been paid to maintaining or extending infrastructure or services. Consequently, the city's growing economy has been fettered by a demoralised and dysfunctional local government. Traffic problems, frequent power failures, and water shortages due to burst pipes are driving investors, businesses and residents from the town. Lawlessness abounds, including traffic offences, illegal development and illegal utility connections. What is worse, the lawlessness extends beyond just residents and small businesses to include some of the major corporations.

Although the region will continue to grow over the medium term because of the current mining boom, the city's long-term growth will depend on the quality of its service delivery and finances and the future prospects of mining and manufacturing. A commitment to improved municipal governance and administration, combined with adequate funds from the national and provincial governments, will be necessary for eMalahleni to resolve its infrastructure crisis and become a developmental local government.

EMalahleni was built on coal mining and power generation, and as long as the coal lasts the economy should do well. Currently, mining contributes 47 per cent of the municipality's GVA, and it will probably continue to make a substantial economic contribution for the next decade or two. However, given revised estimates of South African coal reserves, it is possible that extraction will peak in 10 to 20 years and thereafter decline. The resultant mine downscaling will affect not only the region but the province and the nation as well, as eMalahleni is one of the country's primary coal-producing areas. The resulting social effects are likely to be very similar to those experienced in the Free State Goldfields.

Planning for a future with radically reduced dependence on coal must commence now. Other industries should be developed, preferably those with a smaller ecological footprint than eMalahleni's current major industries. The region should also move away from the current dependence on primary industries and focus more on the secondary and tertiary sectors. Options include going ahead with the Steel and Metals Fabrication Hub, promoting the improvement of steel and iron products and forming a manufacturing cluster. Another option, given its favourable location on the Maputo Development Corridor, is positioning the city as a transport and distribution centre,.

There is a big risk that eMalahleni is heading towards environmental collapse because of the over-exploitation of the ecosystem and the environmental degradation of the past century. Acid mine drainage is one pressing problem that must be confronted. Although the extent of the problem is still being debated, it will increase as mines begin to close, leaving their legacy of environmental degradation. But, although the city is facing a risk of environmental collapse due to resource exploitation, its healthy coal exports mean it has opportunities too. Its fate will depend on strategic role players (the private sector, government and civil society) working together to capitalise on the current economic growth through appropriate planning for a positive future for eMalahleni.

Notes

1 The 'bord' in this method is the 'roadway' between the pillars of the coal seam that are left standing.
2 This last point could be a contributing factor to the positive economic performance of Steve Tshwete Municipality, which showed the biggest growth of all the municipalities in the Mphumalanga Province in GVA between 1996 and 2011 (Borel-Saladin and Turok, 2013).

References

Alexander, P., 2008. Challenging cheap labour theory: Natal and Transvaal coal miners 1890–1950. *Labor History*, 49(1), pp. 47–70.
Allmendinger, P., 2009. *Planning Theory*. Basingstoke: Palgrave MacMillan.
Bell, F., Bullock, S., Hälbach, T. and Lindsay, P., 2001. Environmental impacts associated with an abandoned mine in the Witbank Coalfield, South Africa. *International Journal of Coal Geology*, 45, pp. 195–216.
Binns, T. and Nel, E., 2001. Gold loses its shine: decline and response in the South African goldfields. *Geography*, 86, pp. 255–260.

Blignaut, J., Nkambule, N., Riekert, J. and Lotz, R., 2011. Coal and coal fired power generation in South Africa: the external cost of coal-fired power generation: the case of Kusile. Johannesburg: Greenpeace Africa.

Bloch, A. and Owusu, G., 2012. Linkages in Ghana's gold mining industry: challenging the enclave thesis. *Resources Policy*, 37, pp. 434–442.

Borel-Saladin, J. M. and Turok, I. N., 2013. The green economy: incremental change or Transformation? *Environment, Politics and Governance*, 23, pp. 209–220.

Bryceson, D. and MacKinnon, D., 2012. Eureka and beyond: mining's impact on African urbanisation. *Journal of Contemporary African Studies*, 30(4), pp. 513–537.

Campbell, M., Maritz, J. and Hauptfleisch, A., 2009. The impact of the Maputo Development Corridor on wealth creation within the region it serves. Leuven: Regional Studies Association Conference, Understanding and Shaping Regions: Spatial, Social and Economic Futures.

Caravelis, M. and Russel, I., 2001. From mining community to seasonal visitor destination: The transformation of Sotiras. Thasos, Greece. *European Planning Studies*, 9(2), pp. 187–199.

CDE (Centre for Development and Enterprise), 2006. *Immigrants in South Africa, Perceptions and Reality in Witbank, a Medium-sized Industrial Town.* Johannesburg: CDE.

Cloete, J. and Marais, L., 2009. Mining and housing: the case of the village under the trees. *Town and Regional Planning*, 55, pp. 31–38.

Cloete, J., Venter, A. and Marais, L., 2009. Breaking new ground, social housing and mineworker housing: the missing link. *Town and Regional Planning*, 54, p. 27–36.

Coetzee, J., 2012. The transformation of municipal development planning in South Africa (post-1994): impressions and impasse. *Town and Regional Planning*, 61, pp. 10–20.

CoGTA (Department of Cooperative Governance and Traditional Affairs), 2009. *State of Local Government in South Africa. Overview report.* Pretoria: CoGTA.

De Lange, I., 2011. Tit-for-tat mine spat in court BECSA defunct workings at Witbank Colliery. *Citizen*, 25 August, p. 4.

Dednam, C., 2013. The primary steel industry in South Africa: Business plan proposal for the establishment of the Mpumalanga steel and metal fabrication hub. Presentation on behalf of SAISI to Mpumalanga Provincial Government, 23 July 2013, Nelspruit.

DLA (Department of Land Affairs), 2001. *Wise Land Use: White Paper on spatial planning and land use management.* Pretoria: Department of Land Affairs.

DME (Department of Minerals and Energy), 2010. Mine water management in the Witwatersrand gold fields with special emphasis on acid mine drainage. Unpublished report to the inter-ministerial committee on acid mine drainage, Pretoria: DME.

Du Plessis, D. J., 2013. A critical reflection on urban spatial planning practices and outcomes in post-apartheid South Africa. *Urban Forum*, 25(1), pp. 69–88.

Du Plessis, D. and Boonzaaier, I., 2015. The evolving spatial structure of South African cities: A reflection on the influence of spatial planning policies. *International Planning Studies*, 20(1–2), pp. 87–111.

Eberhard, A., 2011. *The Future of South African Coal: Market, Investment and Policy Challenges.* Stanford: Stanford University Press.

EMalahleni Local Municipality, 2013. Integrated Development Plan, 2011–2016. Witbank: eMalahleni Local Municipality.

Eskom, 2013. *Coal power,* Available at: http://www.eskom.co.za/c/article/200/coal-power (accessed 11 June 2014).

Evraz Highveld Steel and Vanadium, 2012. Integrated Annual report. Available at: http://www.evrazhighveld.co.za/annual_reports/Highveld_Steel_And_Vanadium_2011_Integrated_Annual_Report_2012-04-16.pdf (accessed 21 May 2014).

Gilbert, D., 1995. Imagined communities and mining communities. *Labour History Review*, 60(2), pp. 47–55.

Hague, C., Hague, E. and Breitbach, C., 2011. *Regional and Local Economic Development.* Basingstoke: Palgrave MacMillan.

Haney, M. and Shkaratan, M., 2003. *Mine Closure and its Impact on the Community. Five Years after Mine Closure in Romania, Russia and Ukraine.* Washington: World Bank.

Harrison, P., 2006. Integrated development plans and third way politics. In: U. Pillay, R. Tomlinson and J. Du Toit, eds. *Democracy and Delivery: Urban Policy in South Africa.* Cape Town: HSRC Press, pp. 186–207.

Hartnady, C., 2010. South Africa's diminishing coal reserves. *South African Journal of Science*, 106(9/10), pp. 1–5.

Healey, P., 2007. *Urban Complexity and Spatial Strategies: Towards a Relational Planning for Our Times.* London: Routledge.

Hidalgo, C., Peterson, K., Smith, D. and Foley, H., 2013. AngloAmerican eMalahleni water reclamation plant. Available at: https://sharedvalue.org/groups/anglo-american-emalahleni-water-reclamation-plant (accessed 23 October 2013).

Hiller, J. and Gunder, M., 2003. Planning fantasies? An exploration of a potential Lacanian framework for understanding development. *Planning Theory*, 23(3), pp. 225–248.

Horne, B. 2011. Chief Executive Officer of the Maputo Corridor Logistics Initiative (MCLI). Personal interview on the Maputo Development Corridor. Nelspruit: South Africa, 2 July.

Jackson, T. and Illsley, B., 2006. Tumbler Ridge, British Columbia: the mining town that refused to die. *Journal of Transatlantic Studies*, 4(2), pp. 163–186.

Jacobs, J., 1985. *Cities and the Wealth of Nations: Principles of Economic Life.* New York: Vintage Books.

Kihato, C., 2014. Lost dreams? Tales of the South African city twenty years after apartheid. *African Identities*, 12(3–4), pp. 357–370.

Kumba Iron Ore, 2011. The South African iron ore and steel value chain. Downloaded from: www.kumba.co.za/SIOC/pdf/iron_ steel_sec1.pdf:. Kumba Iron Ore (accessed 15 October 2013).

Le Pere, G. and Ikome, F., 2009. Challenges and prospects for economic development in Africa. *Asia-Pacific Review*, 16(2), pp. 89–144.

Lewis, P., 2003. Housing and occupational health and safety in the South African mining industry. Pretoria: Report prepared for the Safety in Mines Research Advisory Committee (SIMRAC) by CSIR Miningtek.

Lourens, A., 2011. Spatial and temporal assessment of gaseous pollutants in the Highveld of South Africa. *South African Journal of Science*, 107(1/2), pp. 1–8.

Marais, L., 2013a. The impact of mine downscaling on the Free State Goldfields. *Urban Forum*, 24, pp. 503–521.

Marais, L., 2013b. Resources policy and mine closure in South Africa: The case of the Free State Goldfields. *Resources Policy*, 38, pp. 363–372.

Marais, L. and Cloete, J., 2013. Labour migration, settlement and mine closure in South Africa. *Geography*, 98(2), pp. 77–84.

Marais, L. and Venter, A., 2006. Hating the compound, but . . . mineworker housing needs in post-apartheid South Africa. *Africa Insight*, 36(1), pp. 53–62.

McCarthy, J., 2011. The impact of acid mine drainage in South Africa. *South African Journal of Science*, 107(5/6), pp. 1–7.

Mining Weekly, 2010. A brief look at SAs coal mining industry. *Mining Weekly*. Available at: http://www.miningweekly.com/article/a-brief-look-at-sas-coal-mining-industry-2010-09-03 (accessed 12 December 2013).

Morar, C., 2011. Several social impacts of mine closures in the disadvantaged areas of Bihor County, Romania. *Forum Geographic*, 10(2), pp. 303–311.

Mphambukeli, T., 2012. Social justice in planning: A case study of the eThekwini Municipality IDP. Perm, Russia, Social Justice in Planning 48th ISOCARP International Congress, 10–13 September.

Nel, E. and Binns, T., 2002. Decline and response in South Africa's Free State Goldfields: local economic development in Matjhabeng. *International Development Planning Review*, 24(3), pp. 249–269.

Nel, E., Hill, T., Aitchison, K. and Buthelezi, S., 2003. The closure of coal mines and local development responses in the Coal-Rim Cluster, northern KwaZulu-Natal, South Africa. *Development Southern Africa*, 20, pp. 369–385.

Nel, V., 2011. Land-use management system as a tool towards achieving low-carbon cities in South Africa. *Town and Regional Planning*, 58, pp. 1–5.

O'Faircheallaigh, C., 1992. Mine closures in remote regions: policy options and implications. In: C. Neil and M. B. J. Tykkyläinen, eds. *Coping with Closure: an International Comparison of Mine Town Experiences*. London: Routledge, pp. 347–368.

Obeng-Odoom, F., 2014. *Oiling the Urban Economy: Land, Labour Capital and the State in Sekondi-Takoradi, Ghana*. London: Routledge.

Oranje, M., 2014. Back to where it all began . . .? Reflections on injecting the (spiritual) ethos of the early town planning movement into planning, planners and plans in post-1994 South Africa. *HTS Theological Studies*, 70(3), pp. 1–10.

Pattison, G., 2004. Planning for decline: the 'D'-village policy of County Durham, UK. *Planning Perspectives*, 19(3), pp. 311–332.

Petkova, V., Lockie, S., Rolfe, J. and Ivanova, G., 2009. Mining development and social impacts on communities: Bowen Basin case studies. *Rural Society*, 19(3), pp. 211–228.

Pone, J., Hein, K., Stracher, G., Annegram, H., Finkleman, R., Blake, D., McCormack, J., Schroeder, J., 2007. The spontaneous combustion of coal and its by-products in the Witbank and Sasolburg coalfields of South Africa. *International Journal of Coal Geology*, 72, pp. 124–140.

Rodrigues, M., 2010. Import substitution and economic growth. *Journal of Monetary Economics*, 57, pp. 175–188.

Rogerson, C., 2011. Mining enterprise and partnerships for socio-economic development. *African Journal of Business Management*, 5(14), pp. 5405–5417.

Rogerson, C., 2012. Mining-dependent localities in South Africa: the state of partnerships for small town local development. *Urban Forum*, 23, pp. 107–132.

RSA (Republic of South Africa), 2006. *National Spatial Development Perspective*. Pretoria: Government Printer.

RSA (Republic of South Africa), 2012. *National Development Plan*. Pretoria: Government Printer.

SACN (South African Cities Network), 2014. *Outside the Core: Towards Understanding of Intermediate Cities in South Africa*. Johannesburg: SACN.

Samancor Chrome, 2008. Our business – operations and locations. Available at: http://www.samancorcr.com/content.asp?subID=8 (accessed 11 June 2014).

Sandeep, M., 2014. *Economics of South African Townships: Special Focus on Diepsloot*. Washington, DC: World Bank Studies.

Sejake, L., 2013. Witbank air the dirtiest in the world. *City Press*, 25 April, p. 3.

Singer, M., 2011. Towards 'a different kind of beauty': Responses to coal-based pollution in the Witbank Coalfield between 1903 and 1948. *Journal of Southern African Studies*, 37(2), pp. 282–296.

Stats SA (Statistics South Africa), 2012. *Census Data, 1996, 2001 and 2011.* Pretoria: Stats SA.

Stephenson, C. and Wry, D., 2005. Emotional regeneration through community action in post-industrial mining communities: the New Herrington miners' banner partnership. *Capital and Class*, 29(3), pp. 175–199.

Todes, A., 2011. Reinventing planning: Critical reflections. *Urban Forum*, 22, pp. 115–133.

Turok, I., 2010. The prospects of African urban economies. *Urban Research and Africa*, 3(1), pp. 12–24.

UFS (University of the Free State), 2013. *EMalahleni.* Bloemfontein: UFS.

Van Rensburg, D., 2015. Steel industry melts: 'bleeding' ArcelorMittal ponders its future as it joins other role players feeling the heat of China's oversupply. *City Press*, 26 July, p. 1.

Van Vuuren, T., 2013. EMalahleni: assessment, turnaround strategy and progress report. Witbank: Presentation to the eMalahleni Local Council.

Witbank News, 2006. Witbank – the city of black gold. *Witbank News*, 24 November.

World Bank, 2002. *It's Not Over When it's Over: Mine Closure Around the World.* Washington, DC: World Bank Group Mining Department.

World Bank, 2010. *Innovation Policy: A Guide for Development Countries.* Washington, DC: International Bank for Reconstruction and Development / World Bank.

5   Emfuleni

Lochner Marais, Molefi Lenka,
Jan Cloete and Wynand Grobler

Introduction

Emfuleni's past, present and future are closely related to the iron and steel manufacturing industry; in fact, this industry is almost single-handedly responsible for Emfuleni's existence. But this dependence on a single sector leaves the city at the mercy of international economic trends, national policies and programmes, fluctuations in demand for steel, and changes in ownership of the larger firms in Emfuleni. The dependence on steel manufacturing and the lack of a major downstream steel industry represent a long-term threat to both Emfuleni's economy and the city's viability. At the same time, Emfuleni must deal with the environmental consequences of a 'dirty industry' and increasing international pressure to comply with environmental treaties, while struggling to provide and maintain adequate infrastructure and coping with social protests and political in-fighting.

The negative effects of the steel industry's boom-bust cycles have been largely mitigated by increasing linkage with Johannesburg and Pretoria (to which many Emfuleni residents commute on a daily basis), the expansion of the city's two universities and the increase in weekend tourism on the banks of the Vaal River. A positive factor for Emfuleni is the considerable desegregation of its former white suburbs – Emfuleni is one of a handful of places in South Africa where large-scale desegregation is occurring, other notable areas being Polokwane (Donaldson and Kotze, 2006) and Matjhabeng (formerly Welkom) (Marais, 2013). Another is Emfuleni's range of functions, from its international connectivity and national importance (foreign exchange from steel exports) to its regional services (private medical and educational facilities serving the rural hinterland, mainly the northern Free State). Figure 5.1 shows Emfuleni's location in relation to Johannesburg, Tshwane and Ekurhuleni.

Against the above background, this chapter first provides an overview of the iron ore and steel industry and explains Emfuleni's role within this sector. Next is a discussion of four phases in the historical development of Emfuleni, after which comes an overview of internal trends and dynamics. This is followed by a discussion of local responses, focusing mainly on municipality and area-based strategic planning also called an integrated development plan (IDP). Thereafter is a section that considers external pressures facing Emfuleni. Finally, the synthesis section

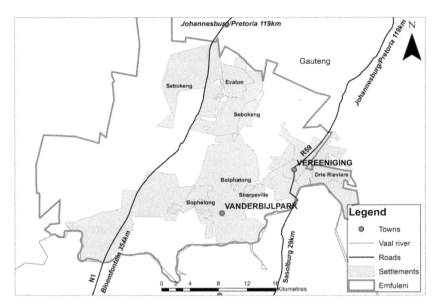

Figure 5.1 Location of Emfuleni

pulls the threads together and comes to some conclusions. The chapter highlights several aspects of Emfuleni that have a bearing on the topic of secondary cities: its capabilities in relation to the steel industry, its links with South Africa's minerals-energy complex, its small but significant global linkages, its reliance on a single-sector global industry, its national and international vulnerability, its lack of institutional capacity and its serious environmental concerns.

The iron and steel industry in South Africa

The two main raw materials used in the steelmaking process are pig iron and scrap metal. Ninety per cent of the pig iron comes from the Northern Cape (90 per cent), while scrap metal is collected countrywide (Kumba Iron Ore, 2011), providing employment to an estimated 425,000 people in South Africa (Cilliers, 2013). The largest producer of pig iron in South Africa is Kumba Iron Ore, and the majority of Kumba's shares are today owned by Anglo American. Kumba was originally part of the state corporation Iscor (Iron and Steel Corporation of South Africa), which was privatised in 1989 as Iscor Ltd and split in 2001 into Iscor (steelmaking) and Kumba (mining). The demand for steel in South Africa was initially a result of the expanding mining industry in the early 1900s. The second big wave of demand came during World War II, followed by renewed demand in the late 1960s to meet the apartheid government's armament requirements. More recently, infrastructure investment in preparation for the 2010 Soccer World Cup was a significant driver of steel production. However, despite some boom periods, the overall demand for steel in South Africa has on average grown by only about 1 per cent for the last 30 years, according to an interviewee in the steel industry.

Although South Africa has the capacity to produce up to 12 Mt (megatonnes) of steel per annum, only 8 Mt were produced in 2008 (Kumba Iron Ore, 2011), and more recent estimates indicate that less than 6 Mt are currently being produced annually. Of this, about 5.5 Mt are consumed by the domestic market, with the remainder being exported, 37 per cent by land to other southern African countries and 63 per cent by sea, mainly to East and West Africa) (Kumba Iron Ore, 2011). At the same time, about 0.8 Mt of steel is imported annually and industry experts say the amount is increasing. In 2008, the industry contributed 0.6 per cent of the country's GDP and R4 billion to the national economy (Kumba Iron Ore, 2011). The steel production industry lost a large number of jobs between 2002 and 2008, but it nevertheless employed nearly 13,000 people in 2008 (Kumba Iron Ore, 2011).

The steel industry has two main components. The first produces primary items such as hot rolled coil and merchant bars and some intermediate products such as wire and tubing. The second, which uses about 30 per cent of South Africa's steel, involves the utilisation in manufacturing. However, South African-made steel is not competitive on the international market. The government believes that the main reason for this is the 'uncompetitive pricing' of steel, which makes it difficult for South Africa to compete in global markets (Filen, 2012).

ArcelorMittal South Africa (formerly Iscor), the largest steelmaker in South Africa, and holding approximately 75 per cent of the market share, has four main plants: Vanderbijlpark and Vereeniging (both in Emfuleni), and Newcastle and Saldanha. Some others are Scaw Metals (owned by Anglo American) in Germiston, DAV Steel in Vanderbijlpark, Cisco in Kuils River, and Evraz Highveld Steel and Vanadium in Witbank. Just over 60 per cent of South Africa's steel production from raw iron ore and 22 per cent of its steel production from scrap metal take place in Emfuleni (Kumba Iron Ore, 2011).

Among the many reasons for the slow growth in demand for steel in South Africa over the past 30 years, three are worth mentioning here. First, the country's technology for producing steel for containers such as cans is outdated – South Africa makes cans of 0.3 mm thickness whereas other countries can make cans of 0.1 mm and less, thus making three times more cans with the same amount of material. And cans are also now being made of other materials, such as plastic. Second, the quality of the steel produced in South Africa is not good enough for some aspects of automotive manufacturing, so automotive companies have started to import steel. And third, South Africa's steel industry has become somewhat unreliable; ArcelorMittal's Vanderbijlpark and Newcastle plants, for example, were closed for significant periods in 2009 and 2011, respectively, because of blast furnace failures (Radebe, 2013). Consequently, South African companies that use steel have started to import.

History of Emfuleni

The history of Emfuleni is bound up with the history of Iscor and the steel industry in South Africa. In turn, the history of Iscor is closely related to

Afrikaner nationalism, which historically ensured jobs for white people, and the availability of low-paid black, mostly migrant, labour. The historical overview below is organised according to four important phases in the development of Emfuleni.

The first phase (1892–1943) began with the founding in 1892 of the settlement now known as Vereeniging. The town was given its name after serving as the location for the signing of the peace treaty between the British and the Afrikaner republics in 1902. The growth of Vereeniging was largely due to the discovery of coal nearby and the establishment of a private steelmaking enterprise near the coal mines shortly after the unification of South Africa. Horace Wright and Sammy Marks received a licence in 1909 to build a steelmaking plant in Vereeniging. Their Union Steel Corporation started production in 1913 using scrap metal from railroads and mines as inputs (ArcelorMittal, 2013). Then in 1929, the government established the Iscor parastatal in an attempt to provide job opportunities for whites and assert Afrikaner control over the iron and steel industry, which up to that point had been dominated by English capital (ArcelorMittal, 2013). Iscor started production in Pretoria in 1934 and became the main supplier of rail infrastructure in the country. Iscor soon established its own mining operation in Thabazimbi in order to ensure sufficient iron ore for its steelmaking efforts. By 1935, Iscor was providing 17 per cent of South Africa's steel.

The second phase (1943–1959) came with the establishment of a steelmaking plant near Vanderbijlpark in 1943. The town of Vanderbijlpark was planned as a modern garden city similar to other new towns such as Welkom and Sasolburg. Although the plant was initially established to provide steel for the war industry (mainly armoured cars), it was planned in such a way that it could adapt its operations and enter the commercial market once the war ended. The reasons for establishing the plant near Vanderbijlpark are not very clear. Factors that may have played a role include the limited expansion possibilities in Pretoria, proximity to the existing steel industry in Vereeniging, ample open space, the availability of water and coal energy, and the general slope which allowed for industry related waste products to be run off into the Vaal River (this was before environmental concerns became prominent), below the pumping stations of the water utility Rand Water.

The third phase (1960–1988) witnessed the growth of Iscor into one of the largest parastatals in South Africa, employing more than 60,000 people at its peak. Three factors influenced this growth. First, the international sanctions prohibiting South Africa from trading war machinery made it strategically important for the apartheid government to have control over the domestic steel industry. Thus, government pressure resulted in further expansion of various steel works in Vanderbijlpark and elsewhere in the country. At the same time, Iscor invested in expanding its range of steel products. Second, the increase in Iscor's steelmaking capacity also resulted in the expansion of their mining operations and the opening of the Sishen mine in what is now the Northern Cape Province; the railway from Sishen to Saldanha also allowed for the export of iron ore. Third, the formation of Sasol (an energy and chemical company) in 1950 resulted in a large demand for steel and steel products and ensured the sustained growth of the steel industry. Although some rationalisation and strategic positioning did take place at intervals, Iscor grew significantly and by the late 1980s had an 85 per cent market share in the South African steel industry and employed about 60,000 people (ArcelorMittal, 2013). However, this growth was largely due to the fact that Iscor received major subsidies from the government and benefited from a protected market position, advantages which were not viable in the long term. This third phase saw considerable economic growth in Emfuleni, and both Vanderbijlpark and Vereeniging expanded rapidly.

The fourth phase (1989 to the present day) began with the privatisation of Iscor as Iscor Ltd in 1989. This privatisation process was part of the apartheid government's changing economic policy and involved other parastatals as well. Although privatisation resulted in significant job losses in Emfuleni (more than 10,000 jobs were lost in about 10 years) and a considerable decline in Emfuleni's economic output (see Table 5.1), the opening up of international markets after the end of apartheid meant an expansion in Iscor Ltd's operations at the Sishen mine. In 1998, the Saldanha steel mills came into operation, the result of a collaboration between Iscor Ltd and the Industrial Development Corporation. Thus, Iscor managed to adapt to the changing times and even experienced growth in various areas around the country. The implications for Emfuleni, however, were disastrous, as the region experienced massive job losses after Iscor was privatised.

Table 5.1 Emfuleni's economic growth by sector, and total economic growth in Gauteng, South African metros and South Africa (1996, 2001 and 2011) (constant 2005 figures, Gross Value Add)

Sector	Gross Value Add, 2005 constant figures (R1000s)			Annual growth rate		
	1996	2001	2011	1996– 2001	2001– 2011	1996– 2011
Agriculture	106,629	108,652	121,444	0.4	1.1	0.9
Mining	66,860	20,366	42,930	−21.2	7.7	−2.9
Manufacturing	7,270,797	5,560,615	7,151,435	−5.2	2.5	−0.1
Construction	312,718	218,100	519,925	−7.0	9.1	3.4
Utilities	494,202	406,792	543,509	−3.8	2.9	0.6
Trade	1,033,842	840,880	1,210,746	−4.0	3.7	1.1
Transport	540,609	547,812	769,838	0.3	3.5	2.4
Finance	1,797,822	2,040,297	3,688,376	2.6	6.1	4.9
Services	2,579,133	2,501,756	3,511,739	−0.6	3.4	2.1
Total (Emfuleni)	14,202,613	12,245,270	17,559,942	−2.9	3.7	1.4
Gauteng	352,002,678	410,324,667	609,050,965	3.1	4.0	3.7
All metros	595,946,896	708,520,914	1,051,872,917	3.5	4.0	3.9
South Africa	1,044,970,331	1,191,041,813	1,700,825,798	2.7	3.6	3.3

Source: UFS (2013).

The 2001 unbundling of Iscor Ltd's steelmaking and mining activities resulted in a long-term agreement between Iscor and Kumba which stipulated that Kumba would provide Iscor with iron ore at cost plus 3 per cent, placing Iscor in an extremely favourable position in respect of its iron ore supply. However, this agreement was overturned by a 2013 court ruling. Despite the advantage it gained from its relationship with Kumba, Iscor struggled to compete both nationally and internationally. The need to be internationally competitive led to Iscor's first international cooperation agreement, with the Dutch LNV Holdings. In exchange for business advice and innovation assistance over a period of three years, LNV Holdings received 10,000 shares in Iscor. By 2004, LNV had obtained a 35 per cent share in Iscor, and the company was renamed Ispat Iscor Ltd. Later in 2004, when Ispat International obtained the majority share in LNV Holdings, Iscor changed its name to Mittal Steel Company. In 2006, Arcelor and Mittal Steel merged to form ArcelorMittal.

In brief, the story of Emfuleni began with the discovery of coal, which was soon used to power privately owned steel mills, providing steel for an ever-growing mining industry. A few decades later, Afrikaner nationalism and the demand for war machinery led to the establishment and growth of Iscor, the major role player in the growth and development of Emfuleni during the apartheid era. The changing economic policies of the apartheid government, coupled with the demise of apartheid, introduced privatisation to Iscor, which in turn resulted in job losses and economic hardship in Emfuleni. Along with privatisation came internationalisation. In the short term, it seems that internationalisation has helped to slow the decline of Emfuleni, but in the long term the Emfuleni's economy will depend increasingly on the volatility of international markets. As later sections in this chapter make clear, the essential question is whether the municipality and the business sector fully understand the risks and are able to support the multi-nationals in their midst.

Internal trends and pressures

Historically, urbanisation in South Africa was heavily influenced by apartheid legislation that minimised black migration to cities (Mabin, 1992). When black labour was allowed in 'white' urban areas, it was generally in the form of a migrant labour system. An important point to note about the history of black settlement in Emfuleni is that the black townships of Bophelong and Boipatong, now suburbs of Vanderbijlpark, were established in 1943 before the National Party's strict segregation policies came into effect and are thus in close proximity to Vanderbijlpark, whereas the black township of Sebokeng, established in 1965 on the principles of apartheid planning, was located, complete with a large number of hostels, some 15 km north of Vanderbijlpark (see Figure 5.1).

Emfuleni's population growth rate has declined over the past 20 years. The annual population growth rate dropped from 2.08 per cent between 1996 and 2001 to 0.92 per cent between 2001 and 2011 (Stats SA, 2013), and the overall rate of 1.29 per cent over the period 1996–2011 is much lower than the 3.44 per cent for the same period in Gauteng (Stats SA, 2013). Among the various reasons for this decrease in Emfuleni's population growth rate are job losses and the increasing economic uncertainty.

From 1996 to 2001 Emfuleni suffered economic decline (see Table 5.1). Between 1996 and 2011 its economy grew by 1.4 per cent annually, a rate considerably lower than that of Gauteng and the country's metros (UFS, 2013). However, Emfuleni's 3.7 per cent annual growth rate between 2001 and 2011 compares much more favourably with Gauteng, the country's metros and South Africa as a whole, suggesting that the 10 years leading up to 2011 were more stable than the 1990s. It seems that the process of internationalisation helped to halt the decline that was caused by privatisation. However, as argued later in this chapter, internationalisation also poses long-term risks, some of which have yet to be experienced.

Compared to Gauteng overall, the manufacturing, water and electricity sectors make up a larger percentage of Emfuleni's economy (SACN, 2013). However, the contribution of manufacturing has slowly declined, from 55 per cent of Emfuleni's economic output in 1996 to 32 per cent in 2011, while that of other sectors, such as trade and finance, has increased considerably, suggesting a 'normalisation' of the regional economy and the development of a more service-orientated economy. This is mainly due to the considerable expansion of private services (such as private hospitals and educational facilities), the increase in students at the two universities, and the increasing popularity of the Vaal River as a recreation and weekend tourism destination.

Some recent trends in manufacturing have had their effect on Emfuleni. Steel manufacturing contributes just over 80 per cent of output and about 75 per cent of all employment in the manufacturing sector (SACN, 2013), which suggests that the steel industry has a significant labour absorption rate. The most significant decline in manufacturing (dominated by steel making) occurred between 1996 and 2001, when the sector shrunk at a rate of 5.2 per cent per year. However, it then grew by 2.5 per cent per annum between 2001 and 2011 (SACN, 2013). One of the biggest drawbacks is that Emfuleni has not managed to create downstream steel manufacturing activities. As a direct result of Iscor's steel transport pricing policy, which made steel available at zero transport cost within a specific distance of Vanderbijlpark, these activities are carried out largely in Johannesburg and Ekurhuleni, the furthest centres where steel manufacturing businesses can still benefit from the zero transport costs.

The economic decline between 1996 and 2001 has had long-term implications for poverty in Emfuleni, which consistently performs worse than Gauteng on a range of poverty and development indicators. The percentage of people living in poverty in Emfuleni increased rapidly between 1996 and 2001, from 28 per cent to 45.2 per cent but then decreased to 35.4 per cent by 2011 (SACN, 2013). Yet this figure is still considerably higher than the 26.3 per cent for Gauteng as a whole. Emfuleni's 2011 score of 0.70 on the Human Development Index is 0.04 index points lower than that of Johannesburg and Tshwane. Inequality has increased more rapidly in Emfuleni than in the metros. In 1996, the Gini coefficient for Emfuleni was only 0.51, significantly lower than that of the rest of Gauteng. It rose 0.12 index points to 0.63 in 2011. It is likely that the economic hardship that Emfuleni has experienced (especially in the 1990s) resulted in increases in the Gini coefficient.

The growing number of students at Emfuleni's two universities (the Vaal Campus of the North West University and the Vaal University of Technology) – from 7,000 at the beginning of the 1990s to 22,000 in 2013 – has resulted in increased retail expenditure and growth in student housing in some suburbs such as Bedworth Park, where many homeowners rent out their properties to students (ELM, 2012). But much of the unofficial student housing is overcrowded and of poor quality, and the growing demand for student housing has placed increasing pressure on the municipality, as there is a greater need for regulation and enforcement. The municipality is considering converting the Bedworth Park suburb into a student village but allowing owners to maintain their Residential One status if they comply with the student village principles. Owners who do not comply will have to pay guest house rates and taxes.

Emfuleni has experienced service delivery protests repeatedly over the past decade, and the increasing frequency of these protests has been identified as a risk factor in the municipal turnaround strategy (ELM, 2010). The following are some examples. In 2004, a memorandum containing 27 service delivery demands was handed to the mayor in Sebokeng (Tempelhoff, 2004). In 2005, shortly before a visit from former President Thabo Mbeki, residents of Sebokeng threatened an uprising on the scale of those from the apartheid era, such as the Vaal Uprising of 1984–1985 (Tabane, 2005). In 2006, residents of Sebokeng took to the streets again and blocked the Golden Highway in Zone 13 (The Star, 2006b), and at the same time another protest took place in the Sonderwater informal settlement (The Star, 2006a). In 2008, Boiketlong residents marched and delivered a memorandum to the mayor, demanding a response by 3 August (Seleka, 2008a). In January 2009, the police had to use rubber bullets to disperse protestors who had barricaded the old Johannesburg road to demonstrate their dissatisfaction at receiving inadequate attention from the municipality (Van Buul, 2009a). In September 2009, the community of Rust-der-Vaal, formerly a coloured area under apartheid legislation, staged a massive demonstration to call the attention of the municipality to their problems and needs (Van Buul, 2009b).

The level of desegregation that occurred in Emfuleni after the abandonment of the Group Areas Act in 1991 is quite remarkable. In Vereeniging the percentage of non-white residents in former white suburbs rose from 27 per cent in 1996 to nearly 60 per cent in 2011 (Stats SA, 2013). The comparative figures in Vanderbijlpark are 25 per cent (1996) and 48 per cent (2011) (Stats SA, 2013). Emfuleni's levels of desegregation are higher those of the metros (Christopher, 2005). The main reason for this is probably Emfuleni's lower house prices. A comparison, made using the 'My Property' website, of 20 houses for sale in Johannesburg with 20 similar units for sale in Emfuleni revealed that Emfuleni's prices were 20 to 30 per cent lower than Johannesburg's (www.myproperty.co.za, accessed 12 August 2013). One reason for Emfuleni's lower prices has been the economic hardship and job losses of the past 20 years Another is that, when Iscor was privatised in the early 1990s, Iscor's property group Vesgrow privatised many houses that had originally been constructed for Iscor workers, thus flooding the property market with houses whose prices were initially much lower than they had been previously. These two factors have enabled desegregation to occur on a larger scale than elsewhere in the country.

Internal responses

Although Emfuleni's overall municipal management has improved considerably over the past five years, it has had its fair share of political turmoil, mainly related to political divisions within the African National Congress (the ruling party in the city council). In 2005, the national structures of the African National Congress intervened, forcing the mayor, speaker and chief whip to resign and suspending a large number of senior officials (Kgosana, 2005a) because of poor service delivery in the region (Tempelhoff, 2005), including a councillor, for allegedly writing off his outstanding debt (Kgosana, 2005b). Despite this, municipal officials received large bonuses in 2006 (Mafela, 2006). Then in 2008 five senior municipal officials were suspended (Mooki, 2008) and the mayor and the municipal manager resigned after further infighting in the African National Congress (Van Buul, 2008a) and the disruption of a council meeting by African National Congress members (Seleka, 2008b). This was the fourth resignation by a mayor in less than three years (Van Buul, 2008b), and by 2009 Emfuleni had had five municipal managers in three years (Tempelhoff and Van Buul, 2009).

In 2009, a municipal turnaround strategy was developed in association with the Department of Cooperative Governance and Traditional Affairs (ELM, 2012). This strategy has resulted in improved compliance with financial regulations, better monitoring of the municipality's key performance indicators and a clearer understanding of the urgency of dealing with non-payment for services. Although the situation has stabilised somewhat, Emfuleni has had two mayors since the last local government elections in 2011. And in 2011 the city council argued about putting R1.3 million aside to purchase 4x4 vehicles for the mayor and speaker (City Press, 2011).

The current IDP, covering the period 2012–2016, builds on previous plans and has an overall vision of 'providing responsive, effective, efficient, and sustainable municipal services in an accountable manner' (ELM, 2012, p. 5). Although the document holds some promise, it also has shortcomings. First, it concentrates mainly on municipal issues; the significant amount of the IDP that is devoted to the municipal turnaround strategy is evidence of this inward focus. Second, there is very little analysis of the current state of development and the risks associated with the current situation. And third, the role of the private sector is narrowly defined in terms of social responsibility programmes. For instance, the economic section of the IDP mentions ArcelorMittal South Africa's role in poverty alleviation and lists the company's social responsibility programmes (ELM, 2012), but neglects to mention Emfuleni's economic trends, the specific risks associated with the steel industry, and the notion of international competitiveness and its implications for the municipality.

When it comes to local economic development, the IDP identifies two main tourism-related economic development opportunities. One of these is heritage tourism in the Sharpeville and Boiphatong, focusing on the history of resistance to apartheid; but, although a creditable plan was developed in the mid-2000s, very little has actually been done. The second is a logistics hub, based on the assumption that Johannesburg's O. R. Tambo International Airport cannot handle the current freight, but discussions with a range of role players revealed that progress on this project is being hampered because no one at the municipality is actively driving local economic development projects (a point that was also made in the 2010 municipal turnaround strategy – ELM, 2010), and because the plan for a logistics hub is apparently not supported at other levels of government. Pretorius (2013) suggests that national policy frameworks are not supportive of regional airports.

Inadequate or inefficient local infrastructure provision for water, sanitation and electricity constitutes a serious problem, not only because of the inconvenience and health threats to residents but also in view of the importance of Emfuleni's steel industry and its international connectivity.

Emfuleni receives 90 per cent of its water from Rand Water, and the municipality has been given 'blue drop' status (that is, its water has been rated as of an acceptable standard) for the past three years (Department of Water Affairs, 2012). According to officials at Metsi-A-Lekoa (the water services authority), Emfuleni provides water to all of its residents in line with government policy. The available data from Stats SA confirm this: fewer than 2 per cent of households have water access further than 200 m from their homes, and 70 per cent have water inside their homes, which is better than Gauteng as a whole (Stats SA, 2013). But there are five main problems with the municipality's current provision of water. First, there seems to be difficulty in ensuring sufficient water pressure. Second, the aging infrastructure has led to a large number of leakages and an increase in maintenance costs. Third, the municipality is unable to account for a significant percentage of its water losses (ELM, 2013). In this respect, the Auditor General found in November 2010 that the municipality lost about R250 million in unrecovered water and electricity income (City Press, 2011), while the IDP estimates that 39 per cent of water is lost due to leakage and poor maintenance (ELM, 2012). Fourth, there is a big problem with non-payment of water bills, complicated by the fact that in some cases the municipality is unable to bill correctly (ELM, 2013). The IDP estimates that 26 per cent of households are not paying their water bills, while consumers owed the municipality R3.2 billion in 2012 (ELM, 2012). Finally, the water supply itself seems to be threatened, and will remain so until the Lesotho Highlands Project Phase Two begins delivering water to Gauteng (which is expected to be in 2018).

As with the improvement in access to water, the municipality has managed to increase the percentage of people who have access to waterborne sanitation since 1996 (Stats SA, 2013). Furthermore, Emfuleni's sanitation system received 'green drop' status (acceptable standards of managing sewage) from the Department of Water Affairs in 2012 (Department of Water Affairs, 2013). However, the municipality is now struggling to manage sanitation. The sewage works operate at up to

150 per cent capacity. This means that any electricity outage or pump breakdown poses health and water pollution risks. It also means that no new major residential or industrial development can take place. Although the situation has improved in 2013/2014, the municipality's sewer system has a poor history. In 2006, the Emfuleni Municipality was in dispute with several NGOs for pumping raw sewage into the Vaal River (*The Star*, 2006b). In 2008, the 'Blue Scorpions' (the authority managing water regulation in South Africa) ordered the municipality to clean up dead fish in the Vanderbijlpark Lake, apparently killed by sewage spills (Bega, 2008, 2009). At the time, the municipality claimed that the spill was due to outdated infrastructure at the sewage works. It appeared that the Sebokeng sewage works in particular were operating above capacity. Also in 2008, the court ordered the municipality to clear the Vaal River of dead fish, agreeing with the environmental groups and the 'scorpions' that the municipality was responsible for the dead fish because of sewage spilling into the river (Schoeman and Scholtz, 2008). A general warning was issued against using the river in any way, and this had negative repercussions for Emfuleni's tourism industry (Skade and Flanagan, 2008). Besides the spills from the sewage plants, on occasions Emfuleni has pumped sewage from its tank lorries into rivers and dams (Tempelhoff, 2009a). The long-standing dispute went to court again in 2009 and Emfuleni was ordered to get its house in order within four months (Tempelhoff, 2009b) something which they managed to do.

ArcelorMittal South Africa receives its electricity directly from Eskom (South Africa's electricity supplier), but Emfuleni is responsible for providing electricity to the remainder of the businesses and all the households. Of the municipality's revenue from electricity, 78 per cent comes from industry and only 22 per cent from households. More importantly, five companies consume 50 per cent of the electricity provided by the municipality. The energy intensity of steel production is the main reason why Emfuleni's electricity is used mostly by industry. This dominance of heavy industry is both an advantage and a risk for the municipality. On the positive side, it is fairly easy to ensure payments from the five businesses that pay 50 per cent of the municipality's electricity bill; on the negative, the possibility of these five main energy users downscaling their operations or becoming more energy efficient carries long-term risks for municipal finance.

To sum up, although Emfuleni has made laudable achievements in ensuring access to water and sanitation, it is struggling to guarantee the water supply, collect payments from households and carry out adequate maintenance and upgrading of infrastructure, and is at risk in the long term because most of its electricity is consumed and paid for by industry.

The management of Emfuleni's municipal finances has been extremely poor since the municipality's inception in 2001. Although some improvements have been made in the last five years, the municipality has not managed to receive even one unqualified audit report. In 2008, the Auditor General could not express an opinion on Emfuleni's finances for the eighth year in a row (Tempelhoff and Van Buul, 2009). Since 2011 there have been considerable improvements, and the 2011/12 report was unqualified with findings (Auditor General, 2013). The Auditor General's report suggests that a number of improvements occurred during the 2011/12 financial year, including the following: improved leadership and responsibility regarding finance management, a positive political tone, prior year qualifications were addressed and a performance audit committee was established (Auditor General, 2013). Despite these improvements, however, the report noted some problems, such as tenders being awarded to state officials, an extremely high staff vacancy rate of 57 per cent (the norm for Gauteng was 20 per cent), a 43 per cent senior official vacancy rate and underspending on capital budgets (Auditor General, 2013).

Emfuleni's revenue is threatened by three main problems. First, the largest portion of Emfuleni's income comes from service charges (61.2 per cent), followed by government grants and subsidies (15.2 per cent) and property rates (9.9 per cent). More importantly, the percentage of income from service charges has increased considerably from about 55 per cent in 2007/08 to 61.2 per cent in 2012. Consequently, Emfuleni is becoming increasingly dependent on service charges, and in particular electricity, which made up 63.8 per cent of service charges in 2011/2012 (ELM, 2013). Given that five of Emfuleni's industries pay about half of the municipal electricity bill and industry overall pays almost 80 per cent of it, there are two threats to the municipal revenue: the pressure to minimise energy costs by using new technologies and machines that consume less energy, and dependence on the global market, which can be quite volatile – any global trend that affects Emfuleni's industries will also affect municipal finances.

Second, Emfuleni receives only a small national Municipal Infrastructure Grant. Partly as a result of this, one of Emfuleni's main problems has been the lack of appropriate capital expenditure, which is essential for continued economic growth. And third, consumers owe the municipality about R3.2 billion, which is roughly equal to the municipality's entire annual operating budget (ELM, 2012). The high levels of debts is due to multiple factors: illegal connections, billing errors and aging infrastructure (Nel, 2012: ELM, 2013)

Emfuleni's municipal expenditure also suffers from three main problems. First, although employment costs have come down as a percentage of total costs since 2008 (from 23.6 per cent to 17.9 per cent), the increase in these costs remains higher than inflation, creating a long-term burden for the municipality. The current percentage of expenditure going to employee costs is lower than that of any of the metros in South Africa, but this is directly related to the large number of vacant posts at the municipality. Second, the percentage spent on maintaining and repairing infrastructure has dropped over the past few years, and in 2012, only 3 per cent of the municipality's total expenditure went for this purpose. In comparison, the figure for metros was 6 per cent (UFS, 2013). In 2011, Emfuleni's expenditure on maintenance and repairs was approximately 30 per cent less than in 2010, while the 2012 amount was 1 per cent less than in 2011 and only R5,000 more than in 2009. Considering the widespread complaints about old infrastructure and the increasing need for maintenance, the decrease in the maintenance and repair budget comes as a surprise. It suggests that not all the necessary maintenance is being carried out (especially preventative maintenance), and this neglect will hurt the municipality in the long run. And third, as regards capital expenditure, although the Municipal Infrastructure Grant constituted on average 3.38 per cent of the municipality's revenue between 2006/07 and 2011/2012, estimates from the financial statements suggest that only 66 per cent of the funds were spent on time, meaning that only 2.2 per cent of Emfuleni's annual budget was allocated to the development of new infrastructure. The municipality's underspending of this grant is confirmed in the IDP (ELM, 2012).

Relations between business and local government can at best be described as ad hoc and dependent on individuals rather than being institutionalised. The historical racial divide remains evident, and racial prejudice was observed during some of the in-depth interviews that were conducted for this chapter. Although Emfuleni's municipal employees are mostly black, its business owners are largely white. Local government encourages an inclusive local economic development forum and regular business breakfasts, but these efforts are mainly superficial. In practice, the local or district municipalities make little coordinated effort to truly engage with businesses. Considering that Emfuleni's steel industry has been globalised (many of its larger steelmaking corporations have factories around the world) and its manufacturing sector is an important part of South Africa's drive to be internationally competitive, a more formalised and institutionalised approach is necessary. The following two examples provide evidence that relations between business and the municipality are less than ideal.

The first example involves ArcelorMittal South Africa. In 2012, one of their steelmaking blast furnaces had mechanical problems due to an industrial accident. To continue producing, the firm needed to revert to older technology, which would have released more harmful particles into the atmosphere. Permission to do this needed to be obtained from local government. The process for granting permission includes extensive public participation and it was slowed down by various factors such as meetings not being constituted legally. When three months later the local government finally made the decision to allow ArcelorMittal South Africa to switch on their old machines, the original mechanical problems had largely been solved. The time that it took the municipality to make the decision is a threat to Emfuleni's economy. Even worse is the fact that nobody foresaw the possibility that such a problem requiring a decision by local government would develop. There was thus no policy or procedure in place to address the problem systematically. A local government that prioritises 'international competitiveness' should have had some kind of guideline in place for such a scenario.

The second example comes from a different company. Unlike ArcelorMittal South Africa, this company depends on the municipality for the provision of electricity. At the time of writing an electrical transformer close to the company's premises started giving sporadic problems. In the company's opinion, the municipality took too long to fix the problem, and besides being slow to respond, it seldom has the necessary spare parts. The company therefore stocks the spare parts itself, in order to speed up the process, thus essentially taking over a municipal function because the municipality lacks capacity.

External pressures

This section describes two external pressures experienced by Emfuleni: first those related to the environment (more specifically the pressures to comply to national and international pressures) and then those related to national planning frameworks.

Threats to the environment

Emfuleni is at risk from industry-related air, water and land pollution. When it comes to controlling air pollution, the industries appear to be largely compliant with environmental regulations, although the level of compliance is being questioned. Global pressure to improve industry's ecological footprint is increasing and consequently legislation and enforcement are likely to become stricter in the future. Planning ahead for this probability, Emfuleni's industries are progressively investing in more energy efficient technology. But although new machines are likely decrease air pollution, they might also reduce the need for labour, thus increasing unemployment in Emfuleni.

There are four main threats to Emfuleni's water. The first is the steel industry's use of water to cool the steel, after which the heated water is returned into the water system. This process seems largely under control and well-managed. The second results from other industry activity. As mentioned above, prior to environmental legislation pollution from the Vanderbijlpark Iscor plant could be drained into the Vaal River. Third, there is a risk to the environment from the over-capacity of the Emfuleni sewage works and other outdated infrastructure. Although on the surface it seems that much has improved since 2009, the over-extension of the sewage works' capacity remains of great concern. An estimated R4 billion is needed to provide an appropriate sewerage system for Emfuleni.

Fourth, there is potential risk associated with plans to release mine water that is supposed to have been treated to neutralise the acid, but which is in fact still acid, from the Johannesburg area into the Klip River, which runs into the Vaal River at Emfuleni. This 'neutral' water would have salt levels higher than the acceptable limit, threatening the ecology of the river and business activities associated with it. It seems that the decision to release this 'neutral' mine water will be made without a proper environmental impact assessment due to the urgency of the matter. Increased pollution of the Vaal River might decrease waterfront property values, which could in turn decrease municipal revenue even though property taxes account for only 10 per cent of the local government's income.

A further environmental threat posed by ArcelorMittal South Africa is possible failure of the blast furnaces and it possible impact on clean air. Local government should have, at the bare minimum, some kind of contingency plan to deal with this eventuality.

The debate about the pollution of land surrounding ArcelorMittal South Africa's activities is well-documented in the media and in court reports. It has been proven that the land adjacent to ArcelorMittal South Africa's Emfuleni plant is polluted and not viable for agriculture. This problem was supposed to be solved when ArcelorMittal South Africa purchased the land surrounding its premises. However, this only resulted in changed ownership of the polluted land – it did not remove the pollution.

Pressures of national planning

Two aspects of national planning could be bad for Emfuleni: the plans for another steel manufacturing plant in South Africa, and the lack of plans for improving transport for Emfuleni's own steel manufacturers.

The Investment Development Corporation are considering the creation of a new steel manufacturing plant in South Africa, mainly because of the uncompetitive pricing of steel (at import parity), which inhibits downstream opportunities in the country and makes South African steel exports uncompetitive on the global market (Fin24, 2015). A new steel plant would compete with those in Emfuleni. Mpumalanga has been mentioned as a possible location for this new plant, but this seems unlikely, as a report produced by the iron and steel industry suggests that a coastal location would be preferable, so as to focus on steel exports (Ensor, 2013). However, since any new investment in the steel industry would be capital intensive, and it is unlikely that the government will be able to find sufficient capital on its own, Emfuleni's steel industry may be safe from the threat of competition for the moment.

Emfuleni's steel industry is seriously affected by the lack of plans for improving rail infrastructure. Historically, some of Emfuleni's steel went by rail to Durban and from there was exported via Durban's harbour. For several reasons, however, steel companies in Emfuleni have been unable to transport steel by rail since 2010 and have had to send it by road instead, increasing the pressure on South Africa's road network, and making steel exports uncompetitive because of the higher cost. In fact, to move steel by road from Emfuleni to Durban costs more than the sea voyage to its final destination.

Synthesis

Several factors make Emfuleni internationally important. Its two large steel manufacturers are multi-national corporations, subject to the volatility of the international market. The plants they own in different parts of the world compete either directly or indirectly with each other, making locational competitiveness an important consideration. ArcelorMittal South Africa's operations contribute only 1 per cent to ArcelorMittal's global steel production, so although this company's steel production in Emfuleni is vital for the local economy, it is insignificant in terms of the company's worldwide production. There is, however, a history of steel and steel products being exported from Emfuleni by companies such as DCD Ringrollers (which manufactures train wheels) and ArcelorMittal South Africa. Finally, international treaties for combating air pollution of course bring Emfuleni directly into the worldwide debates on global warming.

Two factors make Emfuleni nationally important. On the positive side, it produces about 70 per cent of South Africa's domestic steel. But a negative factor is that its location on the banks of the Vaal River means that its industries could damage the ecology of the river, and air pollution generated by its industries is a threat to Gauteng and the northern Free State.

Besides its international and national roles, Emfuleni also fulfils important local and regional functions, as evidenced by the increasing number of private and public medical and educational facilities that serve its hinterland.

Emfuleni's future is threatened by risks related to inefficient municipal governance and service delivery, damage to the environment, and the uncertain future of the steel industry. Although service delivery and municipal governance have improved somewhat, Emfuleni still faces several long-term risks. First, the Emfuleni's aging infrastructure will require increasing maintenance, which will push up costs and affect service delivery. Second, if the current inward-looking approach to strategic and economic planning continues, there will be negative implications for the region's economy and the municipality's revenue stream. Third, poor municipal management leaves much room for improvement in terms of municipal governance and financial management. And fourth, the possibility of a decrease in energy utilisation by industry means that the municipality must have plans in place to deal with the resulting drop in revenue.

Emfuleni faces three specific environmental risks. The first is air pollution, the subject of a longstanding debate. Although the steel companies appear to have made progress in this respect over the past 10 years, battles between environmental groups and ArcelorMittal South Africa are ongoing. And although Emfuleni's industries currently comply with emissions regulations, long-term compliance might be difficult to ensure since environmental laws and regulations will became stricter over time. Improvements in environmental compliance usually go hand in hand with new machinery and technology, which reduce energy use and air pollution, but these improvements might be offset by the negative effect on both municipal revenue and industry's demand for labour.

The second environmental risk relates to the current process for treating acid mine water, which involves cleaning it to some extent and then releasing it into the Klip River, a tributary of the Vaal River. This could have serious implications for Emfuleni and for the agricultural industry downstream. As this is a new process, the long-term implications for the ecosystem are still unknown. However, the probable implications for Emfuleni are two-fold: there may be damage to the tourism industry, which has grown over the past few decades and helped to diversify Emfuleni's economy, and the city's tax base may be reduced, as properties on the Vaal River may lose value.

The third environmental risk is from the raw sewage that ends up in the Vaal River. Although Emfuleni has made progress in reducing spills since 2009, the sewage works currently run well above 100 per cent capacity. Industrial spills are also a possibility that cannot be ruled out.

A number of risks related to the steel industry could have major implications for Emfuleni. First there are the rapidly increasing energy costs. Since local industries, especially the steel manufacturers, are heavily dependent on energy, the rapid increase in electricity prices over the past 10 years has not been good news.

The second risk is related to the second-largest cost driver in the industry: the cost of labour. Industry representatives mentioned both the direct labour costs and the cost of dismissing employees. In addition, the centralised system of determining labour costs through the bargaining council has been singled out as quite problematic by industry representatives. The third risk is the dependence on old (and in many cases energy-dependent) technology for producing steel. The steel industry is in dire need of increased research and development to find alternative production methods that are cheaper and have a smaller environmental impact Ironically, taking action regarding this third risk may lead to a fourth risk. Industry representatives mentioned that their companies are engaging in a long-term process of renewing their old technology. Although this might reduce industry's dependence on energy and labour, it would also reduce municipal revenue.

References

ArcelorMittal, 2013. The history of ArcelorMittal South Africa. Available at: http://www. fundinguniverse. com/company-histories/iscor- limited-history (accessed 12 August 2013).

Auditor General, 2013. *General Report on Audit Outcomes of Local Governments in Gauteng*. Johannesburg: Auditor General (Gauteng).

Bega, S., 2008. Big stink over dead fish in Gauteng lake. *Saturday Star*, 18 October.

Bega, S., 2009. Council disputes the number of fish that died in the Vaal River. *Saturday Star*, 17 January.

Christopher, A., 2005. Further progress in the desegregation of South African towns and cities, 1996–2011. *Development Southern Africa*, 18(4), pp. 267–276.

Cilliers, H., 2013. Skrootmetaalbedryf skop vas. *Rapport*, 27 September.

City Press, 2011. Bling 4x4's for bling towns. *City Press*, 18 December.

Department of Water Affairs, 2012. *Blue Drop Report for Emfuleni, 2012*. Available at: http://www.emfuleni.gov.za/index.php?option=com_content&view=article&id =404: emfuleni-awarded-with-the-blue-drop-certification&catid=1:emfuleni-news& Itemid=2 (accessed 12 August 2013).

Department of Water Affairs, 2013. Green Drop reports, s.l. Available at: www.ewisa. co.za/ewisa waterworks/misc/. . ./ defaultGAUSedibeng.htm (accessed 11 September 2013) (accessed 11 November 2013).

Donaldson, R. and Kotze, N., 2006. Residential desegregation dynamics in the South African city of Polokwane. *Journal of Social and Economic Geography*, 97(5), pp. 567–582.

ELM (Emfuleni Local Municipality), 2010. Emfuleni turnaround strategy, Vanderbijlpark: Emfuleni Local Municipality.

ELM (Emfuleni Local Municipality), 2012. Integrated Development Plan, Vanderbijlpark: Emfuleni Local Municipality.

ELM (Emfuleni Local Municipality), 2013. Annual financial statements, 2011/2012, Vanderbijlpark: Emfuleni Local Municipality.

Ensor, A., 2013. Buoyant mood from focus on steel mill. *Business Day*, 1 April, p. 2.

Filen, C., 2012. South African metalworkers union slams steel maker ArcelorMittal SA. *Mineweb*, 12 April.

Fin24, 2015. IDC in R45bn steel mill project with China. Available at: http://www.fin24. com/Companies/Industrial/IDC-in-R45bn-steel-mill-project-with-China-20150213 (accessed 20 July 2015).

Kgosana, C., 2005a. Cleaning up the municipal mess. *City Press*, 3 April.

Kgosana, C., 2005b. Emfuleni suspends councillor over allegations of corruption. *City Press*, 10 April.

Kumba Iron Ore, 2011. The South African iron ore and steel value chain. Downloaded from: www.kumba.co.za/SIOC/pdf/iron_ steel_sec1.pdf:. Kumba Iron Ore (accessed 15 November 2013).

Mabin, A., 1992. Dispossession, exploitation and struggle: an historical overview of South African urbanization. In: D. Smith, ed. *The Apartheid City and Beyond: Urbanisation and Social Change in South Africa.* London: Routledge, pp. 13–24.

Mafela, N., 2006. Fat bonuses for officials at ailing municipalities. *Sunday Times*, 8 January.

Marais, L., 2013. The impact of mine downscaling in the Free State Goldfields. *Urban Forum*, 24, pp. 503–521.

Mooki, S., 2008. Corrupt municipal officials suspended. *City Press*, 16 March.

Nel, R., 2012. Taakspan pak die wanbetalers. *Beeld*, 30 May.

Pretorius, M., 2013. Logistical cities in peripheral areas. Unpublished doctoral thesis, University of the Free State, Bloemfontein.

Radebe, K., 2013. ArcelorMittal to declare force majeure. *Money Web*, 22 February.

SACN (South African Cities Network), 2013. Database of financials of metropolitan areas in South Africa. Johannesburg: South African Cities Network.

Schoeman, A. and Scholtz, H., 2008. Dooie vise 24 uur per dag uit Vaal gehaal. *Beeld*, 6 December.

Seleka, N., 2008a. ANC members disrupt meeting. *Sowetan*, 20 May.

Seleka, N., 2008b. Council warned. *Sowetan*, 27 July.

Skade, T. and Flanagan, L., 2008. Ecological disaster as municipality allows sewage spill in Vaal. *The Star*, 5 December.

Stats SA (Statistics South Africa), 2013. *Census Data for 1996, 2001 and 2011*. Pretoria: Statistics South Africa.

Tabane, R., 2005. Residents threaten another Vaal Uprising. *Mail and Guardian*, 13 October.

Tempelhoff, E., 2004. Inwoners beplan opstand en stryd in hof. *Beeld*, 19 October.

Tempelhoff, E., 2005. ANC skop munisipale hoes uit. *Volksblad*, 27 April.

Tempelhoff, E., 2009a. Dis glo modder. *Beeld*, 19 November.

Tempelhoff, E., 2009b. Aanlegte moet gou werk. *Volksblad*, 14 April.

Tempelhoff, E. and Van Buul, S., 2009. Armlastiges and wanbetalers skuld Emfuleni meer as 2.6 miljard. *Beeld*, 9 March.

The Star, 2006a. But sewage spills remain a problem. *The Star*, 8 February.

The Star, 2006b. Residents protest against lack of water and electricity. *The Star*, 12 October.

UFS (University of the Free State), 2013. *Emfuleni: Steeling the River City*. Bloemfontein: UFS.

Van Buul, S., 2008a. 1ste burger waai ook na raadmoles. *Die Burger*, 24 May.

Van Buul, S., 2008b. ANC hoofsweep skryf brief en toe sit hy in tronk. *Beeld*, 17 May.

Van Buul, S., 2009a. Rubberkoeels op betogers gevuur. *Beeld*, 9 January.

Van Buul, S., 2009b. Die bruin opstand het begin. *Beeld*, 11 September.

6 George

Daan Toerien and Ronnie Donaldson

Introduction

Worldwide, secondary cities are receiving research attention. Bolay and Rabinovich (2004) identify 10 types of secondary city according to their functions as regional markets, service centres, regional capitals, economic locations, tourist centres, communication hubs, metro periphery, cities at the national or international interface (such as ports), urban regions (comprising several small urban areas), and conurban areas or groups of towns. Roberts and Hohmann (2014) note that secondary cities are either centres of local government, industry, agriculture, tourism and mining, or city clusters associated with expanded, satellite and new towns which surround large metro regions, or form part of economic trade corridors. They note also that lead secondary cities have strong growth paths and dynamic local economies, and are well connected nationally and internationally in systems of competitive trade, development and investment.

Functions and roles increasingly define the status of secondary cities in a global system of cities (Roberts and Hohmann, 2014). Secondary cities furthermore imply functional intermediacy in the flows of power, innovation, people and resources among places (Rondinelli, 1983a). City size and functional complexity may be positively correlated. Multi-functionality (as opposed to mono-functionality) and the degree of dependence on a single economic sector (Van der Merwe, 1992) are important factors in urban settlement development. Arbitrary selection as administrative, political or educational centres has sometimes resulted in settlements becoming secondary cities (Rondinelli, 1983b) and the employment of government officials is important in this regard (Hjort, 1979).

Natural endowments such as mining potential and physical details such as the presence of international borders or locations suitable for bases of armed forces are important factors in the evolution of some secondary cities (Satterthwaite, 2006). The proximity of secondary cities to larger cities facilitates networking and agglomeration (Min, 1990; Van der Merwe, 1992). Some cities serve as important gateways to international markets, and globalisation fundamentally shapes economic flows, investment patterns and local development opportunities (Coe and Yeung, 2015), thereby severely challenging some secondary cities, which have to develop appropriate local plans.

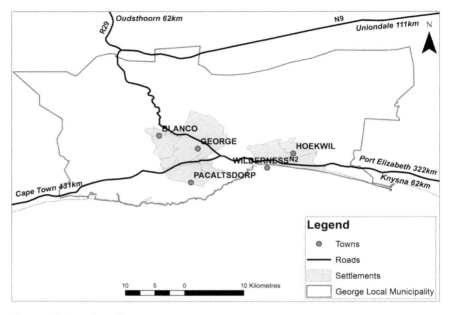

Figure 6.1 Location of George

The above general discussion should be kept in mind as background to this chapter's discussion of the secondary city of George. The city of George straddles the border between the southern Cape and Little Karoo regions of South Africa's Western Cape Province (see Figure 6.1). It is situated approximately halfway between Cape Town and Port Elizabeth. George Municipality is part of the Eden District Municipality. The 2001 South African Census recorded the population of the George Municipality as 150,000 (39,699 households) and the 2011 Census as 193,670 (53,551 households).

Located in one of the most pristine and environmentally sensitive parts of South Africa, George has great tourism potential. It has the feel of a large town rather than a city. It does not have the tall buildings, clearly defined city centre and traffic congestion that are typical of other major cities or metro areas Most of its middle-class suburban houses are not walled or fenced (though this is changing). It still has an old-world charm and a relaxed lifestyle. It is the kind of place where locals complain of parking problems if they cannot park right in front of a shop or their office. It has many long-established retail businesses, though these are now under threat from branded franchises.

This chapter covers the following topics: the development of George com-pared with international experiences of the growth of secondary cities; historical factors that have determined the status of George; the city's demography and economy and the forces that have shaped them; the broad economy of the area and the resources on which it depends; the management of the environment, innovation in planning for the knowledge economy, and the connections with the rural hinterland; and assessment of the current local authority of George in terms of its governance, financial management, service delivery, spatial planning and LED planning. A final 'synthesis' section considers the prognosis for George's future.

Qualitative data for the study were obtained through in-depth interviews with a range of stakeholders in George, comprising senior officials in local government and people from the private sector. Quantitative data were obtained from sources such as the George municipality's IDPs, official census figures, municipal surveys and industry sources.

George as a laboratory for research

Government plans and priorities can have particular consequences for secondary cities, as these cities sometimes serve as test cases for government programmes and policies (Hardoy and Satterthwaite, 1986). The few studies of George and its immediate environs mostly deal with social, environmental, spatial, economic and administrative issues. At the time of major municipal restructuring in 2000, a study was conducted to compare the spatial transformations of George, Pretoria and Cape Town. The study revealed a very positive picture of George in terms of socio-political transformation but spatially the apartheid landscape was very much intact (Lanegran, 2000). The city's proposed integrated transport strategy has been noted as one of the best ways to achieve spatial integration (Page, 2012). Various studies have discussed aspects of the city's LED, such as construction (Terblanche, 2007), SMMEs (Mmbengwa et al., 2013), informal businesses (Smit and Donaldson, 2011) and tourism (Ramukumba, 2012). The city of George has become known for hosting annual sport events such as the President's Cup golf in 2003, a World Sevens rugby tournament (until it was moved to Port Elizabeth in 2013) and an International Under-18 rugby tournament (2013). Several studies have assessed how these events affect the city (Kies, 2005; Rutherford, 2006; Daniels and Swart, 2012; Ramukumba et al., 2012; Biljohn, 2013).

In the Knowledge Age, where knowledge and ideas are the main sources of economic growth, secondary cities face new challenges but can also take advantage of new opportunities (Van Winden et al., 2007). Strong connections between individuals within industries (or clusters of industries) are a prerequisite for success. Higher education institutions play a major role in attracting investment, and since successful cities usually make it possible to enjoy an excellent quality of life they attract educated and skilled people who can create knowledge and use it effectively. Cities that attract the most venture capital for development have benefited from the presence of high densities of enterprises, particularly clusters (Carlso and Chakrabarti, 2007). Some factors that make a city successful are incentives for entrepreneurship, efficient use of existing knowledge, creation of new knowledge, and infrastructure that facilitates the effective communication, dissemination and processing of information (Van Winden et al., 2007). A network of research centres, universities, think-tanks, consultants and firms can tap into the growing stock of global knowledge, assimilate it and adapt it to local needs and opportunities (Levy and Jegou, 2013). Interviewees suggested that the presence of a number of higher education facilities, including a campus of the Nelson Mandela University, positions George well for the Knowledge Age.

Secondary cities have to respond to climate change and other environmental concerns (UNCHS, 2014) but these concerns have received scant research attention (Véron, 2010). The drought in the George region from 2009 to 2011 prompted research into how authorities dealt with the disaster (Lottering et al., 2015; Raju and Van Niekerk, 2013). The opposite risk of floods has also been examined (Benjamin, 2008). The possibility of extreme weather events has prompted a debate on the effects of climate change (Midgley, 2009; Faling and Tempelhoff, 2012), particularly on areas of sensitive biodiversity such as the Eden district (Pauw, 2009; Vromans et al., 2010). The gated residential golf estates in George have been studied as an example of how urban growth and development affect the environment (Van Zyl, 2006; Van der Merwe, 2006).

As George has become an example of a municipality exhibiting good governance and performance, it has been the subject of studies of internal communication strategies (Opperman, 2007), management competence (Krapohl, 2007) and government-subsidised housing (Nell et al., 2011), and social issues such as food security (Modirwa and Oladele, 2012), teenage pregnancies (Sethosa, 2007), crime (Pockpas, 2010) and primary health care (Kapp et al., 2013).

Forces that have shaped Outeniqualand and George

History

'Outeniqualand' is the name given to the region by Khoikhoi settlers. The origin of the name is debated (Thompson, 2013), but all agree that it indicates the presence of honey. The translated title of a book about the history of George is 'George: Land of Milk and Honey' (Van Waart, 1998), suggesting a lush and productive area. For tens of thousands of years, the hunter-gatherer people now known as the San were the only inhabitants of Outeniqualand. Some two to three thousand years ago, Khoikhoi herders moved into this area and the strife that followed, because the San stole Khoikhoi livestock, continued for many centuries (Marean, 2010). In 1652 the Dutch East India Company (Vereenigde Oost-Indische Compagnie, VOC) established a victualling station for its fleets at Table Bay (now Cape Town). By 1713 the first colonist farmers had settled in Outeniqualand, the VOC having assumed the right to allocate land used by the San and Khoikhoi to the colonists. Colonisation continued and more inter-group strife followed. In 1777 the VOC founded a settlement to exploit the forests of Outeniqualand, some 250 to 300 km from Cape Town (Fransen, 2006).

In 1795 and again in 1806 the British occupied the Cape and in 1814 it became formally a British colony. Over the next decades Dutch settlers – for a variety of reasons – became dissatisfied with British rule (Elphick and Giliomee 1989). The town of George, formally founded by the British in 1811, and named after the reigning British monarch, George III, did not escape the British-Dutch colonist tensions that led to the Great Trek in 1836. At the time of the Anglo-Boer War (1899–1902) tensions were high because of British reprisals against Dutch-speaking colonists in the George area who sympathised with the Boer cause (Van Waart, 1998). After 1948 the policies of the apartheid government caused white–black racial tension, which was exacerbated by the eventual development of three separate municipalities: George Municipality for white people, Pacaltsdorp Municipality for coloured people and Thembalethu Municipality for black people. Accusations of white privilege followed.

Since the 1970s George has experienced new waves of immigration. The creation in 1977 of the George airport and in 1996 of an internationally known golf resort (Fancourt) enhanced the reputation of the city and led to an inflow of many wealthy foreigners and white South Africans. These groups are still derogatively called 'inkommers' (incomers) by the original residents, many of whom resent their presence. Many wealthy Europeans (the so-called 'swallows') have bought properties in George to escape the European winters. Their presence is also resented by some. The completion in 1987 of the Mossgas (now PetroSA) gas-to-liquid fuel facility at Mossel Bay brought an inflow of work-seekers into the southern Cape, mostly poor rural blacks from the Eastern Cape. Some settled in George. Those who did not find a job have added to the numbers of the unemployed and are in need of housing and often dependent on welfare. Some people resent their presence too. Other new settlers include foreigners such as Somalis, many of whom work as traders in places like Thembalethu, a suburb of George. This is yet another group whose presence is resented by some, and George did not escape the spate of xenophobic attacks in South Africa in the late 2000s.

Holidaying and retirement

The beaches of Outeniqualand, including those of George, have long been popular holiday spots. In former times, families were transported by ox-wagon to these summer holiday destinations. Later, automobiles, better roads, passenger trains and commercial airlines brought an even larger influx of holidaymakers in the peak summer period (Van Waart, 1998). Many of the visitors own second homes in the area and these have been a major stimulus to the local construction industry. The huge influx of summer visitors is also a boon to the trade and hospitality sectors but puts pressure on the George municipality to provide services for peak demand periods. Because of its scenic beauty and mild climate, George and its surrounds have become a sought-after retirement destination, especially since 1994. Three factors in particular have aided the process: the substantial growth in retirement villages, the increase in high-quality medical facilities (for example a medical business cluster around the hospital), and the safer lifestyle, compared with metros, particularly in the golf estates and in residential expansions such as Eskom Park and Loerie Park. Our interviewees agreed that it was the Fancourt golf development that had put George on the map as a destination of choice for the affluent, and it had become a symbol of what George was standing for at the time – a high-quality, safe lifestyle. Many owners of retirement homes in George and the surrounding coastal areas are now moving to retirement villages with frail-care facilities. The building of such facilities is currently an important stimulus to the construction industry.

Distant markets

Since its early history, Outeniqualand, and thus George, has to a large extent depended on links to distant markets. Once the route around the Cape of Good Hope had been discovered by Bartolomeu Dias in 1488, passing sailors began to trade beads, copper and other goods for livestock with the Khoikhoi. Not long after the Table Bay victualling station had been established, Dutch trading expeditions were sent to barter for livestock to supply the passing ships. Once it became clear that the Khoikhoi were unable or unwilling to supply enough livestock to the VOC, colonist farmers were allowed to move further and further into southern Africa. Part of their agricultural produce, particularly livestock, was marketed in Cape Town. The wood harvested in the forests of the southern Cape was sought after in Cape Town and elsewhere to make carts and wagons, build houses and repair ships. The Great Trek during the 1830s and 1840s, the discovery of diamonds at Kimberley in 1867 and the production of merino wool (especially after the 1830s) opened new inland markets for the George farmers and forest workers. By the middle of the nineteenth century some George farmers were exporting wool to the wool industry in Britain and at the end of that century some were also supplying the booming international ostrich feather market.

Technology, especially transport technology, plays a role in the evolution of a secondary city. Airports, seaports, high speed rail systems and national roads all contribute to its economic growth. The rugged mountain ranges to the north and the deep ravines of the streams draining the Outeniqua mountains have always made it difficult to transport goods and passengers to and from George. In the nineteenth and twentieth centuries much effort went into building passes through the mountains, constructing bridges and building better roads. By 1907 George was linked to Cape Town by rail and in 1977 the new airport gave access to countrywide air traffic. Three important national roads, the N2, N9 and N12, pass through or by George. The improvement to the Outeniqua Pass (carrying the N9 and N12) in the 1990s has helped to position George as a regional service centre. Access to distant markets is much improved but high transport costs limit the profitability of exports and, according to some interviewees, make it difficult for some George businesses to compete on price. The economy of Outeniqualand, including that of George, is thus sensitive to competition and the state of the world economy.

Natural and man-made disasters

A smallpox outbreak in 1713 that may have originated from a Dutch ship at Cape Town considerably reduced the Khoikhoi population of the Cape Colony, including that of Outeniqualand. Encroachment by colonist farmers reduced the area available to the Khoikhoi, many of whom eventually became workers on colonist farms. In 1869 a fire destroyed huge tracts of forest between what are now the towns of Riversdale and Uitenhage, a stretch of over 400 km. Outeniqualand has often been drought stricken, most recently from 2009 to 2011 when the water supply to George struggled to cope (Lottering et al., 2015; Holloway et al., 2012). In 2004/2005 Outeniqualand suffered floods (Tempelhoff et al., 2009) and in 2006 another flood caused severe damage to the rail track on which the famous Choo-Tjoe train ran between George and Knysna, putting an end to that tourist attraction (Friends of the Choo-Tjoe, n.d.).

Leadership and politics

Leadership is an important determinant of successful communities. Various leaders have contributed substantially to the development of George (Van Waart, 1998). Two notable examples are Charles Pacalt of the London Mission Society and the Khoikhoi captain 'Dikkop', who together served the Khoikhoi community at Hoogekraal (now Pacaltsdorp). Their efforts led to the founding of Pacaltsdorp, which in 1975 became an independent municipality and is today still an important part of the city of George (Van Waart, 1998). Another is the magistrate Van Kervel, who started the process of building the first, but dangerous, Cradock Pass across the Outeniqua Mountains. John Montagu, the Colonial Secretary, was a driving force for the construction of the safer Montagu Pass, which was completed in 1848 by Henry Fancourt White. White also played an important role in the development of the town of Blanco (now part of George), which became a manufacturing centre. In the 1990s a German married couple, the Plattners, provided the initiative for the development of the Fancourt golf resort, which helped to position George internationally.

A succession of political processes and changes may be largely responsible for the growth of George since the 1980s. Before that George was not the major role-player in the region that it is today. Its importance began to grow from 1977 with the construction of the airport, originally named after P. W. Botha, later the state president, who lived in the area and secured this development. As part of the apartheid government's 1982 Regional Industrial Development Programme, the city was identified as one of some 50 industrial development points. Growth points and concomitant concessions were planned so as to distribute economic activities more evenly in the country, while at the same time compensating for the lack of agglomeration advantages that entrepreneurs could have gained in metros (Van der Merwe et al., 1987). George was the only identified growth point in the southern Cape, and one of two within the Western Cape provincial boundary. However, when the apartheid system began to fail and P. W. Botha was ousted as president of the country, the anticipated state-driven support for George did not materialise. During the transition to democracy and immediately after 1994 the city's growth process, as has been the case in most secondary cities in the country, was driven and dictated entirely by the private sector. In George, the current lack of visionary leadership has at times resulted in a fractious community working against itself.

Demographic and social conditions in George today

In studies of the growth potential of Western Cape towns (Donaldson et al., 2012a; Van Niekerk and Du Plessis, 2013), George is classified as having a very high overall growth potential and is ranked as the settlement with the highest growth potential in the Western Cape (excluding the Cape Town metro area). It achieved a very high rating on the economic, infrastructure and institutional thematic indexes and a high rating on the human capital and physical indexes. On the economic index it achieved the highest overall score in the province and the highest score for three of the indicators on this index (total personal income, value of property transactions and number of formal retail outlets and service sector businesses). Its infrastructure is of high quality, giving it high and very high scores for most of the indicators on the infrastructure index. It also performed exceptionally well on the institutional index, although it still needs to reduce its basic infrastructure backlogs, as can be seen by its score on the socio-economic needs index, where it is classified as having very high levels of socio-economic needs (Van Niekerk and Du Plessis, 2013).

Racial geography and population growth

The racial geography of settlements in the Western Cape is typically dominated by coloured residents. George is no exception. In 2011 the largest proportion of its residents were coloured (47 per cent) followed by blacks (32 per cent) and whites (19 per cent). Unlike the situation in other secondary cities such as Polokwane (Donaldson and Kotze, 2006), the racial geography of George's living areas is strongly intact according to our interviewees. However, the 2011 Census shows that, according to population group and suburb, integration has been quite substantial in several areas, such as Glenwood, Groeneweide Park, George Central, Blanco and Fancourt (the highest percentage integration is in Fancourt, probably due to a big labour force staying on the estate).

Compared with the immediate post-apartheid period (1994–2001), all three main population groups in George saw a decline in growth rate between 2001 and 2011. The 2005 IDP predicted that the municipal area would have a population growth rate of 2.5 per cent until 2015. The actual 10-year growth rate between 2001 and 2011 is in line with this prediction.

Many of our interviewees agreed that the growing population is putting pressure on land use because of increased demand for housing and the need to provide basic infrastructure. The population growth can be attributed to natural increases and in-migration. The interviewees named two specific in-migrant groups: people from the impoverished rural areas of the Eastern Cape in search of work (leading to an increased demand for subsidised housing) and an affluent socio-economic group, mostly elderly, drawn by the lifestyle possibilities of George, as evidenced by the increase in the number of luxury residential estates. A noticeable feature of George is the way that demand for land responds to robust economic development elsewhere in South Africa. This can be seen in particular in the market for holiday homes.

Household conditions and development

The 2011 broad household income profile of George is similar to those of the Western Cape Province and the Eden district. The highest income group is made up almost entirely of whites, although whites are the smallest of George's population groups. The middle income group comprises blacks, coloureds and whites. Approximately 88 per cent of George's households live in informal housing, a percentage slightly higher than that for the Eden District Municipality and the Western Cape. In 2011/2012, water of a quality that met or exceeded minimum standards was delivered to 41,272 households (99.88 per cent of the total).

Economy of George

Economic structure and growth

Table 6.1 shows the changes from 1996 to 2011 in the GVA contributions of various sectors to the George economy. By 2011 the finance and insurance sector was by far the dominant sector, adding about half a billion rand (constant 2005 rand) per annum more in 2011 than in 1996. Financial courses offered by the Nelson Mandela Metropolitan University's satellite campus in George may have played a role in creating the capacity of George's financial services sector to deliver services. The success of this sector lends credence to the suggestion by an interviewee that George could endeavour to become a 'college town' and it raises the question why this sector has not received more attention in the city's municipal LED strategies.

In 1996 the real estate and retail trade sectors dominated, but by 2011 they had lost their advantages. Both sectors were apparently hard hit by the economic slump after 2007. For example, according to a real estate interviewee, real estate

Table 6.1 Business sectors in George whose annual GVA increased by more than R100 million, 1996–2011 (values in constant 2005 rand)

Business sector	1996	2011	Increase
Finance and insurance	168.3	729.8	561.5
Retail trade	233.0	507.0	274.0
Other business activities	104.3	357.8	253.5
Construction	128.8	375.7	246.9
Posts and telecommunications	54.8	225.4	170.7
Motor vehicle services	62.7	211.1	148.4
Air transport and services	71.7	211.6	139.9
Real estate	291.2	407.2	116.1
Food, beverages and tobacco	200.6	316.5	115.9
Furniture manufacturing and recycling	170.9	284.2	113.3
Health and social work	139.0	240.4	101.4

Source: UFS (2013).

transactions declined in the part of George that he serves from R105.5 million in 2007 to R58.5 million in 2008 and approximately R36 million in 2009, and since then have remained at this level or below.

George and the surrounding region have a diverse economic base which, in addition to agriculture and tourism, is well developed with respect to industries, government and civil service functions, as well as financial, educational and medical services. Its tourism sector is strong and is a driver of the construction sector. The demand for second homes, holiday homes, retirement villages and low-cost houses provides employment and supports a strong local property market. Agriculture, a labour-intensive sector, has a good potential for the cultivation and agro-processing of high-quality products. Currently, a number of agricultural products of the district (such as berries) have been destined for overseas markets, which increases the geographical gross product (total GVA in the region). However, distance from the large metro markets and high transport costs are holding back exports of produce and products.

Does George's economic structure differ from that of metros and other secondary cities? If we compare the ratio of population size to GVA for George with the ratios for a selection of South African secondary cities, we find that George falls within the dataset, albeit in the lower part of it (Figure 6.2). George's ratio is also not out of step with the ratios for metros, though again it is in the lower part (Figure 6.3). The structure of George's economy, as profiled in terms of GVA, is very similar to those of Johannesburg and Cape Town (Figure 6.4) and the dominance of the finance and insurance sector differentiates these three cities from the rest in Figure 6.4.

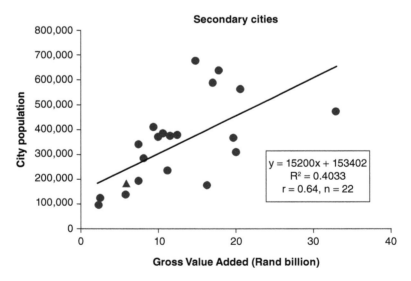

Figure 6.2 The Gross Value Added–population relationship of secondary cities in South Africa (George indicated as a triangle)

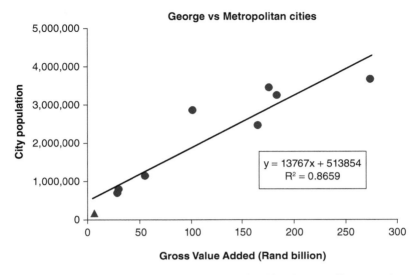

Figure 6.3 The Gross Value Added–population relationship of metropolitan areas in South Africa (George indicated as a triangle)

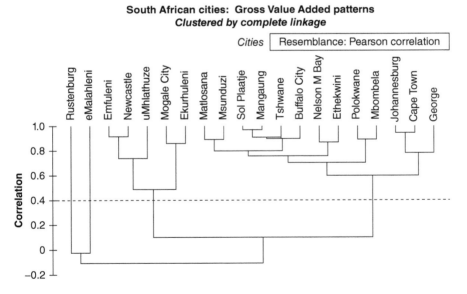

Figure 6.4 Cluster analysis for GVA contribution per sector in secondary cities and metropolitan areas in South Africa

Employment

According to the 2011 Census there were 50,405 people in formal employment in George. Seventeen sectors together contributed at least 80 per cent of the GVA and formal employment in George in 2011 (Figure 6.5). There is a clear mismatch between value addition and employment in some sectors (e.g. finance and insurance, real estate, construction). Sectors that contribute more to the GVA than to employment are necessary to compensate for sectors that contribute little to GVA (such as hotels and restaurants) or nothing (such as households) but which contribute quite large percentages of employment opportunities (hotels and restaurants 6.5 per cent, households 5.7 per cent).

The normalised sector employment profile of George was compared to those of other secondary and metros in a cluster analysis (Figure 6.6). At a correlation level of 0.68, four clusters and three outliers (Rustenburg, eMalahleni and Matlosana) could be discerned. George and Cape Town had very similar formal employment profiles. The same 12 business sectors provided at least 80 per cent of the formal employment opportunities in George and almost 70 per cent of those in Cape Town.

In 2011 George had close on 2,900 people in informal employment. Unemployment numbers for blacks in George in 2011 were 7,399 and a further 2,195 were discouraged jobseekers. The corresponding figures for coloureds were 8,187 and 2,670, for whites 706 and 215, and for Indians (only 0.5 per cent of the city's total population) 56 and 18. Interviewees said the unemployment figures for black and coloureds are obviously a matter for concern.

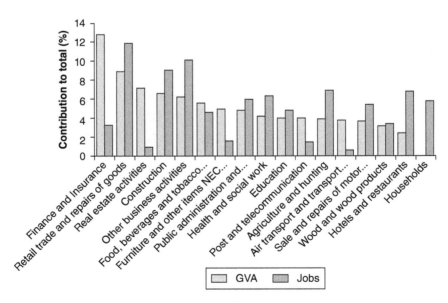

Figure 6.5 Formal GVA and employment contributions per sector

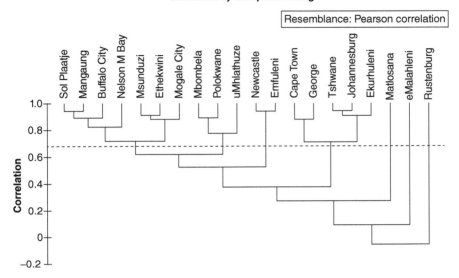

Similarity of formal employment patterns of South African cities
Clustered by complete linkage

Resemblance: Pearson correlation

Figure 6.6 Normalised sector employment profile of George compared to those of other secondary and metropolitan cities

Natural resources and the environment

George is situated in a diverse geographical area, being located on the temperate Garden Route but having the dry and climatically extreme Little Karoo to the north. It is an area of considerable natural assets and scenic beauty, with mountains and forests, wilderness areas, a varied coastline, and extensive lakes, rivers and estuaries. Its natural assets include parts of the Garden Route National Park and the Baviaanskloof Wilderness Area. The municipal area also includes fertile farmlands and timber plantations along the coastal plain, fruit orchards in the Langkloof and arid grazing areas in the Little Karoo.

It is a biodiversity hotspot (Vromans et al., 2010; Page, 2012; George Municipality, 2013a). A study by Faling and Tempelhoff (2012) of the potential effect of climate change on the environment of George revealed that the natural vegetation of George (part of the Cape Floral Kingdom) is threatened by reduction in water quality and quantity, pollution and eutrophication, introduction of invasive alien species, agricultural activities and urban expansion. Traditionally the economy of George was based on forestry and agriculture. Large areas were cleared of natural vegetation to make room for commercial forests, transforming the natural environment that protected the steep slopes of river gorges. Forestry and agriculture are now threatened by urban expansion into the few remaining areas of high-potential farmland, the development of golf estates, the provision of land for small farmers, and an increase in the demand for water (Faling and Tempelhoff, 2012).

Managing its natural resources wisely and preserving the natural environment are priorities for George that have been stated in many statutory documents related to integrated development and LED planning. A Biodiversity Sector Plan provides a synthesis of prioritised information to planners and land use managers, enabling the integration of biodiversity into land use planning and decision making (Vromans et al., 2010).

Some interviewees were of the opinion that the Eden district has effectively reached its carrying capacity in terms of water availability. Serious water shortages may well recur during drought years, like those experienced in George during the severe droughts of 2009–2011. However, based on water availability in 2013 and predicted consumption levels, George has 45 per cent spare capacity. The municipal manager suggested in an interview that increasing the Garden Route dam overflow would give George sufficient water to meet anticipated growth and demand until 2025.

Regional services

George is increasingly serving as a regional service centre, as can be seen by the growing number of shopping malls, private and public educational facilities, and private medical facilities. Some financial firms use George as a regional and even national base.

Internal responses

Municipal governance

The city of George is divided into 25 wards and is served by 49 councillors, of whom 25 are elected in wards and 24 are proportionally appointed. The party political composition after the 2011 municipal election was as follows: Democratic Alliance (DA) 25, African National Congress (ANC) 19, African Christian Democratic Party (ACDP) 1, Congress of the People (COPE) 1, George Independent Ratepayers Forum (GIRF) 1, Independent Civic Organisation of South Africa (ICOSA) 1, Plaaslike Besorgde Inwoners (PBI) 1. Since the election the media have reported many political squabbles; however, interviewees did not consider them serious, believing there was a reasonable amount of cooperation between parties and between councillors.

The municipality's independent four-person audit committee, whose job is to assess risks, met six times in the 2011/2012 financial year. The top 10 possible risks it identified for the city were lack of financial viability, inadequate standards of service delivery, community dissatisfaction, poorly maintained infrastructure, lack of staff skills and capacity, municipal officials' poor levels of compliance with municipal strategies and regulations, weaknesses in governance and accountability, increasing poverty and numbers of indigents, failure or non-integration of IT systems, and inefficient investment in capital expenditure.

Of George municipality's 68 key performance indicators (KPIs) in 2011/2012, 8 were not met (11.8 per cent), 5 were almost met (7.4 per cent), 38 were met

(55.9 per cent), 10 were well met (14.7 per cent) and 7 were extremely well met (10.3 per cent). The KPIs that were not met were in the areas of basic service deliveries, good governance and public participation, LED and financial viability and management. Overall the performance has been good but some areas still need attention.

Strategic planning, LED and spatial planning

George has been described as having an optimistic view of the future (Lanegran, 2000). Its catchy slogan, 'The city for all reasons', captures the spirit of its five strategic goals: to deliver quality services in George, ensure good governance in George, grow George, keep George safe and green, and participate in George. Economic development is essential to achieving these goals, and the IDP stresses the importance of providing resources to improve the lot of the poor and the previously disadvantaged. The current IDP, covering the period 2012 to 2016, builds on previous IDPs and is summed up as follows: 'To build on George's status as the pace-setting destination in the region and utilising all resources available to us to the benefit of our Community in our growing and thriving city' (George Municipality, 2013b).

To ensure equitable and sustainable development of the municipal area, the municipality's plans are as follows: to make the services economy, particularly the technology, tourism, and business and financial sectors, the local economic base; to prioritise the needs of vulnerable communities and develop the human capital for a service economy; to create humane and living environments by delivering services to all households, upgrading informal settlements and degraded neighbourhoods, providing houses to the subsidy market, promoting 'green' household technologies and protecting the municipal area's natural and cultural heritage; to build institutional excellence by providing a high standard of services to consumers and functioning effectively as a developmental local government; and to ensure that all members of public, organised business and other organisations have the opportunity to participate in the decision-making process and that a culture of participation is nurtured. It is interesting to note that interviewees at the municipality saw the possibility of receiving metro status as an opportunity to grow George further.

LED was identified as one of the challenges for the municipality and its planning has received much attention, as it is a national requirement (George Municipality, 2013a, 2013b). A small but energetic Economic Development Unit has driven a planning process that combines the participatory appraisal of competitive advantage (PACA) and Genesys processes, both of which are internationally proven methodologies. This combined process was implemented largely by a few senior municipal officials with the assistance of local representatives of the public, some of whom were volunteers trained in the PACA methodology by an expert. The local team was then supported by experienced external facilitators to ensure capability transfer. Important relationships were built that will help to bridge the gap between the public and private sectors.

Deliberations during the PACA process led to a decisive policy statement for economic development. The George Municipality:

> recognises the important role it plays in ensuring an enabling environment for economic development as a means to sustainable livelihoods for its residents. In aggressively pursuing economic growth a multi-faceted, cross-sectoral, participatory approach will be followed. At the centre of this will be cooperation and the building of lasting, productive relationships with civil society, business, NGOs and other stakeholders in the pursuit of common goals. Although a structured approach is envisioned, sufficient flexibility will be incorporated to allow for the identification and pursuit of ad hoc opportunities.
>
> (George Municipality, 2013a)

The PACA process led to two questions about George's socio-economic future: Is there a shared transformational view of the future? Will the 'haves' continue an overall patronising, largely exploitative business model? The answers to these questions will depend on the extent to which stakeholders share a common vision of the future and cooperate to achieve LED goals. Advantages that George enjoys over other cities are its natural endowments (arable land, a climate favourable for agricultural development, and usually adequate and predictable availability of water), and its well-developed (but improvable) social infrastructure, recreational potential and generally good quality of life.

An LED maturity assessment in 2012 ranked George eighth out of 29 Western Cape municipalities (Hadingham, 2013). The report suggested that a functional LED leadership and governance system should be established, the LED facilitation capacity should be broadened across a range of people, coherent strategies should be ensured and the focus should be on making George a better place for the poor to access economic opportunities. Compared to metros such as Cape Town, the Economic Development Unit of George municipality is very small and has limited capacity to address LED. Plans to expand the Unit have not yet been formally accepted – this will require political, financial and infrastructural support. It makes little sense, given the importance of the tourism and hospitality sector for George, that there is a separate tourism office in the George Municipality and that tourism does not form part of the mandate of the Economic Development Unit. It is surprising that LED planning for George seems to ignore certain sectors that are important to the George economy. For instance, it lacks information about how much money is being brought into the George economy by retired and elderly people. Similarly, it has not adequately quantified the revenue from tourism and the so-called 'swallows' (Europeans who spend their winter months in George). Interviewees who owned businesses said that the huge influx of South African visitors during peak summer holiday periods contributes substantially to their turnover, but this has not been properly quantified.

In South African cities, spatial planning and development are tied up with local politics and George is not an exception. The city does not have an identifiable centre. As the need for office and retail space increased after the 1980s, houses in the residential areas close to the CBD were transformed into business spaces and office parks sprang up. Evidence of decentralisation and de-concentration can be seen in the regional shopping centre and business area that developed from 2005 next to the N2 national road to the east of the CBD, increasing the vacancies in the CBD, and the smaller shopping centres scattered throughout the town. A corridor development has taken shape along the main roads leading from the CBD in the directions of Oudtshoorn and the N2. Developers appear to have dictated the spatial development since 2000 and have been the de facto planners of the city. According to some interviewees, George 'did not see this coming'. Interviewees (from both public and private sectors) expressed a fear that the businesses still located in the CBD will not be able to compete against the big branded shops of the new regional mall and will ultimately close down, as happened elsewhere in South Africa 20 years ago.

Gated developments that contrast with the general open character of the city are also proliferating. A study in the Western Cape of non-metro areas showed that gated residential security estates are most abundant in George, which has 35 such developments (Spocter, 2013). This form of development has been criticised by academics (Spocter, 2013) as fuelling spatial segregation and disrupting the spatial flow of the city. The Spatial Development Framework (SDF) interviewees and interviewees are in agreement that it must be curtailed.

Synthesis

The importance of George as a national economic and development role-player has been evident since the 1980s. Recognised as a secondary city, George has been variously identified as part of the development of a decentralisation programme, as a growth point, and as part of projected policy formulation for national urbanisation. Similarly, in 2003 the National Spatial Development Perspective (NSDP) identified the city and its region as areas of national economic significance. The city is located in one of the most pristine and environmentally sensitive parts of South Africa. It is without doubt the main service centre of the Garden Route region, which is located halfway between the two metros of Cape Town and Nelson Mandela Bay, yet it still maintains its 'large town' character.

Several other slightly smaller cities in the southern Cape, such as Mossel Bay, Knysna and Oudtshoorn, show an equally high potential for growth and are all located within the daily urban system of George (Donaldson et al., 2012b). This urban system could be described as a 'dispersed city', which is one that has a number of 'discrete or physically (but not necessarily politically) separate urban centres in close proximity to each other and functionally interrelated, although usually separated by tracts of non-urban land' (Burton, 1963). This might be a future for George, Mossel Bay, Knysna and Oudtshoorn to consider.

Some other secondary cities are provincial capitals (e.g. Polokwane, Mbombela). George could perhaps play a bigger role as one of the decentralised regional headquarters of the Western Cape government. Decentralised provincial offices have already opened in George and more are apparently in the pipeline.

A study of the growth potential of Western Cape towns conducted by Stellenbosch University (Donaldson et al., 2012a) indicated that George has a high growth potential. The question is whether this potential can be realised. The study revealed a lot of positives but also some negatives. George is a supportive and productive municipality but its efforts are limited by the size of financial and other resources at its disposal. Some of its structural decisions do not make much economic sense, for example having LED and tourism managed by separate departments. Common problems of secondary cities are lack of long-term vision, with a resulting focus on short-term benefits leading to disappointing performance; less ability than metros to plan in a global context, often because they lack international experience; and dependence on a single industry, which increases the risks in a complex world. George does have a long-term vision but lacks clear globally focused development strategies. Its economy is reasonably well balanced, being dependent on several business sectors: agriculture, tourism, some manufacturing, the retirement industry, retail, financial services and construction. It should have more resilience when the global economy goes awry.

Industrial cluster planning has had some success (e.g. Ferguson, 1992; Wilson, 1992). George does not have a strong industrial base or a large agricultural sector but it has potential for cluster planning within the knowledge-based economy, as Rodríguez-Pose and Fitjar (2013) suggest, in the form of industrial parks, learning regions or regional innovation. To do this it will be important to create networks and interact with external actors. The idea of a knowledge-based economy growth-path is, however, viewed with both scepticism and optimism in George. Nevertheless, from a macro-economic policy point of view George shows that it is possible for a South African town without the benefits of mineral exploitation to grow into a secondary city with a balanced economy.

The racial geography of George resembles that of other Western Cape secondary cities but is distinctly different from that of secondary cities in the other provinces of South Africa. This geography makes for more complex racial arrangements in all spheres of life in George, such as in local politics, where the nationally leading African Nation Congress political party is not in power specifically because it is not supported by George's large proportion of coloured voters. Although the Western Cape is under the same political authority as George, any change in power would create tension between the city and its second-tier governance structures. This is not the situation in most other secondary cities in South Africa.

Historically George has been, and still is, far removed from the large national and international markets. Its position midway between two metros and the difficult topography of its surroundings necessitate good road and air connections. It is prone to flooding, which can cut off road access. These factors, which can make it difficult for entrepreneurs in George to compete in external markets, were responsible for a recent decision by a food company to terminate production in George and focus rather on the large Gauteng market. LED decisions are therefore more difficult for George than for other secondary cities that are closer to large South African markets or that have ports that can handle international trade.

All our interviewees agreed that, socially, economically and developmentally, George is largely a retirement destination. Like all other South African secondary cities, George has to overcome the legacies of the apartheid years. Yet, at the same time, it has to ensure that the people and economic sector-drivers who have contributed to its rapid growth over the past two decades are not neglected. It is therefore surprising that, while acknowledging the economic contributions of elderly, affluent 'inkommers' (incomers), foreign 'swallows' and large numbers of tourists and holidaymakers, the city planners do not have accurate figures showing the size of these contributions. Much of the city's spatial planning and marketing is aimed at promoting the city as a retirement destination. To learn international lessons on how to plan for such city growth, the city should look at the so-called 'sunbelt' region of the US, where people at retirement age have sought protected environments, away from violent urban areas and located in warmer climate zones. Targeting South Africa's growing black middle class (the so-called 'black diamonds') would perhaps be a way to grow the retirement market. This could, of course, encourage a situation where South African 'haves' continue a patronising largely exploitative business model. Frank policy discussion of this issue is needed.

What makes George more difficult to manage than other South African secondary cities is its location in an area noted for its sensitive biodiversity. It is potentially a fast-growing area, facing pressure for land to be developed. But developments encroach on the biodiversity areas and threaten the ecology. Managing this will require comprehensive and sustainable strategies. Although strategies are in place, they will need continual upgrading to cope with further pressures for development and to deal with the increasing urbanisation of George. A biodiversity sector plan has been formulated; and George is the only secondary city in the country that has such a plan. Secondary cities faced with rapid growth have the option to reshape themselves for the better. George has to some extent failed in this regard, merely mimicking failed responses to urban integration challenges of bigger cities and metros, such as decentralisation of business space, class-based segregation and gated developments. Transport planning is often considered a weak form of post-apartheid restructuring strategy, but George's new Integrated Public Transport Plan was considered by our interviewees to have set the city apart from other secondary cities. To have succeeded in negotiating buy-in from all role-players, including the temperamental taxi industry, is indeed a sign of a city authority and civil society that are functioning well.

The net result of the growth experienced in George has been rapid in-migration of mostly unskilled and unemployed people from the Eastern Cape. Increasing unemployment, the growing number of indigent welfare recipients and an increasing rate of HIV infection are policy issues that need to be addressed as a matter of urgency. Today George has about 23,000 people on the waiting list for state-subsidised housing. Since 2009 the economic recession has obstructed growth in the construction industry, complicating the problem. At the other end of the market, 29,000 serviced residential plots for middle- and upper-income groups are standing empty.

On an institutional level, the city cannot compete with metros. The lack of funding to employ more qualified and experienced staff in important departments is seen as a major inhibitor of further growth. The city authority acknowledges that George's socio-economic future will be largely determined by shared ideas on transformation. Communities that have a shared vision of their future do better than communities that lack such vision. Strong leadership is essential for developing this vision, aligning people to it and getting them to commit to achieving it. Leaders in George will have to rise to this challenge.

References

Benjamn, M.A., 2008. Analysing urban flood risk in low-cost settlements of George, Western Cape, South Africa: investigating physical and social dimensions. Unpublished master's thesis, University of Cape Town, Cape Town.

Biljohn, M., 2013. Analysis of interventions in support of small tourism businesses in the Eden District Municipality. Unpublished master's thesis, Stellenbosch University, Stellenbosch.

Bolay, J., and Rabinovich, A., 2004. Intermediate cities in Latin America: risk and opportunities of coherent urban development. *Cities*, 21(5), pp. 407–421.

Burton, I., 1963. A restatement of the dispersed city hypothesis. *Annals of the Association of American Geographers*, 53(3), pp. 285–289.

Carlso, C., and Chakrabarti, P., 2007. Venture capital in New England secondary cities. *New England Community Developments*, 1 (1), pp. 1–7.

Coe, N., and Yeung, H., 2015. *Global Production Networks.*, Oxford: Oxford University Press.

Daniels, T., and Swart, K., 2012. The 2010 FIFA World Cup and the Eden District Municipality. *African Journal for Physical Health Education*, 18(1), pp. 152–161.

Donaldson, R., and Kotze, N., 2006. Residential desegregation dynamics in the South African city of Polokwane. *Journal of Social and Economic Geography*, 97(5), pp. 567–582.

Donaldson, R., Van Niekerk, A., Du Plessis, D., and Spocter, M., 2012a. Non-metropolitan growth potential of Western Cape municipalities. *Urban Forum*, 23(3), pp. 367–389.

Donaldson, R., Ferreira, S., and Spocter, M., 2012b. Growth potential of towns in the Western Cape. Qualitative phase: unlocking latent potential and recommendations for appropriate interventions for regional development. Unpublished report, University of Stellenbosch, Stellenbosch.

Elphick, R., and Giliomee, H., 1989. *The Shaping of South African Society, 1652–1840*. Cape Town: Maskew Miller Longman.

Faling, W., and Tempelhoff, J.W.N., 2012. Rhetoric or action: are South African municipalities planning for climate change? *Development Southern Africa*, 29(2), pp. 241–257.

Ferguson, B., 1992. Inducing local growth: two intermediate-sized cities in the state of Parana, Brazil. *Third World Planning Review*, 14(3), pp. 245–265.

Fransen, H., 2006. *Old Towns and Villages of the Cape.*, Johannesburg: Jonathan Ball Publishers.

Friends of the Choo-Tjoe (n.d.). History of the line and current status. www.friend-softhechoo-tjoe.co.za/history-of-the-line-and-current-status (accessed 12 May 2015).

George Municipality, 2013a. Participatory appraisal of competitive advantage (PACA). Economic development initiative. Unpublished report from the George Municipality, George.

George Municipality, 2013b. *Annual report 2012/13*. George: George Municipality.

Hadingham, T., 2013. *Municipalities Are Growing Horns. A Reflection on the Outcomes of the Western Cape LED Maturity Assessments.* LED case study. Cape Town: SALGA Western Cape.

Hardoy, J. and Satterthwaite, D., 1986. *Small and Intermediate Urban Centres: Their Role in National and Regional Development in the Third World.* London: Hodder & Stoughton.

Hjort, A., 1979. Sedentary pastoralists and peasants. The inhabitants of a small towns. In: A. Southall, ed. *Small Urban Centres in Rural Development in Africa.* Madison: University of Wisconsin, pp. 45–55.

Holloway, A., Fortune, G., Zweig, P., Barrett, L., Benjamin, A., Chasi, V. and de Waal, J., 2012. Eden and Central Karoo drought disaster 2009–2011: the scramble for water. www.westerncape.gov.za/text/2012/11/eden-and-central-karoo-drought-disaster-2009–2011.pdf (accessed 11 April 2015).

Kapp, P.A., Klop, A.C., and Jenkins, L.S., 2013. Drug interactions in primary health care in the George sub-district, South Africa: a cross-sectional study. *South African Family Practice*, 55(1), pp. 78–84.

Kies, C., 2005. The local impact of the President's Cup 2003. What lessons for sports tourism and development in South Africa? Unpublished master's thesis, Stellenbosch University, Stellenbosch.

Krapohl, J., 2007. Assessing management competencies in selected southern cape municipalities. Unpublished master's thesis, Nelson Mandela Metropolitan University, Port Elizabeth.

Lanegran, D., 2000. The post-apartheid city and the globalization of eroding the landscape of apartheid. *Macalester International*, 9(9), pp. 269–278.

Levy, R. and Jegou, L., 2013. Diversity and location of knowledge production in small cities in France. *City, Culture and Society*, 4(4), pp. 203–216.

Lottering, N., Du Plessis, D. and Donaldson, R., 2015. Coping with drought: the experience of water sensitive urban design (WSUD) in the George Municipality. *Water SA*, 41(1), pp. 1–6.

Marean, C.M., 2010. Pinnacle Point Cave 13B (Western Cape Province, South Africa) in context: the Cape Floral kingdom, shellfish, and modern human origins. *Journal of Human Evolution*, 59(3–4), pp. 425–443.

Midgley, S.H., 2009. Climate change and agriculture: impacts and opportunities. The impact of climate change on coastal and little Karoo living. Eden District Municipality conference, Mossel Bay, 2–4 February 2009.

Min, M., 1990. Growth of small and intermediate cities in Korea, 1975–1980. *Korea Journal of Population and Development*, 19(1), pp. 47–70.

Mmbengwa, V.M., Groenewald, J.A., and Van Schalkwyk, H., 2013. Evaluation of the entrepreneurial success factors of small, micro and medium farming enterprises (SMMEs) in the peri-urban poor communities of George municipality, Western Cape Province, RSA. *African Journal of Business Management*, 7(2), pp. 2459–2474.

Modirwa, S., and Oladele, O.I., 2012. Food security among male and female-headed households in Eden District Municipality of the Western Cape, South Africa. *Journal of Human Ecology*, 37(1), pp. 29–35.

Nell, M., Bertoldi, A., Taljaard, R., Gordon, R., Holmes, T. and Pretorius, R., 2011. Report on a qualitative study on three communities. Johannesburg: Shisaka Development Management Services. www.housingfinanceafrica.org/wp-content/uploads/2011/12/RDP-Assets-Qualitative-Report_Final_May11.pdf (accessed 23 February 2015).

Opperman, Y., 2007. An internal communication assessment of the George municipality. Unpublished master's thesis, University of South Africa, Pretoria.

Page, J. H., 2012. A comparison of integrated transport and spatial planning instruments: a case study of the Eden district municipality, Hermanus local municipality and Cape Town metropolitan areas. Unpublished master's thesis, North-West University, Poptchefstrooom.

Pauw, J., 2009. Challenges to sustainability in the Garden Route: Water, Land and Economy. Report. Nelson Mandela Metropolitan University. Available at: http://sru.nmmu.ac.za/sru/media/ Store/documents/Publications%20and%20Reports/Pauw,-2009--Challenges-to-sustainability-in-the-Garden-Route---.pdf (accessed 13 December 2014).

Pockpas, M.L., 2010. An operational analysis of known rape cases in the greater George area. Unpublished master's thesis, University of South Africa, Pretoria.

Raju, E. and Van Niekerk, D., 2013. Intra-governmental coordination for sustainable disaster recovery: a case-study of the Eden District Municipality, South Africa. *International Journal of Disaster Risk Reduction*, 4, pp. 92–99.

Ramukumba, T., 2012. The local economic development in the Eden District Municipality, Western Cape Province, South Africa: a case study of emerging entrepreneurs in tourism industry. *American Journal of Tourism Research*, 1(1), pp. 9–15.

Ramukumba, T., Mmbengwa, V.M., Mwamayi, K.A. and Groenewald, J., 2012. Analysis of the socio-economic impacts of tourism for emerging tourism entrepreneurs: the case of George municipality in the Western Cape Province, South Africa. *Journal of Hospitality Management and Tourism*, 3(3), pp. 39–45.

Roberts, B. and Hohmann, R., 2014. *The Systems of Secondary Cities: The Neglected Drivers of Urbanising Economies.* Brussels: Cities Alliance.

Rodríguez-Pose, A. and Fitjar, R., 2013. Buzz, archipelago economics and the future of intermediate and peripheral areas in a spiky world. *European Planning Studies*, 21 (3), pp. 355–372.

Rondinelli, D., 1983a. *Secondary Cities in Developing Countries. Policies for Diffusing Urbanisation.* Beverley Hills: SAGE.

Rondinelli, D., 1983b. Towns and small cities in developing countries. *Geographical Review*, 73 (4), pp. 379–395.

Rutherford, D.L., 2006 Towards a development strategy for small businesses in the tourism industry of the Southern Cape. Unpublished doctoral thesis, University of Pretoria, Pretoria.

SACN (South African Cities Network), 2014. *Outside the Core: Towards Understanding of Intermediate Cities in South Africa.* Johannesburg: SACN.

Satterthwaite, D., 2006. Outside the large cities: The demographic importance of small urban centres and large villages in Africa, Asia and Latin America. UNCHS. Human Settlements Discussion Paper. Retrieved from: http://www.iied.org/pubs/display.php?o=10537IIED (accessed 12 April 2014).

Sethosa, G.S., 2007. Teenage pregnancies as a management issue in townships in George. Unpublished master's thesis, Nelson Mandela Metropolitan University, Port Elizabeth.

Smit, E., and Donaldson, R., 2011. The home as informal business location: home-based business (HBB) dynamics in the medium-sized city of George. *Town and Regional Planning*, 59 (1), pp. 26–35.

Spocter, M., 2013. Non-metropolitan gated developments in the Western Cape. Patterns, process, purpose. Unpublished doctoral thesis, Stellenbosch University, Stellenbosch.

Tempelhoff, J., Van Niekerk, D., Van Eeden, E., Gouws, I, Botha K, and Wurige, R., 2009. The December 2004–January 2005 floods in the Garden Route region of the Southern Cape, South Africa. *Journal of Disaster Risk Studies*, 2 (2), pp. 93–112.

Terblanche, J.C., 2007. Construction and infrastructure development in local economic development: a Southern Cape perspective. Unpublished master's thesis. Stellenbosch University, Stellenbosch.

Thompson, L., 2013. Outeniqualand: What's in a Name? www.historycape.co.za/files/5513/9798/3720/OUTENIQUALAND_-_meaning.pdf (accessed 31 May 2015).

UFS (University of the Free State), 2013. *George: Land of milk and h(m)oney*. Bloemfontein: UFS.

UNCHS (United Nations Centre for Human Settlements), 2014. *State of the African Cities: Re-imagining Sustainable Urban Transitions*. Nairobi: UN Habitat.

Van der Merwe, I. J., 1992. In search of an urbanization policy for SA: towards a secondary city strategy. *Geography Research Forum*, 12, 102–127.

Van der Merwe, I. J., Van der Merwe, J. H., and de Necker, P. H., 1987. *The Regional Industrial Development Programme and the White Paper on Urbanization viewed against the spatial realities of urbanization in Southern Africa*. Report of the Institute for Cartographic Analysis, Stellenbosch University, Stellenbosch.

Van der Merwe, S.W.J., 2006. Local and sub-regional socio-economic and environmental impact of large-scale resort development. Unpublished master's thesis, Stellenbosch University, Stellenbosch.

Van Niekerk, A., and du Plessis, D., 2013. *Growth Potential of Towns in the Western Cape Quantitative Analysis of Growth Potential at Settlement and Municipal Level*. Report of the Department of Environmental Affairs and Development Planning. Cape Town: Western Cape Provincial Government.

Van Waart, S., 1998. *Outeniqualand: Plek van Melk en Heuning*. Pretoria: J. P. van der Walt.

Van Winden, W., van den Berg, L., and Pol, P., 2007. European cities in the knowledge economy: towards a typology. *Urban Studies*, 44 (3), pp. 525–549.

Van Zyl, L. M., 2006. The Garden Route golfscape: a golfing destination in the rough. Unpublished master's thesis, Stellenbosch University, Stellenbosch.

Véron, R., 2010. Small cities, neoliberal governance and sustainable development in the global south: A conceptual framework and research agenda. *Sustainability*, 2 (9), pp. 2833–2848.

Vromans, D. C., Maree, K. S., Holness, S., Job, N., and Brown, A. E., 2010. The Garden Route biodiversity sector plan for the George, Knysna and Bitou municipalities. Available at: http://bgis.sanbi.org/GardenRoute/GardenRoute_BiodiversitySectorPlan_WesternCape.pdf (accessed 11 February 2014).

Wilson, P., 1992. Secondary cities in the global economy: the growth of export-oriented small and medium-sized producers: the case of Mexico. *Investigaciones Geograficas: Boletin del Instituto de Geografia, Universidad Nacional Autonoma de Mexico*, Special Issue, pp. 215–218.

7 Polokwane

John Ntema and Anita Venter

Introduction

Polokwane, situated 270 km north of Pretoria, was historically Pietersburg, a bastion of white conservatism in the northern part of South Africa. Today it is the capital of the Limpopo province and the largest urban area in the province (see Figure 7.1). Pietersburg/ Polokwane has changed considerably over the past two to three decades. This chapter describes these changes against the background of the secondary city literature reviewed in Chapter 2.

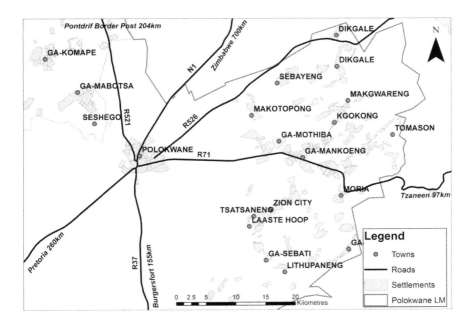

Figure 7.1 Location of Polokwane

Established in 1886, Pietersburg developed as a regional service centre. Under apartheid, the town provided schools, hospitals, financial and other services, and trading spaces to its inhabitants and the surrounding commercial farming communities, and increasingly to the rural population in traditional areas. The creation of the University of the North (now the University of Limpopo) in 1959 further boosted the development of the city. It was in 1994, with the switch to democracy, that Polokwane City became the administrative capital of the newly created Northern Province (later renamed Limpopo Province), a status that led to its increasing development as a public sector town and the relocation of a large number of provincial government departments from former homeland areas. There were three such homeland governments in place: Lebowa and Gazankulu self-governing territories, and Venda, a so-called independent state. The transition to democracy, coupled with the provincial capital status, has given rise to a prominent black middle class in Polokwane.

Economic decline in Zimbabwe (a mere 220 km away) has brought medium-term advantages to Polokwane. The city has become an important trading space for Zimbabweans who cannot obtain basic household products in their own country. Polokwane is also important from a social perspective: since the repeal of the Group Areas Act in 1991 it has become one of the most desegregated urban areas in South Africa (Donaldson and Kotze, 2006). The latest census shows that there is a mix of racial groups in every ward in Polokwane Municipality, particularly in Polokwane City (Stats SA, 2011). However, despite rapid urbanisation after 1994, Polokwane remains predominantly rural and impoverished (Wichmann et al., 2009; SACN, 2012). The latest census data show that an astonishing 63 per cent of the municipal population still live in rural areas (Stats SA, 2011; SACN, 2012).

We may reasonably assume that Polokwane will follow the growth and development trajectories of secondary cities in other developing countries (Hardoy and Satterthwaite, 1986; Bolay and Rabinovich, 2004; Satterthwaite, 2006). As its population and its economy are growing (Global Insight, 2014), it will probably play an increasingly crucial role as an administrative and public sector service centre and a regional market centre and economic hub.

South African research on urban spaces, as elsewhere in the world (Bell and Jayne, 2006), is concentrated on metros, leaving secondary cities and other small towns under-researched. As with most secondary cities, only a few studies have been done of Polokwane (see Chapter 1).

Historical development: from Pietersburg to Polokwane City

The history of Polokwane must be understood against the background of apartheid policy. Originally, the city was named after a prominent Afrikaner, Petrus (Piet) Joubert, Commandant-General of the South African Republic from 1880 to 1900. Pietersburg's residence and business activities were racially segregated and exclusively managed by the Pietersburg Town Council (Donaldson, 1999; Ngoatje, 2003; Molema, 2011). The city's history also cannot be understood separately from the development of the neighbouring 'homeland' of Lebowa and its two border townships, Seshego and Mankweng (Platzky and Walker, 1985;

Donaldson, 1999; Donaldson and Van der Merwe, 2000; Christopher, 2005). Apartheid planning redirected black urbanisation from the main urban area of Pietersburg to these townships. Seshego township, close to the city, accommodated black people who were forcibly removed from Pietersburg. It functioned as a labour reserve for the city, conveniently close for daily commuting (Donaldson, 2000). Mankweng township, 30 km from the city, hosts various institutions such as the University of Limpopo (formerly known as University of the North), the Mankweng Regional Hospital and a regional magistrate court. Black migration to Pietersburg, as to other cities in South Africa, was strictly controlled under apartheid legislation (Mabin, 1992; Donaldson and Kotze, 2006).

By the late 1980s Pietersburg had created a small but noteworthy manufacturing industry, expanding its regional services function through an industrial hub that supported a regional market concentrating mainly on food products. The construction of a two-lane highway from Pretoria to Pietersburg in the 1980s further assisted the development of the city and promoted access and connectivity, particularly facilitating trade with Zimbabwe. From the early 1990s, Pietersburg began preparing itself to become the public administrative centre of the Limpopo province. By 1999 a decision had been made to change the name to Polokwane City and the official declaration was made by government in 2005.

Internal pressures

This section describes some internal pressures Polokwane is undergoing and shows how far the city's socio-economic significance extends beyond its municipal and provincial borders.

Demographic trends

Apartheid planning shaped migration in and around Polokwane. Post-apartheid demographic and population patterns usually stand in direct contrast to these patterns. Unsurprisingly, Polokwane is the fastest growing urban area in the Limpopo province (Stats SA, 2011). Table 7.1 shows that its population increased by 2.4 per cent per annum from 2001 to 2011. This fast growth rate is a result of Polokwane's strategic location as a gateway to southern African countries to the north and its status as the provincial administrative capital (SACN, 2012). Polokwane City recorded an annual average growth of 9.2 per cent over this period and the rural areas 1.2 per cent (Stats SA, 2013). Yet villages in close proximity to Polokwane City are growing faster. The number of households in Moletji Blood River village, for example, increased from 7,006 to 8,406 and in Ga-Chuene village from 4,964 to 5,488 over the period 2001 to 2011 (Stats SA, 2001, 2011). Seshego township, however, recorded an average annual growth of 0.05 per cent over this period. This low growth rate is unsurprising, as many former Seshego residents, attracted by Polokwane City's infrastructure development and the rapid desegregation in the former white suburbs, have moved to the more desirable areas closer to the city centre or in the city itself.

Table 7.1 Differential population growth rates in Polokwane, 2001–2011 (Statistics South Africa census data)

Places	2001 Population	2011 Population	Average annual growth %
Polokwane City	86,580	166,403	9.2
Seshego	71,835	72,181	0.05
Mankweng	23,180	25,869	1.2
Rural areas	326,675	364,547	1.2
Polokwane total	508,270	629,000	2.4
Capricorn District Municipality	1,154,690	1,261,228	
Limpopo	**5,273,639**	**5,404,033**	**0.82**

Source: UFS (2013).

Migration has boosted the population of Polokwane City, from Seshego township to Polokwane City's former white suburbs because of desegregation and from rural villages around Polokwane, and the population of Polokwane Municipality more generally, from other parts of the Limpopo province and from neighbouring Zimbabwe and Mozambique (Donaldson, 2001; Wilkin, 2010; Molema, 2011; Chipu, 2011; Sebola, 2011; Stats SA, 2011, 2013). Three main factors have encouraged this influx: the relocation of provincial government departments and some decentralised national government departments from the former Lebowa homeland to Polokwane City; the provincial capital status, which has boosted the economy and employment opportunities, particularly in the service sectors; and the employment of especially Zimbabweans in the education sector (university and private schools).

Not all migration is in the direction of central Polokwane City. Some people are migrating to the rural villages, especially those within a 30 km radius of the centre. Polokwane municipality consists of nearly one hundred small villages spread over more than a 100 km radius and split into two municipalities, Polokwane local municipality and Aganang local municipality. Moletji Blood River village, west of the city, and Ga-Chuene village, east of the city, have basic services and easy access to central Polokwane City. These two villages attract Zimbabweans and some Mozambicans. The attractions are largely the services, the close proximity to the central city and the sense of personal security and respect for human rights and dignity that they gain from living here (Wilkin, 2010). Against the background of the 2008 xenophobic attacks, an interviewee from the traditional authority said Moletji Blood River village has become a haven for non-South Africans. The village's proximity to central Polokwane City enables villagers to commute daily and send their children to better resourced schools.

Economic trends

Evidence of the city's role as a regional shopping and logistics hub are the regional shopping mall (the Mall of the North), the regional offices of various large national financial institutions (banks and insurance companies), various companies and businesses (such as BMW and South African Breweries) and a growing number of private medical facilities. The establishment of Polokwane International Airport (originally used for defence) has further contributed to economic growth in the city and external connectivity.

Compared to Limpopo province overall, the services, household, trade, transport and finance sectors make up a larger percentage of Polokwane's economy, but there has been a proportional decline in the manufacturing and agricultural sectors since 1996. Despite this decline, however, Polokwane's economy is growing, recording an annual average growth of 3.7 per cent between 1996 and 2011. This is lower than Johannesburg's annual average economic growth rate of 4.1 per cent for the same period, but slightly higher than that of Mangaung metro (2.9 per cent), Mbombela local municipality (2.9 per cent), Sol Plaatjie local municipality (3.1 per cent) and the national average of 3.2 per cent (Stats SA, 2011; Harrison and Todes, 2015). Polokwane's contribution to the province's total economy grew by 1 per cent in that period, from 14.4 per cent to 15.4 per cent (Stats SA, 2011, 2013). Factors largely responsible for this high economic growth rate have been the capital status, which brought the head offices of almost all the provincial departments and state agencies to the city, and the subsequent growth in the services sector. From 2001 to 2011 the services sector recorded a 4.2 per cent growth. The agricultural sector, however, recorded a negative growth of -1.5 per cent for this period. According to an interviewee at the municipality, this decline could to a large extent be attributed to the widespread conversion of commercial farming into game farming, greater emphasis on subsistence farming, and uncertainty in agricultural policy (Stats SA, 2001, 2011). The growing demand for private accommodation for students studying at the University of Limpopo is giving the city an additional economic boost. And Polokwane's central and strategic location in relation to southern African countries is also an economic advantage.

Spatial integration and the rising black middle class

Post-apartheid policies have struggled to redress South Africa's apartheid spatial patterns (Department of Cooperative Governance, 2014; Harrison and Todes, 2015). Polokwane is proving to be the exception to the rule, emerging as one of very few thoroughly desegregated post-1994 cities (Donaldson and Kotze, 2006). Seshego has been well integrated into the former white city of Pietersburg (Polokwane City) and infill residential development between Seshego and Polokwane gives the feeling of a spatially integrated city. And the black middle class is rising, coincidentally with civic pride and what we may describe as 'bling', i.e. the delight in wearing expensive and ostentatious clothing and jewellery, and the materialistic attitude associated with this style (Donaldson et al, 2013). This outlook on life was evident from interviews conducted during our visits to Polokwane, particularly at some of the city's popular night clubs. There is a sense of importance and power, coupled with a vision of Polokwane developing into an important city – some interviewees even suggested that it would become a metro.

Infrastructure problems

Polokwane has two main infrastructure problems. The first has to do with the incorporation of rural villages into the Polokwane municipal area. The traditional land arrangements that apply in most of these villages make formal township development difficult, and the municipality is expected to provide services to these villages even if formal development is not possible. It has been argued that the pace and level of infrastructure development in Polokwane have taken a knock from the incorporation of the many surrounding rural villages (Ngoatje, 2003). The insufficient revenue base in these traditional areas means that cross-subsidisation is necessary – that is, charging the more affluent areas a higher price for services in order to subsidise services in the traditional areas. Some of the interviewees suggested that the municipality did not have sufficient capacity to deal with this situation. On top of this, ageing infrastructure is adding to maintenance costs, particularly for repairing leaking water pipes. Many farms and villages in rural Polokwane have no, or only rudimentary, water infrastructure, and development will be costly.

The second infrastructure problem has to do with water shortage, which has obliged Polokwane to put land development on hold. Some interviewees said one of the unintended consequences of this embargo has been increased development on traditional land. This circumvents the embargo but also means that, in terms of municipal policy for indigent households, land tax cannot be collected on these developments. The blanket exemption from water payment for households in all surrounding rural areas puts pressure on municipal finances. Further water-related problems for the municipality are the growing official list of registered urban-based indigent households in Seshego, Mankweng and Polokwane, the increasing municipal debt because of non-payment for services, and a 5 per cent underestimation by the National Department of Water Affairs in its 2010/11 projections for residential water consumption.

External pressures

Two pertinent external pressures require attention. First, Polokwane is coming under pressure from the influx of foreign nationals. Both the literature and the community interviews show how the improvements in Polokwane's economy and infrastructure have sparked the influx of economic migrants from Zimbabwe (Wilkin, 2010). For example, a number of interviewees confirmed that the informal sector is dominated by Zimbabweans. The influx of Zimbabwean informal traders in particular could put further strain on limited business opportunities for semi-skilled South Africans struggling to survive in a competitive informal business environment. A second pressure pertains to the regional service role that Polokwane plays. This role is highly dependent on swift access to Polokwane. The current deterioration in road access means that getting to specialised services such as air transport, car services, financial services and exclusive shopping may become more difficult in future.

Responses

In this section we discuss Polokwane's internal responses to problems and the pressures that come with these problems. We consider municipal governance, strategic planning and LED, municipal infrastructure, municipal finance, and relations between business and local government and between traditional leaders and local government.

Municipal governance

Polokwane is more than just an administrative capital for the local municipality and provincial government; it is also home to most of the province's senior political principals and leaders across political parties. The city acquired international political significance in 2007 from media reports about politician Julius Malema and the 52nd National Elective Conference of the African National Congress, held in Polokwane. Polokwane's capital status in particular means that political and administrative stability are important for good and sustainable governance, both in the Capricorn district, of which it is the largest municipality, and the province as a whole. From the transition to democracy in the mid-1990s until 2010, Polokwane went through a period of politically related administrative instability. According to municipal and business interviewees, the high vacancy rate in several senior and strategic positions is probably a consequence of this, and the vacancies may also have contributed to the instability. The Polokwane municipality's failure to fill some strategic positions has meant that several strategic areas, such as municipal project management across various Directorates, have been negatively affected (Mojapelo, 2010). This has led in turn to some municipal projects with economic potential being either delayed, derailed or completely stalled (Polokwane Local Municipality, 2012a).

With the appointment of the executive mayor in 2010 and the municipal manager and chief financial officer in 2012, the municipality began to acquire the much-needed political stability and administrative capacity to turn the situation around. This helped to restore trust in especially the tender system. Financial management also improved. Polokwane municipality could, for the first time, mobilise extra financial support from the National Treasury, enabling the appointment of a funded temporary municipal financial advisor to support the recently appointed chief financial officer and the entire finance section (Polokwane Local Municipality, 2012a). This intervention has improved compliance with financial regulations (see the section on municipal finances below), and the formulation and adoption of an extensively revised IDP and Municipal Finance Policy in 2012 has further bolstered municipal governance in project management. These and other initiatives, according to interviewees, have increased municipal income and investment in infrastructure and also boosted the confidence of stakeholders, such as ordinary community members, the business community and the private sector, in the municipality. According to an official at the municipality, growing business confidence in Polokwane is confirmed by a growing number of outside bidders. Further reflecting the improved governance since 2010, one interviewee from the business community noted that:

> the appointment of the current executive-mayor has boosted business confidence and, unlike before, there are constant and regular consultations between organized business, such as the Polokwane Business Chamber and the Black Management Forum, and the municipality ... in fact we collectively agreed that there should be no discussion about business issues without business people involved.

Notwithstanding the strides made in turning around municipal governance since 2010, there are still governance-related challenges to be faced. Concerns are regularly expressed about the lack of long-term planning and, according to our interviewees, continued interference in the administrative systems by politicians remains a problem (see also Mahlakoane, 2010; Chipu, 2011). Polokwane has for many years struggled to retain professionals with scarce skills, such as those needed in the financial sector and engineering (Ngoatje, 2003).

Strategic planning and LED

The absence of an efficient and effective LED directorate and strategy since 2008 has had far-reaching economic implications. It has affected municipal planning, among other things, and has perpetuated marginalisation, as very little attention is paid to enterprise development and the informal sector. The municipal 2013 organogram shows that provision is made for separate Directorates for the IDP and LED strategy. At the time of this research, Polokwane was basing its strategy on a revised IDP, covering the period 2012 to 2015, which built on previous IDPs but also made some fundamental changes. But despite some positive aspects, the new IDP also has some shortcomings. Although the Polokwane municipal area is predominantly rural, the IDP focuses on urban Polokwane, Seshego and Mankweng, and commercial farming areas, rural villages and traditional areas are excluded, despite their economic potential – some, for example, may be heritage sites that could be tourist attractions. And the plan underplays the importance of capacity building programmes or initiatives for stakeholders other than full-time municipal employees and officials (Polokwane Local Municipality, 2012a).

Municipal infrastructure

To strengthen the city's regional role as an economic and services centre, Polokwane municipality has had to take a more focused approach to providing and developing infrastructure. As regards water provision, Polokwane municipality is currently the only municipality in the Capricorn District, and in Limpopo as a whole, that has a water services authority. As a municipality with the accreditation or licence to provide water services, Polokwane municipality receives its bulk water from Lepelle Northern Water. Since 1994 Polokwane municipality has made significant progress in water provision, reducing the percentage of households with no access to water from 20 per cent in 1996 to 4 per cent in 2011 (Stats SA, 2011, 2013). Given its predominantly rural nature, it is unsurprising to find that 86 per cent of rural households are without access to a piped water supply on their individual stands and are at times obliged to use rivers, dams and stagnant water. An attempt is, however, being made to provide communal taps not more than 100 m from dwellings (Chipu, 2011). Notwithstanding the progress made in water provision since 1996 and the consistent 'blue drop' water status[1] from 1996 to 2013, the municipality has some difficulties in fulfilling its mandate to provide residents with water. According to interviewees, the water problems are of three kinds: those that cut across the entire municipality, those that are specifically urban, and those that are specifically rural. The first type, affecting both urban and rural communities, is the result of the Municipal Water Services Development Plan being based on the Department of Water Affairs' 5 per cent underestimation of the water demand for residential consumption in the Polokwane Municipality. Specific problems for the urban dwellers are the need to provide for some 8,000 registered urban indigent households in Seshego, Mankweng and Polokwane City (Polokwane Local Municipality, 2012a) and the increasing municipal debt due to non-payment for services, R450 million at the time of writing (Polokwane Local Municipal, 2012b).

The water provision problems suffered by rural Polokwane residents are more serious and have different causes from those in the urban areas. One cause is the municipality's official indigent policy that prohibits cost recovery in these areas. This automatically exempts every household, regardless of financial status, from paying for municipal services (Polokwane Local Municipality, 2012a), despite the fact that some rural villages, particularly those adjacent to the city, have several privately financed middle-income housing developments.

As regards electricity provision, the providers are Polokwane municipality and Eskom, separately, with the municipality being responsible for urban Polokwane (Seshego, Mankweng and Polokwane City) and Eskom for all rural villages, commercial farming areas and traditional areas. The percentage of households with access to electricity for lighting increased from 43 per cent in 1996 to 83 per cent in 2011 (Stats SA, 2011, 2013). However, while almost every household in the urban areas has been provided with electricity, there are backlogs in the rural areas of the municipality. In an attempt to reduce the rural backlog by at least 2,200 households annually, the municipality has set aside R25 million for the 2014/15 financial year (Polokwane Observer, 2014).

Sanitation provision is affected by Polokwane's water shortage. The municipality is facing backlogs in the provision of sanitation, but the percentage of households with access to flush or chemical toilets increased from 27 per cent in 1996 to 44 per cent in 2011 (Stats SA, 2011, 2013). The 52 per cent of households still using pit latrines and the 4 per cent with no access to any form of sanitation

(Stats SA, 2011) are indicative not only of water related backlogs in the provision of sanitation but of daily health and safety hazards faced by households, particularly in rural areas. In the absence of water-borne sanitation, households are left with no option but to make use of bushes and, in some places, poorly built pit latrines (Chipu, 2011). In an attempt to solve the problems caused by both water scarcity and financial constraints and to speed up the clearing of the provision backlog, the local municipality, in partnership with Department of Water Affairs and Lepelle Northern Water Board, set targets of 4,000 and 2,000 ventilated improved pit toilets in rural areas for the 2013/14 and 2014/15 financial years respectively (Polokwane Observer, 2014).

Municipal finance

The financial management of Polokwane local municipality has been weak (with exception of the 2008/09 and 2009/10 financial years). Since 2011, the municipality has never received an unqualified audit report from the Auditor General. According to most of the senior municipal officials we interviewed, and the official report by the Auditor General (2012), the main reason the municipality received a qualified audit report in 2010/11 was the absence of a permanent Chief Financial Officer. Lack of leadership and oversight in this critical portfolio led, among other things, to unauthorised spending to the value of R30.4 million and a poor internal audit due to a dysfunctional internal audit committee (Auditor-General, 2012; Polokwane Local Municipality, 2012b).

Polokwane's municipal revenue comes mostly from three sources: services charges (43 per cent), government grants and subsidies (20 per cent) and property rates (13 per cent). The large contribution of services charges could be ascribed to, among other things, the sound relationship between local municipality and big businesses; the recent improvement in the municipal collection rate, with an impressive 95 per cent collection being achieved over the past financial year (2011/12); and the contribution of the Municipal Infrastructure Grant, especially in 2009 when it made up nearly one-third of the total municipal budget (Polokwane Local Municipality, 2009). This grant was a national government initiative to cover the capital cost of basic infrastructure for the poor so as to give all South Africans at least a basic level of service by the year 2013 (Department of Provincial and Local Government, 2007). In 2009 this grant was increased for Polokwane partly because the city was preparing to host the FIFA 2010 World Cup.

Relations between business and local government

The relationship between local government and the business community takes two forms. Relations between local government and the big formal businesses in Polokwane are formalised and institutionalised. Despite the LED forum, relations between local government and the small informal businesses are not yet formalised, although some of these businesses are affiliates of the National African Federated Chamber of Commerce. The municipal executive council has made it compulsory for every senior official (the mayor, municipal manager and chief financial officer included) to adopt several businesses identified by the council as top-performing in terms of turnover. At the time of this research, one hundred of these businesses were being divided equally among these senior municipal officials for special attention. One aim of this arrangement is to ensure a quick municipal turnaround time in responding to the needs of these businesses. The municipality has also officially resolved to hold regular business breakfasts and gala dinners where both sides can air their views and discuss any problems. A senior municipal official said this had been 'one of the most successful municipal initiatives' and that the events are 'always able to draw no less than 90% attendance by these big businesses'. It seems reasonable to assume that the arrangements have so far worked well for the municipality and business community in Polokwane.

Further complementing the sound relations between the municipality and big business is the active involvement of some of the provincial agencies, particularly those based in Polokwane City, such as the Limpopo Economic Development Agency. Our interviewees explained that, in collaboration with the local municipality, the Black Management Forum and the Polokwane Chamber of Business, the Agency coordinates and facilitates municipal support to create a successful business environment for these local businesses, in particular an environment conducive to forging ties internationally. The same success has not, however, been achieved in the relations between the municipality and the small informal business sector in Polokwane's urban and rural areas. If complaints by National African Federated Chamber of Commerce about marginalisation and lack of recognition by the municipality, especially during policy and programme implementation, are anything to go by, we may conclude that relations between the small informal businesses and the municipality are less than ideal and in sharp contrast with what is set out in the IDP strategy.

Relations between traditional leaders and local government

Whether in mobilising resources, implementing policy or attaining political stability, despite modernisation and the introduction of shared rural governance, traditional leaders are still influential actors in the life of South African rural communities and, as such, play a vital role in the government's agenda for rural development (Tlhoaele, 2012). Polokwane is no exception in this respect. Yet, despite the IDP's detailed acknowledgment of programmes and processes to involve traditional leadership in municipal planning and decision-making, in practice the relations between that leadership and the municipality appear to be weak (Ngoatje, 2003; Segooa, 2006; Manamela, 2010), and not much different from relations between the municipality and the National African Federated Chamber of Commerce and its affiliates, where there is also little real engagement or consultation. Relations between the local municipality and the traditional leadership are strained for various reasons. The two bodies are involved in land-related disputes and they do not have a common system for allocating land earmarked for development initiatives in rural villages (Ngoatje, 2003; Mmola, 2012), The municipality fails to consult the traditional leadership when planning and implementing projects in rural villages and traditional areas (Manamela, 2010; Mmola, 2012). For example, an interview confirmed that in 2012 the municipality obtained a restraining order from the court against the traditional leadership and local community members who opposed the implementation of a municipally funded project in Ga-Chuene village. Both the traditional leadership and the community complained of being marginalised when the municipality took a decision to implement the project.

Synthesis

This chapter traced the historical development of Polokwane and the adjacent former 'homeland' townships of Seshego and Mankweng and the traditional villages, particularly the two adjacent villages of Moletji Blood River and Ga-Chuene. Our research into the socio-economic and administrative significance of the city in relation to a largely impoverished surrounding rural and regional community produced mixed findings, the following being the most notable.

Polokwane City is centrally located in Limpopo province and the infrastructure, although not perfect, is in place for the city to be used as the administrative capital, economic hub, and shopping and service centre for the surrounding rural areas, the neighbouring province of Mpumalanga, and southern African countries such as Zimbabwe. Despite its economic significance for these areas, Polokwane plays an administrative and political role in a mostly rural area where the traditional leadership is acknowledged as a viable governance model. The mass relocation of public services from the former Lebowa homeland to Polokwane has brought a rapid improvement in the living standards of previously disadvantaged citizens. The centralisation of various government departments has not only created opportunities for infrastructure development, it has also created sustainable job opportunities, particularly for black professionals in the city and neighbouring areas. Many residents we interviewed described Polokwane as a city of middle-class bliss.

Unemployment is increasing among former mine and farm workers, but there is a large distribution of wealth among the middle-class working as professionals in various sectors, private and public. The growth in the city's black middle class may have directly or indirectly contributed to the rapid post-1994 spatial transformation of previously racially segregated residential areas in former white suburbs. Attainment of political freedom (to some extent) and the subsequent distribution of wealth among the black middle class in the post-1994 era have been two of the forces driving what is widely known in the South African literature today as the 'highly desegregated Polokwane'. Besides the residential desegregation in the city, the growing influence of the middle class is also evident in the city's adjacent but peripheral areas. An example in this respect is the privately financed housing development in Moletji Blood River village. Thanks to improvements in, among other things, roads and services infrastructure, this development has attracted not only immigrants from less resourced outlying small villages (rural to rural migration) and Zimbabwean economic migrants, but also a certain number of middle-class people. Other than Moletji Blood River village, the significance of Polokwane to adjacent villages is also evident in the level of government investment in infrastructure development, particularly improved roads and adequately resourced public clinics and schools, in Ga–Chuene village.

The political and administrative changes effected in the Polokwane municipality in 2010 have helped to sustain the city's economic and spatial transformation. There has been a turnaround in municipal strategic planning for finance, procurement, the tender system and infrastructure development. The appointment of an executive mayor, chief financial officer and municipal manager in the 2009/10 financial year has helped to create much-needed political and administrative stability and an enabling environment for the city's businesses to recover their faith in the local municipality and begin to flourish, with some businesses extending their services to the Mpumalanga province.

In sum, Polokwane's small but significant industrial base and its administrative capital status in both local and provincial government have not only attracted economic migrants from surrounding and neighbouring areas but also boosted the economy and the growth of a black middle class. Polokwane has been a beacon of economic hope, particularly for Zimbabweans visiting the shops, operating as informal traders, lecturing at the university and teaching in several private schools in Polokwane. However, the reliance on Zimbabweans will remain economically sound only until Zimbabwe recovers from the 2008 political turmoil and the subsequent economic downturn. Shortage of resources, particularly water, is a threat to the city and should be taken much more seriously. A further possible long-term threat to Polokwane's development and economic growth is the difficulty in attracting and retaining professionals with scarce skills and in persuading the youth to remain.

Note

1 This indicates compliance by a water service authority (e.g. a local municipality) with drinking water quality and safety standards as determined by the National Department of Water Affairs

References

Auditor General, 2012. *Auditor General Annual Report for Polokwane Local Municipality.* Johannesburg: Auditor General (Polokwane).

Bell, D. and Jayne, M., 2006. *Small Cities: Urban Experience Beyond the Metropolis.* New York: Routledge.

Bolay, J. C. and Rabinovich, A., 2004. Intermediate cities in Latin America risk and opportunities of coherent urban development. *Cities*, 21(5), pp. 407–421.

Chipu, S. T. L., 2011. Institutional capacity of local municipalities in the delivery of services to communities: a case study of the Polokwane municipality in Limpopo Province. Unpublished master's thesis, University of Limpopo, Polokwane.

Christopher, A., 2005. Further step in the desegregation of South African towns and cities, 1996–2011. *Development Southern Africa*, 18(4), pp. 267–276.

Department of Cooperative Governance, 2014. *Integrated Urban Development Framework: Draft for Discussion.* Department of Cooperative Governance, Pretoria.

Department of Provincial and Local Government, 2007. *The Municipal Infrastructure Grant 2004–2007.* Department of Provincial and Local Government, Pretoria.

Donaldson, R., 1999. Restructuring in a South African city during transition: urban development and transformation in Pietersburg during the 1990s. Unpublished doctoral thesis, Stellenbosch University, Stellenbosch.

Donaldson, R., 2000. Urban restructuring through land development objectives in Pietersburg: an assessment. *Journal of Public Administration*, 35(1), pp. 22–39.

Donaldson, R., 2001. An overview of urban integration and restructuring of Seshego during transition. *South African Geographical Journal*, 83(3), pp. 208–213.

Donaldson, R. and Kotze, N. J., 2006. Residential desegregation dynamics in the South African city of Polokwane (Pietersburg). *Tijdschrift voor Economische en Sociale Geografie*, 97(5), pp. 567–582.

Donaldson, R., Mehlomakhulu, T., Darkey, D., Dyssel M. and Siyongwana, P., 2013. Relocation: to be or not to be a black diamond in the township? *Habitat International*, 39, pp. 114–118.

Donaldson, R. and Van der Merwe, I. J., 2000. Apartheid urban development and transitional restructuring in Pietersburg and environs. *Historia*, 1, pp. 118–134.

Global Insight. (2014). *Global Insight.* Pretoria: Global Insight.

Hardoy, J. and Satterthwaite, D., 1986. *Small and Intermediate Urban Centres: Their Role in National and Regional Development in the Third World.* London: Hodder and Stoughton.

Harrison, P. and Todes, A., 2015. Spatial transformations in a 'loosening state': South Africa in a comparative perspective. *Geoforum*, 61, pp. 148–162.

Mabin, A., 1992. Dispossession, exploitation and struggle: an historical overview of South African urbanisation. In: D. Smith, ed. *The Apartheid City and Beyond: Urbanisation and Social Change in South Africa.* London: Routledge, pp. 13–24.

Mahlakoane, N. N., 2010. Vulnerability to brown environmental problems within informal settlements in Seshego, Limpopo province. Unpublished master's thesis, University of Limpopo, Polokwane.

Manamela, K. F., 2010. An investigation of water delivery constraints at Mabokelele Village, Limpopo Province, South Africa. Unpublished master's thesis, University of Limpopo, Polokwane.

Mmola, D. M., 2012. An assessment of the role played by Polokwane local municipality in service delivery within Manthorwane community of Limpopo Province. Unpublished master's thesis, University of Limpopo, Polokwane.

Mojapelo, H. L., 2010. Basic infrastructure services provision by Polokwane local municipality in Limpopo Province. Unpublished master's thesis, University of Limpopo, Polokwane.

Molema, T. M., 2011. Educational needs of domestic workers in Pietersburg circuit-Polokwane. Unpublished master's thesis, University of Limpopo, Polokwane.

Ngoatje, M. F., 2003. Capacity building and sustainable development with reference to the Pietersburg/Polokwane municipality. Unpublished master's thesis, Rand Afrikaans University. Johannesburg.

Platzky, L. and Walker, C., 1985. *The Surplus People: Forced Removals in South Africa.* Johannesburg: Ravan Press.

Polokwane Local Municipality, 2009. *Annual Financial Statement*. Polokwane: Polokwane Local Municipality.

Polokwane Local Municipality, 2012a. *Integrated Development Plan*. Polokwane: Polokwane Local Municipality.

Polokwane Local Municipality, 2012b. *Annual Financial Statement*. Polokwane: Polokwane Local Municipality.

Polokwane Observer, 2014. State of city address: Greaver's promises. *Polokwane Observer*, 19 June.

SACN (South African Cities Network), 2012. *Secondary Cities in South Africa: The Start of Conversation*. SACN: Johannesburg.

Satterthwaite, D., 2006. Outside the large cities. The demographic importance of small urban centres and large villages in Africa, Asia and Latin America. UNCHS: Human Settlements Discussion Paper – Urban Change 3.

Sebola, M., 2011. The socio-economic impact of illegal immigrants: a case of Zimbabweans in the city of Polokwane. *Journal of Public Administration*, 46(3), pp. 1055–1072.

Segooa, R.W., 2006. The impact of service delivery in Mankweng Township by Polokwane municipality as a third sphere of government. Unpublished master's thesis, University of Limpopo, Polokwane.

Stats SA (Statistics South Africa), 2001. *Census Data*. Pretoria: Statistics South Africa.

Stats SA (Statistics South Africa), 2011. *Census Data: Population Dynamics in South Africa*. Pretoria: Statistics South Africa.

Stats SA (Statistics South Africa), 2013. *Census Data for 1996, 2001 and 2011*. Pretoria: Statistics South Africa.

Tlhoaele, C.T., 2012. The interface between traditional leadership in shared rural local governance. Unpublished master's thesis, University of Johannesburg, Johannesburg.

Wichmann, J., Wolvaardt, J., Maritz, C. and Voyi, K., 2009. Household conditions, eczema symptoms and rhinitis symptoms: relationship with wheeze and severe wheeze in children living in Polokwane area, South Africa. *Maternal Child Health Journal*, 13, pp. 107–118.

Wilkin, R.L., 2010. Zimbabweans in Moletji: a rural alternative. Unpublished master's thesis, University of the Witwatersrand, Johannesburg.

8 UMhlathuze

Johannes Wessels and Kholisa Rani

Introduction

The City of uMhlathuze (the name of the whole municipal area) is a largely rural municipality in the north-eastern part of KwaZulu-Natal. It is known for its harbour at Richards Bay, from which coal and other commodities are exported. The two main urban areas of uMhlathuze are Richards Bay, founded in the late 1960s, and the much older Empangeni (first established as a mission station in 1851). This chapter focuses largely on Richards Bay. Depending heavily on national infrastructure decisions, the town benefited from the apartheid government's industrial decentralisation policies. With the backing of these policies, and the energy and vision of local role-players, it quickly developed a significant industrial base (Goodenough, 2003; Hill and Goodenough, 2005; Hall, 2009; Nel et al., 2009). Before the port was constructed, Richards Bay was a rural area under traditional land regimes. The only permanent settlements, other than the villages along the coast, were a fishing community at Richards Bay that also served as a holiday resort, mainly for campers, and the inland town of Empangeni, which was then quite small (see Figure 8.1).

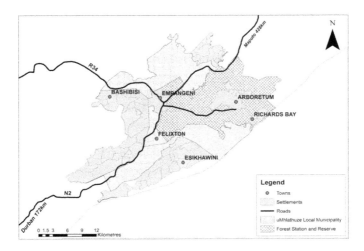

Figure 8.1 Location of uMhlathuze

UMhlathuze makes an excellent case study of three concerns for secondary cities in South Africa today: the positive and negative effects of national policies and political preferences on the city's economy, the conflicts between modernity and traditionalism in the urban–rural links, and the challenges of globalisation. This last is a particular concern for the future of Richards Bay – precariously poised between 'gateway to globalisation' and 'forgotten harbour town'. The reason for the existence of Richards Bay, the mining, manufacturing and logistics hub, could become the reason for its decline, in a period of lower demand for commodities.

The chapter starts with the history of uMhlathuze, which is essential for understanding its current development problems. We then discuss the internal pressures experienced by uMhlathuze over the past 20 to 25 years, in the process expanding on some of the trends discussed in the post-1990 section of the historical overview. This is followed by a discussion of external pressures, and the chapter concludes with a brief synthesis and recommendations for the area's future.

Historical overview

This section describes three phases of uMhlathuze's history up to 1990: the early years, colonisation, and apartheid and the development of Richards Bay.

Early years up to colonisation of Zululand (up to 1879)

The early history is predominantly that of the Zulu Kingdom. Between 1817 and 1819 Shaka Zulu defeated the Ndwandwe tribe of Zwide in a series of battles, the decisive one being at the Mhlathuze River not far from Nongoma. Over the next nine years Shaka consolidated various smaller tribes into a larger unit and the Zulu Kingdom took root, with the area between the Pongola and Tugela rivers as its heartland. The Kingdom's focus was mostly on the interior rather than the coastal stretch that was not suitable for herding cattle. The coastal wetlands with their swamps, mosquitoes and crocodiles were sparsely settled.

The Zulu Kingdom's economy consisted of subsistence farming, hunting, cattle herding and bartering, but wealth accumulation happened mainly through conquest of other tribes. The consolidation of the Zulu Kingdom resulted in increased centralisation, with Shaka establishing agents of the royal kraal in the kraals of the conquered tribes. From the main royal kraal close to modern day Eshowe, Shaka organised Zulu regiments that required spoils of war and conflict.

During Shaka's reign, the British established a trading post at Port Natal. Shaka in response established a new royal kraal in the vicinity of KwaDukuza (today called Stanger). After the murder of Shaka in 1828, Dingane as new king moved the royal kraal to near Melmoth, where it stayed until after the Zulu defeat at the Battle of Blood River in 1838.

After the British forces destroyed the Voortrekkers' dream of an independent Republic when a frigate relieved the siege of Port Natal in 1842, a colony (originally ruled from Cape Town) was declared, with a permanent British military contingent. The European population more than doubled between 1848 and 1850 when more than 4,000 British immigrants were settled and 188 German settlers landed in Port Natal in 1848, lured by the prospect of cotton cultivation. By 1850 the cultivation of sugarcane resulted in labourers from Mauritius and India being brought into Natal, which largely adhered to the Tugela River as the boundary between the colony and the Zulu Kingdom. Although the British Government was opposed to a war with the Zulus, Sir Henry Bartle Frere, the High Commissioner for Southern Africa, issued an ultimatum to the Zulu king Cetshwayo in 1878 to disband his army and accept a British resident administrator. Cetshwayo refused, and a force of 7,000 British soldiers and 1,000 volunteers crossed the Tugela River in January 1879. On 22 January 1879 the Zulu army surprised the British at Isandlwana, leading to the loss of 1,600 British soldiers (Greaves, 2012). Shortly thereafter the Zulu army suffered large losses at Rorke's Drift, and British reinforcements were landed at what is now Richards Bay. After the Zulu capital of Ulundi was conquered by the British, King Cetshwayo was exiled first to the Cape and then to London. The Zulu Kingdom was thus effectively colonised before 1880.

Colonisation and early development (1880–1948)

Colonisation brought immediate changes. The area's forests and fertile land attracted settlers and commercial farming began in the fertile valleys between the swampy coastal belt and the drier interior. Empangeni began to function as a regional service centre for the social and commercial needs of the frontier farming community. In 1894 a magistrate was installed and in 1903 the Zululand railway linked the village with Durban. After the success of an experimental eucalyptus plantation that led to large afforestation and construction of saw mills, large-scale sugar plantations were also established. These expanded rapidly after a sugar mill was constructed at Felixton in 1911 (Tongaat Hulett Sugar, 2014). Empangeni was officially proclaimed as a town in 1931.

Development in the first half of the twentieth century was driven by sugarcane farming, sugar mills, the timber industry, saw mills, paper pulp mills, and dairy and beef production (mainly to supply the growing demand in Durban) as well as trade with the Zulu population in the traditional authority areas. The economic thrust provided by agro-processing and commercial farming led to public investment in schools, hospitals and municipal infrastructure, and Empangeni soon contained a growing number of traders, professional services (doctors, dentists, attorneys, and so on) and light engineering businesses.

Richards Bay remained a small community of fishermen and a place to camp during the December and January holiday.

Apartheid and the development of Richards Bay (1948–1990)

Under the apartheid government, separate development was to be achieved partly through industrialisation, providing job opportunities for Africans commuting daily from independent 'homelands'. In 1965 the national Department of Planning proposed the development of a new harbour at Richards Bay.

This was the closest South African port to Johannesburg and the mining industry in the eastern Transvaal. A rail link from Ermelo to Richards Bay would be more energy-efficient than the existing railway from Johannesburg to Durban, which traversed steep inclines. In addition, job opportunities would be created close to a homeland with an expanding population.

The CSIR conducted studies to investigate the possibility of draining the wetlands and diverting the Mhlatuze river. It also investigated the structure of the underlying rock foundations (for piling purposes), the most appropriate harbour mouth and the environmental impact of the proposed industries. Since aluminium was considered a crucial strategic metal and South Africa had no bauxite, the Industrial Development Corporation gave the Swiss company Alusuisse a 22 per cent share in the Alusaf aluminium smelter in exchange for its expertise and management of the design and construction of the smelter since its involvement also assured a constant supply of bauxite. Another anchor industry for the new industrial and logistics hub was the Triomf fertiliser plant.

The South African Railways and Harbours constructed the port and the railway line, which involved more than 80 bridges by the mid-1970s.

Richards Bay was proclaimed as a town in 1969. In line with apartheid planning, the R293 black township of eSikhawini was established behind homeland boundaries, close to the N2.[1]

The establishment of Richards Bay and eSikhawini and the construction of the harbour, railway lines, electricity and water supply and the first industrial plants (Alusaf and Triomf Fertilizer) brought significant changes to the area. In addition to the influx of temporary construction teams, highly skilled professionals (e.g. chemical and mechanical engineers) and a large array of tradesmen settled permanently in the area, creating a dynamic very different from that of the earlier sparsely populated rural and agricultural settlements.

The economic sanctions of the 1980s made South Africa increasingly isolated. The aluminium smelter at Richards Bay was thus critical for ensuring a supply of aluminium to South African companies such as Hulamin (in the Tongaat Hulett group) and Wispeco (in the Remgro group) which manufactured aluminium products for the domestic market that could no longer be sourced from abroad.

Challenges of globalisation and the financial crisis

This section first provides an overview of the changes that came to the fore after the demise of apartheid. It then describes the pressures faced by uMhlathuze over the past two and a half decades, making reference also to some longer-term processes and dynamics. The section covers demographic and population changes; economic trends (under three headings: the port of Richards Bay, the Richards Bay Industrial Development Zone, and uMhlathuze overall); relations between business and government; municipal plans; and municipal governance, management and finance.

The early 1990s were a time of increasing international interest in South African enterprises and an outward drive by large South African companies.

Gencor (which had taken over Alusaf) became part of BHP Billiton, and they developed a state of the art additional aluminium smelter (Hillside), also at Richards Bay. Tata Steel established their KwaZulu-Natal plant in Richards Bay in 2006, adding steel to the group of industries that call the area home. The Richards Bay Coal Terminal (a private sector development by a consortium of mining companies) was enlarged to meet the anticipated higher demand for South Africa's coal exports. However, this increased capacity cannot be fully utilised because Transnet failed to increase the capacity on the Ermelo-Richards Bay rail. There have been several calls to increase rail capacity, but the expansion will only be in place in 2019 at the earliest.

With the opening of BHP Billiton's new Hillside Smelter in 1996, things were looking good for uMhlathuze. However, rather than ushering in a golden era, 1996 saw the beginning of a succession of obstacles. Pulp United began engaging with the municipality in 2007/8 to obtain land for a factory that would produce pulp from eucalyptus trees. The investors would have consisted of a Swedish company, the Industrial Development Corporation and NCT Forestry. After six years of struggling with difficulties (land zoning, environmental impact assessments, bulk services, and so on), the Swedish investor is no longer interested. The inability of the local authority to act decisively stands in contrast to the dedicated, targeted approach that enabled the necessary decisions in the early 1990s that resulted in the opening of the Hillside smelter.

The KwaZulu-Natal provincial government and the local authority also established the Richards Bay Industrial Development Zone Company in 2002, but there have been no visible economic benefits to date. Separate land parcels (problematic for an IDZ that aims to have one overall import-export duty regime) and insufficient electricity supplies are contributing factors.

Demographic and population changes

Empangeni appeared in the South African census for the first time in 1921, with a total population of 337. By 1936 its population had grown to 2,117 and Felixton had a population of 818. It was only in 1946 that a permanent population was recorded at Richards Bay, then a fishing community of 240 people. In 1970, after construction had begun on Alusaf, the harbour and the town's infrastructure, Richards Bay had a population of 594. At about the same time, an R293 township was established and proclaimed in the Mkwanazi South traditional authority. Throughout the 1970s and 1980s, Richards Bay grew enormously, and by 2011 the population had reached 330,000. Since the abolition of influx control in 1986 and especially since 1994, the racial composition of Richards Bay has changed significantly – whereas the town was mainly white and Indian prior to 1986, it now has a mixture of all racial groups.

Against this background, a number of important trends should be noted. The population growth rate in uMhlathuze is significantly higher than that of KwaZulu-Natal as a whole. For example, between 2001 and 2011 the KwaZulu-Natal population increased by 8.6 per cent, whereas the population of uMhlathuze grew by 15.4 per cent – almost double the provincial rate (Stats SA, 2013). UMhlathuze's population growth rate is also significantly higher than that of the uThungulu District Municipality, of which uMhlathuze is a part. The other municipalities in the uThungulu District together had 23,764 fewer residents in 2011 than in 2001 (Stats SA, 2013). UMhlathuze is clearly a focal point for population growth.

South Africa's population as a whole is 63.6 per cent urban, with 4.89 per cent of people living on commercial farms and 31.5 per cent in traditional authority areas. The population of KwaZulu-Natal, on the other hand, is only 47.5 per cent urban, with 45.7 per cent of the population living in traditional authority areas and 6.8 per cent on commercial farms (Stats SA, 2013). UThungulu District Municipality is predominantly rural, with only 18.1 per cent of its population living in urban areas, 2.6 per cent on commercial farms and 79.3 per cent in traditional authority areas. Although uMhlathuze is more urban (35 per cent) than the rest of the district, the majority of its population (62.5 per cent) live on traditional authority land, which in itself raises some questions about the name of the municipality: City of uMhlathuze. The urban settlement of Richards Bay, with its significant international and national economic linkages, is thus the exception in an area where most people live on traditional land. Relatively dense settlements in unplanned traditional authority areas are rapidly growing on the boundaries of the formally proclaimed urban areas. This probably indicates increased urbanisation from the rural hinterland. The municipality of uMhlathuze is rolling out water connections to such areas, but formal township establishment is not being considered because of the complexities inherent in dealing with Ingonyama Trust land. (The trust is the legal owner of all the land in traditional authority areas in KwaZulu-Natal, with the Zulu King as main trustee.)

An important question to consider is whether people view uMhlathuze's main urban areas (Richards Bay, Empangeni and eSikhawini) as permanent places to settle, or just stepping stones from the rural hinterland to Durban. There appears to be a distinct difference between the informal settlements surrounding Empangeni and eSikhawini and those closer to Richards Bay. There is evidence that, perhaps because of the convenient proximity of the N2, some residents of Empangeni and eSikhawini work in Durban (in places such as KwaMashu, Inanda and Ntuzuma) and return home at the weekends.

Economic trends: the port of Richards Bay

Richards Bay and its port contribute most of the area's GVA. Before the port and the town of Richards Bay were established, Empangeni was the main town. It was a commercial and administrative town servicing the commercial farmers and the important agro-processors located there (the sugar mills and saw mills) as well as the homeland hinterlands. But the development of the port and the accompanying industry dramatically changed the character of the whole uMhlathuze area.

Richards Bay is sometimes referred to as 'Secunda-by-the-Sea' because of the air pollution it suffers from the Foskor fertiliser factory, the Mondi paper pulp plant, the Tata Steel factory and the aluminium smelters.[2] Ironically, however, the port's biggest economic thrust has little to do with these local industries (Goodenough, 2003; Nel et al., 2004). The main activity at the port is exporting the coal that arrives via rail from Mpumalanga and Limpopo. The coal terminal (a private sector development) initially had the capacity to handle 24 million tons of coal per annum (mtpa). This has since been expanded to 91 mtpa. With the current average of 74 mtpa, the privately owned Richards Bay Coal Terminal (a consortium of Anglo American, BHP Billiton, Sasol, Exxaro, Glencore and Xstrata) has spare capacity; the bottleneck is the rail line that Transnet as state-owned enterprise did not improve in time to handle increased capacity. This obstacle is effectively an opportunity tax on the private sector investment in the coal terminal, resulting in South Africa not being able to supply China and Europe when there was high demand for coal imports from those countries.

Exports make up 92 per cent of the cargo handled in the port. The remaining 8 per cent consists of imports of sulphur (for Foskor and other fertiliser producers), alumina (for the BHP smelters), poking coal for furnaces, liquids and petroleum products. Apart from coal, other exports include chrome, ferrochrome and wood chips. Despite handling approximately 18,000 containers per annum the harbour has no dedicated container terminal, and most locally manufactured exports use the Durban harbour. The senior planning manager at the National Ports Authority at Richards Bay said in an interview that Durban, Cape Town and the port of Ngqura (part of the Coega Industrial Development Zone) are Transnet's preferred container-handling ports. According to the ports capacity planner, South Africa's ports are complementary rather than competitive, and the National Ports Authority is 'careful not to plan and develop capacity that will not be utilised since then the public could criticise the Ports Authority for developing white elephants'. This is an interesting comment given that the development of the deep water Coega port proceeded without even an anchor industry or any investors for terminal developments.

It appears that Coega was a political attempt to boost economic development in the Eastern Cape at all costs. Negative impacts such as wasteful expenditure and the lost opportunity to increase coal exports from Richards Bay (by investing in the Richards Bay rather than Coega port) were apparently disregarded. One interviewee quoted a study that said more than 80,000 containers are trucked annually from Richards Bay to Durban and vice versa on the N2 because of the absence of a dedicated container terminal at Richards Bay. Containers can be loaded and off-loaded by cranes in Durban. In Richards Bay harbour, containers can only be handled if there is a freight ship with a container hoist on the ship itself. Approximately 18,000 containers are handled at Richards Bay (loading and off-loading) but the further 80,000 containers per annum travel by road from Richards Bay to Durban or vice versa.

Table 8.1 summarises expansions of the port that were planned in 2013 and the situation two years later. There are no current plans to increase the capacity of the bulk liquid terminal (currently 3 mtpa). The Ports Authority is engaged in negotiations to acquire land for possible future expansion of the Richards Bay port.

Table 8.1 Comparison of progress made in respect of plans for the harbour at Richards Bay

Planned expansion as documented in 2013[a]	*State of progress two years later*[b]
The construction of an additional coal terminal to provide export facilities to small black coal mining companies, with a capacity of 14 mtpa.[c]	Not mentioned in the May 2015 Ports Development Framework Plan of the National Port Authority
Increasing the capacity of the existing Richards Bay Coal Terminal to 97 mtpa (from its current 84 mpta) capacity by 2017. The private consortium will commence work on this project once the rail line capacity has been increased, as the current rail capacity is only 76 mtpa.	Private consortium is holding back on this since: i Transnet is late with their rail upgrade and the current capacity of 85 mpta cannot be used. ii The demand for coal export from South Africa has dropped substantially and Germany (procuring more coal to replace in the interim energy lost by the closure of the nuclear reactors) has sourced coal from Canada and the US.
The expansion of the Transnet port terminals from a current capacity of 28 mtpa to 59 mtpa by 2024.	Expansion to a specific capacity is not mentioned in the May 2015 Ports Development Framework Plan.
The development of a floating dry dock.	A call for tenders was made in 2014 but no bids were received. The project is on hold.

Sources: a Hills (2013); b Van der Walt (2015) and Portnet (2015); c Maharaj (2013).

This would approximately double the port's capacity, and the docks would stretch almost to the N2. However, this will not happen before 2050, and even then only if there is an assessed need for expansion.

An environmental impact assessment of the upgrading of the rail link between Ermelo and Richards Bay was completed and submitted to the Department of Environmental Affairs for scrutiny (Aurecon, 2014). Transnet Freight Rail put out a call for tenders in 2014, with the expansion to be operational by 2018. By mid-2015 the expected completion date had already shifted to 2020. The planned upgrade would increase the carrying capacity to 97 mtpa (two trains of approximately 200 bulk wagons daily). To achieve this, the existing heavy haul rail line must be upgraded and freed from other rail traffic as much as possible. In addition, a new line will be built from Richards Bay through Swaziland to Mpumalanga, ending at Davel. The cost estimate for these two developments is R12.2 billion.

Meanwhile, the Richards Bay port is also facing increasing competition from outside South Africa. After years of neglect, the port of Maputo is benefiting from major investment by a multi-national consortium that includes Grindrod, which is linked to the massive Remgro Group. This privatisation of the Maputo port coincides with the privatisation of the rail link from the South African border to Maputo. Although the capacity of Maputo's existing coal export terminal is far below that of the Richards Bay terminal, multiple export contracts (both market and shipping contracts) are being sealed with Maputo. These contracts might have gone instead to Richards Bay if Transnet had enabled the establishment of a dedicated container terminal at Richards Bay.

Maputo's Matola coal terminal has already been upgraded to a capacity of 6 mtpa and the next upgrade will bring it up to 26 mtpa. Besides the Matola coal terminal, Grindrod also has a 48,000 m² footprint in the Maputo main port where sized coal is loaded by skip and either vessel or shore cranes. In 2012 Grindrod sold a 35 per cent stake in the Matola Coal Terminal Concession Company to the Vitol Group, which is the world's largest independent energy trader and one of the top five coal traders in the world. These strategic developments in Maputo and the involvement of large international conglomerates stand in sharp contrast to the wasted opportunities in Richards Bay and the apparent white elephant of Coega.

The boom in demand for commodities, caused especially by the extraordinary growth of China up to 2012 (a massive investment in infrastructure, the construction of several major cities, and large-scale industrialisation), has driven production of commodities (coal and steel) as well as commodity prices to previously unheard-of levels. Richards Bay's lack of a container terminal and the inadequate rail line have prevented the mining companies from maximising their potential exports. And the decline in the demand for commodities because of the lower economic growth rate in China since 2014 has increased this port's vulnerability.

Economic trends: Richards Bay Industrial Development Zone

The Richards Bay Industrial Development Zone (RBIDZ) company was established in 2002 by the KwaZulu-Natal Provincial Government. The two main stakeholders were the Ithala Development Finance Corporation (60 per cent) and the uMhlathuze Municipality (40 per cent) (Hall, 2009). The plan was for Ithala to provide the capital and uMhlathuze to provide the land. However, the land provided by uMhlathuze consisted of five non-contiguous pieces and was therefore not very suitable. Eventually, three pieces were given back to uMhlathuze and the provincial government purchased the other two. The reconstituted RBIDZ is now a wholly owned public enterprise with the KwaZulu-Natal Provincial Government as the only shareholder.

The larger of the two pieces of land is now being serviced, with water and sanitation already in place, but only a portion of the 95 hectares can be developed since one section contains a wetland with a variety of bird life, and only light industries can be established because of the already high level of air pollution. At the time of writing, there was also no rail link between the site and the adjacent harbour. So far, not a single investor has been lured to this development zone, but the hope is that a company can be found to lease the land.

A 50-year master plan was developed and released. Despite 3,500 ha of development land next to the port being available, the RBIDZ company received Cabinet approval to buy 1,100 ha 20 km from the port. Officials who were interviewed made two criticisms. Firstly, they observed that it is difficult to compete with industrial development zones abroad that offer better incentives such as existing buildings; simply providing serviced land may not be enough to attract development. Secondly, they noted that the port of Richards Bay lacks a container terminal, but expressed the hope that the Ports Authority might address this at some point. These issues aside, they noted that creating an industrial development zone is a long-term project and that returns would have to be measured in the form of eventual job creation and investment. The current state of play, however, does not inspire confidence: in the 2011/12 financial year, in addition to money already earmarked for capital expenditure, the RBIDZ company received a grant of R26 million from the provincial government and R6.6 million in investment income (earned on seed capital provided by the government). Operating expenditures for the year totalled R30 million. Of this, the financial statements show that the cost of the 28 staff members was R19,163,358, although in the human resource component of the report this amount is listed as R10,281,000 (RBIDZ, 2012). It must be concluded that this company has made little headway to date, and there is little evidence that positive benefits will be realised in the future.

Economic trends: uMhlathuze overall

Eight important points can be made in respect of economic trends in uMhlathuze. First, from 1996 to 2001 uMhlathuze's economic growth rate was higher than that of most of the rest of the country. This was due to international investment such as BHP's new Hillside smelter and the expansion of Mondi's operations. Second, economic growth was slower between 2001 and 2011, largely due to the drop in commodity prices as a result of the global financial crisis of 2007/8. Third, the estimated 17 per cent to 32 per cent worldwide surplus production of iron ore and steel has had a negative impact on the steel manufacturing companies, RBM, Tronox and Tata Steel. Tata Steel is in business rescue and the plant is up for sale. Irregular electricity supply and the rapid electricity rate hikes have rendered the plant unviable, given the world oversupply of steel.

Fourth, the aluminium smelter played an important role in the original development of Richards Bay. Yet, current and future downscaling have and will have negative impacts in uMhlathuze. BHP Billiton will continue smelting aluminium in South Africa only if it remains economically viable to do so. The current closure suggest that the smelter is not economically viable. Furthermore, Eskom's provision of low-cost electricity to BHP Billiton's smelters is under close scrutiny. Large hikes in electricity tariffs and Eskom's continuing struggle to meet the current electricity demand are all future problems of industrial development in uMhlathuze.

Fifth, in 2015 BHP Billiton closed the Bayside smelter and placed the modern Hillside smelter (together with many of their South African assets that are no longer considered as core by this multi-national corporation) into a separate South Africa-based company. Consequently, the aluminium smelter is now effectively delinked from the BHP multi-national value chain.

Sixth, Bell Industries, which makes heavy industrial and transport equipment, is also situated in Richards Bay. Machinery manufactured by Bell is used in the mining and forestry industries. According to an interview with the manager at the Richards Bay plant, the downsizing of mining internationally has considerably reduced the number of orders received by Bell.

Seventh, because wood is a renewable resource, forestry and wood product businesses are more sustainable in the long run than mining or coal-related industries (this also applies to sugarcane growers and other farmers). In 1984, Mondi established a large plant at Richards Bay to produce Baycel (a bleached hardwood pulp made from eucalyptus fibre) and Baywhite (white linerboard). The plant was expanded and modernised in 2005 and, despite doubling its output to 720,000 tonnes per annum, now uses only 75 megalitres of water a day, compared to 150 megalitres in the 1980s. Nevertheless, the shortage of water in the area is having a negative effect on the Mondi plants. However, Mondi is succeeding in keeping costs under control, but the company is under threat from land reform pressures and urbanisation pressures. In uMhlathuze, large tracts of fertile river valley land and the undulating hills on both sides of the N2 highway have been used for sugarcane production for decades. Most of this sugarcane is processed at the Felixton mill. Land reform projects since the early 2000s have caused the disappearance of vast tracts of commercial sugarcane, leading to lower production and job losses at the mill. The municipality has earmarked all the commercial farms and afforested areas as potential urban expansion areas, since it is easy to establish townships in these areas but difficult to do so in the traditional areas.

Finally, the international links of Richards Bay based enterprises create potential but also increase vulnerability. One drawback is that the financial performance of such factories and mines is meticulously scrutinised against the firms' operations in other countries. When we consider South Africa's restrictive labour practices and the high incidence of strikes, relatively low productivity levels, massive increases in electricity tariffs and property tax hikes, it becomes clear that the situation is risky. If a multinational corporation experiences lower profit margins, it might scale back or even close its South African operations. The advantage of international linkages for local businesses is that access to multi-national research and development findings as well as best practice can improve local productivity.

Relations between business and government

It seems that relations are less than ideal. In interviews, individuals from the private sector expressed major concerns about the public sector. The reverse was also the case. Members of uMhlathuze's LED division said their interactions with the business sector were not positive: 'Why should I go to the business chamber meetings if they are always just criticising the municipality?' asked one official. Criticisms from business people were related to procurement procedures, lengthy processes and informal traders. The uMhlathuze LED Strategy 2013–2017 lists the following complaints from stakeholders (UMhlathuze, 2013b):

- the municipality is not effectively engaging the business community around development issues;
- the municipality's ad hoc and arbitrary mode of operation creates uncertainties for the business community; and
- proposals from the business community are often ignored – for example, there was no reaction to the proposal submitted for a Business Retention and Expansion process.

In terms of the National Ports Act, there must be a port consultative committee comprising the harbour master, two representatives of the Ports Authority, three representatives of local port users (the private sector), two persons representing organised labour, and one person each from the local and provincial authorities of the area where the port is situated (RSA, 2005). This committee is a forum for exchanging views and advising the Minister, and it must be consulted on any port development scheme. From the interviews, it was clear that the Richards Bay port consultative committee does not function effectively – further proof of the damaged relationships between the public and private sectors.

Municipal plans

This section considers uMhlathuze's IDP (UMhlathuze Local Municipality, 2012) and Spatial Development Framework (SDF) (UMhlathuze, 2013a). Perhaps because the IDP is a five-year plan, the importance of the Richards Bay port is overlooked. In the entire IDP there are only two references to the port: the vision statement refers to a port city and the social and economic development section contains a statement about 'the promotion of the dry dock and container terminal developments' (UMhlathuze, 2012, p. 37). But in all the lengthy project lists, there is not a single initiative to pursue this action plan. This is despite the fact that the Constitution gives municipalities executive authority over harbours (RSA 1996, Schedule 4). By not focusing on how the harbour's potential can be maximised for the development of the locality, the IDP ignores the urgent need to diversify uMhlathuze's economy. Neither coal exports nor aluminium smelters are secured activities, so the municipality should be attempting to diversify the economy now. Unfortunately, instead of focusing on the port, the IDP contains the idealistic notion of an International Convention Centre – but without an operational airport this idea is unlikely to succeed.

In contrast to the IDP, uMhlathuze's SDF is logically structured. It offers a 50-year perspective while simultaneously identifying some immediate priorities (UMhlathuze, 2013a). The Richards Bay port and its potential expansion inland towards the N2 are at the heart of the SDF. The land identified for residential, commercial and industrial development consists mostly of privately owned commercial farms (high-yielding sugarcane plantations in the vicinity of the N2 and forests that are under long-term leases). Traditional Authority Land is not included because of the untested processes and potential problems with township establishment in such areas (UMhlathuze Local Municipality, 2010).

Local authorities seem to be waiting for provincial or national directives and guidance for developing traditional land. Meanwhile, national and provincial authorities appear to be too indecisive to deal with such a sensitive issue in a comprehensive manner, choosing instead to make ad hoc decisions in order to avoid policy changes that could be politically detrimental.

Municipal governance, management and finance

The municipality has had its share of political instability since it was formed in 2001. The Inkatha Freedom Party was originally the majority party, but a tenuous coalition government was formed between 2006 and 2011. The 2011 local elections then put the African National Congress firmly in control. Recently, rumours have spread about excessive expenditure on security measures for councillors and senior officials. Suspicions are running so high between councillors from the African National Congress and the Inkatha Freedom Party that they even refuse to contract the same security firm to provide protection services to councillors.

There are, however, some positive indicators regarding local government. UMhlathuze Municipality has been very successful in rolling out access to potable water, with 97 per cent of households being connected to the municipal water supply. In 2012 uMhlathuze was ranked sixth in KwaZulu-Natal in the Department of Water Affairs' 'Blue Drop' evaluation (which measures clean water supply). The National Treasury named uMhlathuze the local municipality with the best debt collection record in 2011. And uMhlathuze received a clean audit for five years up to 2012 (Auditor General, 2013).

However, some concerns must be mentioned. UMhlathuze has been in the news since August 2013, when the Public Protector visited the municipality to begin an investigation into a range of complaints. Residents had submitted a 12-page document to her office claiming nepotism, collusion between senior municipal figures and regional political heavyweights, and irregular and unauthorised expenditure. There have also been numerous conflicts between senior municipal management and the municipal council, most of which were won by management (Ramsamy, 2013, p. 4).[3]

Some concerns have also been expressed about the municipality's financial situation. Among these concerns are the high municipal salary bill and the increase in the equitable share of capital grants and underspending of these grants. In addition, the reason that uMhlathuze Local Municipality does so well at collecting debts is that the 100 largest ratepayers and consumers of electricity and water make reliable payments. This heavy dependence on a small number of large users holds long-term risks should these industries relocate or consume less electricity.

UMhlathuze's record of rolling out water infrastructure is good, but it is not investing concurrently in additional bulk supply capacity and it is not ensuring ongoing maintenance of existing infrastructure. Its mode of providing sparsely settled traditional authority areas with waterborne connections is inefficient. This could be made efficient if the municipality implemented proper township establishment procedures with dense and compact settlement patterns.

External pressures

Political pressures

Politics in KwaZulu-Natal have been messy since the 1980s, mainly because of tension and conflict between the African National Congress and the Inkatha Freedom Party. The province experienced high levels of violence in the late 1980s and early 1990s, and although the situation has greatly improved, there are still occasional incidents of political violence. In the early post-apartheid period, KwaZulu-Natal was one of only two provinces not under African National Congress rule (the other being the Western Cape). Thus, despite growing international interest in the port of Richards Bay, the national African National Congress leadership was not very interested in supporting Richards Bay since this would strengthen the economy of KwaZulu-Natal – and thus give a boost to a main political rival. Rather than investing in the upgrade of the Ermelo–Richards Bay rail and improving the harbour of Richards Bay, the government invested, against Transnet's own advice, in developing the new port of Ngqura (Coega) in the Eastern Cape.

Unfortunately for Richards Bay, this situation is likely to repeat itself. It looks as though the next major national infrastructure investment will be at the old Durban airport. This will again put major port development in Richards Bay on the back burner. Given international concerns about global warming and the fact that the US is becoming an energy exporter, the demand for and price of coal may decrease in the near future. Unless the Richards Bay port is diversified through the development of a modern container terminal to transform it into a container-importing harbour as well, it may become much less lucrative by 2025.

On a related note, although globalisation has brought opportunities, it has also exposed uMhlathuze to competition from world markets. During the apartheid years, aluminium smelters played an important local and national role. But globalisation has transformed the South African operations into mere production units within an international network. Important future decisions about these plants are now made in the boardrooms of multinational corporations because of the decision by BHP Billiton to close the Bayside smelter and to transfer the Hillside smelter to South 32.

Natural resources and the environment

In the late 1960s, when the deep sea harbour, the industrial zone and the new town were conceptualised, the Richards Bay area was thoroughly researched by the CSIR. Geological studies were completed to determine how the harbour pilings should be constructed; the rock in some areas was so deep that specialised piling methods were required. The CSIR continues to monitor and evaluate the area, making Richards Bay one of the best-documented localities regarding the impact of development on the environment. The town, port and industrial sites were all built on virgin territory – the river was re-routed to create the deep sea harbour, excavated soil was used to fill in the surrounding wetlands and drainage canals were constructed to create developable land. It is therefore likely that, if current environmental legislation had been in place in the 1960s, Richards Bay would never have been developed.

Although the Richards Bay Nature Reserve is a bird paradise, the area's ecology faces multiple risks. Many of its wetlands have been destroyed, reducing the habitat for birds and other wildlife, and the Foskor fertiliser plant discards gypsum through a pipeline 5 km from the coast. Meanwhile, Richards Bay Minerals is conducting dune mining activities, despite environmental studies that warned about the negative impact of this mining and an expensive process of rehabilitation of dune vegetation is in place.

Dependence on Transnet

The Richards Bay economy is highly dependent on rail and port activities. It was mentioned in interviews that international logistics firms wanted to invest in the port of Richards Bay, but Transnet could not provide a meaningful framework for such investment. This is yet another example of Transnet hindering the economic growth of uMhlathuze. Transnet's mistake has been to put all its eggs in one basket, by bargaining on coal exports, but then in effect to 'drop the basket' by neglecting to provide the necessary rail capacity when demand for coal exports was at its height. Rather than building a local economy on one sector, it is better to diversify by creating new value chains. Diversifying the port of Richards Bay by developing a dedicated container terminal would give the port life apart from coal, help local industries to import and export through the harbour, and contribute to the regional and national economy.

Both rail and port activities have contributed to the economy of Richards Bay. The real question is whether Richards Bay has benefited as much from Transnet as it could have done. The answer to that question might be found by asking two additional questions:

1   Did the commitment of capital to create the Port of Ngcura contribute to Transnet's acknowledged inability to provide timeous and required maintenance to both rail and rolling stock that clearly has a negative impact on maximising the export potential of Richards Bay?
2   Did the commitment of capital to the Port of Ngcura also make it impossible for Transnet to start sooner on the plan to strengthen the Ermelo–Richards Bay rail link (for example by widening the tunnel that is a major bottleneck)?

The answer has to be 'yes' in both cases, which implies that the politically-driven development of Coega (despite the initial documented objections by Portnet's management) has resulted in investment in what is still largely a white elephant whilst penalising not only large mining companies who had invested in capacity in Richards Bay Coal Terminal that cannot be utilised since the Transnet trains and railroad cannot meet that capacity, but also penalising the small black mining companies who also could have benefited from the international demand for coal. The attack made at the end of October 2013 by Brian Molefe, then CEO of Transnet, on BHP Billiton and other companies in the area, saying that they do not want to provide opportunities for emerging black miners to benefit from coal export opportunities, can only be interpreted as searching for another scapegoat because all the indicators are pointing to Transnet as the guilty party. Transnet's lack of planning succeeded in slowing down the country's economic growth rate and enabled other coal exporters to grow their market share faster than South Africa could. It was therefore a decision that still has a very negative effect on BEE as well as on job creation. Molefe is now arguing that BHP Billiton and others should be generous and assist these emerging miners, but the state-owned enterprises that he is heading will be able to provide sufficient rail capacity for the Richards Bay Coal Terminal Consortium to export coal only at the level that they created some years ago.

Synthesis

A big part of the story of uMhlathuze is the tale of Richards Bay. Developed in the late 1960s to export coal, the port now faces the uncertain long-term prospects of coal. Given the additional concerns about the future of the remaining aluminium smelter and the Tata Steel Plant as well as the mining operations of RBM and Tronox, there is uncertainty about the future of uMhlathuze and Richards Bay. Although internal pressures play a role, the most important factor is national planning processes. UMhlathuze still has significant international linkages, but the internal and external pressures put the area's international competitiveness at risk.

UMhlathuze should use the window of opportunity as long as coal is being exported to diversify the area's economy. The existing multinational linkages would be strengthened by the construction of a dedicated modern container terminal. To achieve this, there has to be a concerted effort to promote this terminal in Richards Bay before work begins on the dig-out port at Durban's old airport. Proponents should emphasise that rail transport costs from Gauteng and Mpumalanga via the Ermelo–Richards Bay line are lower than those via the Johannesburg–Durban line. Imports would also be cheaper to transport from the Richards Bay port than from Durban. For this to happen, the local government and private sector will need to join forces. If Transnet will not provide the capital, an international port operator (such as DP World or Maersk) could be approached to develop the port and the necessary rail linkages on a privatised basis. If this were to happen, local role players should play an important role.

The story of uMhlathuze confirms the economic vulnerability of secondary cities associated with the minerals-energy complex in South Africa. The decline in the demand for commodities could well continue in the short and medium term. The case study also suggested that local planning and thinking have been unable to diversify the economy over the past decade. In fact, national policies and investments have ignored uMhlathuze in favour of investing in metros. Finally, although the regional services role of Richards Bay and Empangeni should not be ignored, land pressures suggest that urgent plans are required to address increasing urbanisation. The mere fact that formal agricultural land and not traditional land parcels are earmarked in this regard could well be reconsidered.

Notes

1 R293 township establishment was the administrative process to proclaim land in a traditional authority area as a formal township with residential, commercial and institutional (e.g. education) land uses. The townships thus established were no longer under the direct administration of the chieftainships.
2 Secunda is an inland Mpumalanga town known for pollution from the Sasol processing plants that convert coal into oil.
3 Dladla v Council of Mbombela Local Municipality and Another (1) (2008) 29 ILJ 1983.

References

Auditor General, 2013. *General Report on Audit Outcomes of Local Government in KwaZulu-Natal and Feedback from Hilton Renald in the uMhlathuze LM Finance Management Division.* Pietermaritzburg: Auditor General.

Aurecon, 2014. *Environmental Impact Assessment: The Proposed Upgrade and New Construction Related to the Development of the Swaziland Rail Link Project, for the Davel Rail Yard in Mpumalanga.* Durban: Transnet.

Goodenough, C. K., 2003. The local global nexus: a case study of Richards Bay. Unpublished master's thesis, University of KwaZulu-Natal, Pietermaritzburg.

Greaves, A., 2012. *Crossing the Buffalo: the Zulu War of 1879.* Durban: Adrian Greaves.

Hall, P. V., 2009. Regional institutional structure and industrial strategy: Richards Bay and the spatial development initiatives. Development Policy Research Unit, University of Cape Town.

Hill, T. and Goodenough, C., 2005. A case study of local economic development in Richards Bay. Pietermaritzburg: Unpublished report conducted for pro-poor LED project funded by the World Bank.

Nel, E., Hill, T. and Goodenough, C., 2004. Global coal demand, South Africa's coal industry and the Richards Bay coal terminal. *Geography,* 89, 292–297.

Nel, E., Hill, T. and Goodenough, C., 2009. Multi-stakeholder driven local economic development: reflections on the experience of Richards Bay and the uMhlathuze municipality. *Urban Forum,* 18, 31–47.

Ramsamy, R., 2013. Complaints about councillor. *Zululand Observer,* 4 September.

RBIDZ (Richards Bay Industrial Development Zone), 2012. *Annual Report 2011/12.* Richards Bay: RBIDZ Company.

RSA (Republic of South Africa), 1996. *Constitution of the Republic of South Africa. Schedule 4 – Functional Areas of Concurrent National and Provincial Legislative Competence.* Pretoria: Government Printers.

RSA (Republic of South Africa), 2005. *National Ports Act, Act No. 12 of 2005.* Pretoria: Pretoria: Government Printer.

SACN (South African Cities Network), 2014. *Outside the Core: Towards Understanding of Intermediate Cities in South Africa.* Johannesburg: SACN.

Stats SA (Statistics South Africa), 2013. *Census Data for 1996, 2001 and 2011*. Pretoria: Stats SA.

Tongaat Hulett Sugar, 2014. South Africa: Sugar Mills: Felixton Mill. Available at: www.huletts.co.za/ops/south_africa/mills/felixton.asp (accessed 12 December 2013).

UMhlathuze, 2013a. *Draft Spatial Development Framework*. Richards Bay: UMhlathuze.

UMhlathuze, 2013b. *Local Economic Development Strategy*. Richards Bay: UMhlathuze.

UMhlathuze Local Municipality, 2010. *Spatial Development Framework*. Richards Bay: UMhlathuze Local Municipality.

UMhlathuze Local Municipality, 2012. *Integrated Development Plan, 2012–2017*. Richards Bay: Umhlathuze Local Municipality.

9 The role of secondary cities in South Africa's development

Lochner Marais, Etienne Nel and
Ronnie Donaldson

Size, functions, places and strategies

This chapter concludes the first reflection in book form on secondary cities in South Africa. Hitherto, urban research in South Africa has generally focused on the three main metros, Cape Town, Johannesburg and Durban/eThekwini (Visser, 2013), and more recently on smaller towns (Donaldson and Marais, 2012). In this book we have looked at evidence from six case studies of secondary cities in South Africa.

We mirrored this evidence against the literature in Chapter 2. In Chapter 1 we set up a conceptual framework of the four main attributes of the six cities: size, function, location and locational interdependence, and strategic planning (Table 1.4). This final chapter consolidates the case study findings from the preceding chapters. It has four objectives: to compare the findings from the six case studies with each other, to compare them with the attributes of secondary cities internationally (listed in Table 2.2), to consider what secondary cities have contributed to the development of South Africa, and to draw policy lessons from the six studies.

The chapter begins by discussing issues of city size, particularly in relation to population and the economy. We then consider city function, location and locational interdependence. This is followed by a discussion of strategies the six cities have adopted, comparing them with strategies described in the literature. Next we turn to the question of how important secondary cities are to South Africa. The chapter concludes with an examination of uniquely South African policy issues.

Size

Internationally, the size of urban areas is increasingly acknowledged as a basic determinant of economic development (Rodríguez-Pose and Dahl Fitjar, 2013). The label 'secondary' implies that a city is secondary to a country's main (usually larger) cities. We have seen that definitions of secondary cities emphasise size, with common indicators being the size of the population or the economy, population density and the extent of the built-up area (Van der Merwe, 1992). The criteria for size can be expanded to include such factors as municipal revenue and expenditure, infrastructure networks (roads, water supply and so on), the property tax base, and charges for water, electricity and other utilities. 'Secondary' also means the city is big enough to manage self-generated growth but small enough to avoid some of the negative aspects of massive urban agglomerations, such as urban sprawl, social problems and environmental damage. In looking at *how* cities reach a particular size, we need to consider two contrasting mechanisms: 'self-generated' growth (to study this we need to know both the historical and the current reasons), and planned growth or decentralisation of growth activity to second-tier cities.

Table 9.1 compares the size-related indicators of the six case study cities with the averages for the main South African metros. The table reminds us that a range of size indicators should be considered rather than just one. For example, Polokwane's population is 24 per cent of the metro average, and almost as big as the population of some of the smaller metros (for example Mangaung/ Bloemfontein and Buffalo City/East London), but its revenue is only 11 per cent of the metro average. None of the case study cities have size indicators larger than the metro average but some do come close to the size of the smaller metros. For example, Emfuleni's population of 721,000 is not much below that of Mangaung at 747,000 (Stats SA, 2013). More importantly, size indicators must be viewed in conjunction with a city's functions and location. Finally, it is important to note that size indicators are not always meaningful on their own – we also need to know the associated trends and risks.

Functions

Our six case study cities have a variety of important functions, such as being linked to the South African mineral-energy complex, or providing important regional services, or serving as politically driven administrative centres. As is explained further in the section below on strategy, these secondary cities are mostly mono- rather than multi-functional. Their mono-functional roles are in mining (City of Matlosana and eMalahleni), steel production (Emfuleni), coal exporting (uMhlathuze), tourism (George) and being a provincial capital (Polokwane). All six are linked to national roads, and uMhlathuze is linked to an export harbour. Three of them have their own airports (George, Polokwane and uMhlathuze). Essentially, these cities are well connected transport-wise.

Besides their main functions, these cities have important subsidiary functions. George and the City of Matlosana are historically important service centres for their rural hinterlands, providing inputs for commercial agriculture as well as educational, medical and other social services. The Polokwane case study shows that these services are also being provided for people living on rural communal land that extends far into the province. In uMhlathuze municipality, Richards Bay and Empangeni provide similar services to surrounding rural communal land in KwaZulu-Natal. The connections between the urban areas in eMalahleni and Emfuleni and their rural hinterlands are less direct, but an assessment of migration patterns shows that Emfuleni is closely connected to rural areas in the northern parts of the Free State province.

Table 9.1 Sizes of the six secondary cities compared with the average for the metropolitan areas (2011)

	Matlosana	eMalahleni	Emfuleni	George	Polokwane	uMhlathuze	Metro average
Population size	398,676	395,466	721,567	193,672	628,999	334,450	2,546,000
Population density (people per sq km)	110	148	747	37	167	420	957
GVA (R1000)	9,397,796	39,000,000	17,600,000	5,800,000	15,800,000	9,758,715	203,000,000
Municipal revenue (R1000)	1,616,000	n.a.	3,555,000	920,830	1,787,000	2,040,655	15,314,000
Municipal expenditure (R1000)	1,466,638	n.a	3,815,000	1,049,006	1,622,000	1,860,854	13,908,000

Source: Compiled from data provided by SACN (2014).

Note: Municipal figures for eMalahleni were unobtainable due to the fact that audit financial statements were not available.

Over the past 20 years, the regional service role of the six cities has expanded (in geographic terms), probably because political transformation after apartheid has enabled freedom of movement and choice of relocation, improvements in transport infrastructure, the parallel demise of the service character of smaller urban areas and the ability of secondary cities to provide services at scale. These cities have also all become home to new privatised medical and educational institutions. For example, all six have private hospitals (medical care franchises such as mediclinics) that located there in the past 20 years, and a number of private schools. Banks and other financial services have chosen these secondary cities to serve as regional hubs, with many banks closing down full banking services in smaller urban settlements but increasing the range of services offered in these cities.

Although Gauteng and the Cape Town area are experiencing the highest levels of urbanisation in the country, the importance of secondary cities in managing urbanisation should not be underestimated. Figure 9.1 shows the distribution of South Africa's population across small towns, secondary cities and metros.

Considering their small number, secondary cities (the 21 identified by the National Treasury) are home to a relatively large percentage (15 per cent) of the South African population, and although metros are growing the fastest, secondary cities are also increasing their share. They thus take some of the pressure off the big cities. This seems to be occurring naturally in South Africa, which is a positive trend considering that the international literature and South Africa's own history warn against trying to prevent urbanisation.

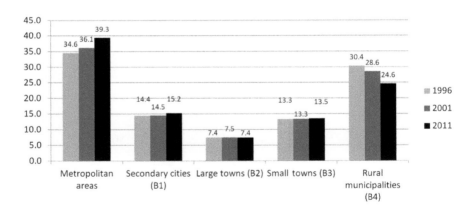

Figure 9.1 Percentage distribution of South African population by settlement type (1996, 2001, 2011)

Source: Stats SA (2013)

Note: Settlement types according to National Treasury definitions and categorisation.

Location and locational interdependence

A factor that must be taken into account when categorising secondary cities is their strategic location in relation to large metros, infrastructure, and resources such as agriculture, mining and the environment. Important components of location include transport and communication networks linking a city to the rural hinterland and larger urban areas. In the 1970s and 1980s it was assumed that the 'small city near the large metropolis gains most of the benefits of agglomeration without the pains of large size' (Van der Merwe, 1992). Ideally, a secondary city should be close enough to a large urban centre to benefit from developments in that centre but far enough away to avoid full integration with it.

Table 9.2 shows five locational aspects of the case study cities. It shows that all six cities have a direct link with either agricultural or mining resources, or both. Their location near major transport infrastructure (road, rail, sea and air) has helped to make them larger than small towns. Four of them have direct links with larger metros, and they all have important connections with the environment.

Size, location and function are interrelated. A locational aspect that particularly distinguishes these cities is that they are more directly related to primary sector industries and the environment than the larger metros with their diversified, service sector-focused economies. Mining-related activities, for example, play a crucial role in four of the six case study cities (City of Matlosana, eMalahleni, uMhlathuze and Emfuleni). And because of their large rural hinterlands all six have substantial agricultural production under their jurisdiction.

Strategies

This section summarises seven characteristics of secondary cities, as identified in Chapter 1 and expanded on in Chapter 2, that are related to or affect their strategies: institutional capacity and decentralisation; small but significant international links, and global links usually by means of one sector (these two characteristics have been condensed into one discussion point); high levels of vulnerability; LED strategies and spatial planning; strategic planning and the knowledge economy; and environmental confrontations.

Institutional capacity and decentralisation

The quality of municipal management varies across the six case studies. It is difficult to determine objectively whether the municipal management of these six cities is overall better or worse than that of metros. But, because these cities have a narrow economic base and are particularly vulnerable to economic change, it is likely that poor local government will have a disproportionly larger impact than in metros.

Table 9.2 Locational attributes for the six secondary cities

City	Dependence on agriculture	Dependence on resources	Proximity of a metropolitan area / degree of isolation	Proximity to transport infrastructure	Dependence on and links with environment
City of Matlosana	Regional service centre; historical links with agriculture.	Gold; uranium; agricultural products.	Almost an extension of the West Rand. Linked to the platinum belt.	N12 highway.	Linked to farmland and Vaal River.
eMalahleni	Limited agricultural links.	Coal/energy.	Close to Tshwane.	N4 highway; railway link to uMhlathuze and Maputo.	Linked to farmland and Olifants River.
Emfuleni	Limited agricultural links.	Coal/energy; steel.	Linked with Johannesburg and Ekurhuleni.	N1 and N3 highways; railway link	Linked to Vaal River.
George	Regional service centre; historical links with timber.	Wood.	Halfway between Cape Town and Port Elizabeth – fairly isolated.	N2 highway; airport.	Sensitive biodiversity in surrounding area.
Polokwane	Regional service centre; historical links with agriculture.	Agricultural products.	Linked with Gauteng but fairly peripheral location.	N1 highway; airport.	Water shortage.
uMhlathuze	Limited agricultural links.	Port for coal exports.	To some degree delinked from the KwaZulu-Natal economy.	N2 highway; port.	Sensitive biodiversity in surrounding area.

Source: SACN (2014).

We found many examples of poor governance and management in our six cities: eMalahleni is currently under government administration; Emfuleni has suffered much instability, having had four mayors and five municipal managers between 2005 and 2009; management and governance problems were reported in the City of Matlosana; and Polokwane has historically had its fair share of municipal problems. Furthermore, only two of the cities (George and uMhlathuze) received a clean local government audit for 2013/14. This is clearly not ideal, especially since some of these cities are experiencing either rapid population growth or rapid economic decline, or both, and are thus particularly in need of effective municipal management. Weak local capacity hampers long-term planning and holds back economic growth. South Africa's increased energy requirements have led to increased coal mining, which has boosted populations in coal mining areas such as eMalahleni and put heavy pressure on local government infrastructure. Areas experiencing economic decline are also under pressure. The City of Matlosana, for example, has been unable to set up an appropriate billing system for its municipal accounts. A particular problem is that, because of mine downscaling, many houses formerly owned by mining companies have been privatised and the city is now struggling to bill them individually.

The management of municipal finances is usually (although not always) a reliable indicator of the quality of overall municipal management. It is a matter for concern that during the 2011/12 financial year George was the only one of the six cities to receive an unqualified municipal audit from the Auditor General, while eMalahleni could not even provide financial statements. In contrast, five of the nine metros received unqualified municipal audits in 2011/12. It seems that the secondary cities, apart from George, do not yet have the capacity to manage large budgets.

As expected, given their smaller size, total municipal income and expenditure in the secondary cities is lower than the average for metros. Service charges (especially electricity) make up a large percentage of municipal income in uMhlathuze, Emfuleni and eMalahleni. This is directly related to the heavy industries that use old technologies and consume large amounts of electricity. This makes credit control easier for these cities, but relying on major energy-dependent industries is a long-term risk for municipal income.

Three of the cities (Emfuleni, City of Matlosana and uMhlathuze) were under-spending on infrastructure maintenance and repairs (3 per cent or less of their total annual expenditure). This is a big problem for Emfuleni and the City of Matlosana because of their ageing infrastructure. Emfuleni's underspending is a direct result of cash flow problems. UMhlathuze has newer infrastructure, so the fact that it spends less than 5 per cent of its budget on maintenance and repairs is not as troubling. Overall, the average expenditure on maintenance and repairs for the five secondary cities (3.1 per cent) is considerably lower than the average for metros (5.2 per cent).

Small but significant international links, usually by means of one sector

International competitiveness has increased substantially since South Africa returned to the global economy in the early 1990s. All six case study cities are connected to the global economy but, unlike South Africa's five biggest metros, their international links are based on only one or two economic sectors, which makes them more vulnerable to international shocks.

International connections are pertinent to our six cities in various ways and to differing degrees. In George, for example, the international tourism sector and the phenomenon of European 'swallows' visiting there during the South African summer are important. The City of Matlosana and Polokwane have started to transcend international boundaries by doing business with Botswana and Zimbabwe, respectively, and attracting foreign buying power from them. The City of Matlosana's international connectivity is mainly a result of the extraction and export of gold and uranium and its mining companies are mainly multinational corporations. Approximately 20 per cent of eMalahleni's coal is exported, and its steel industry also has some minor links to markets in southern and eastern Africa. UMhlathuze, through its port at Richards Bay, has major links to the international aluminium and coal markets and is home to many multinational corporations. Emfuleni also has a number of multinational corporations, particularly in the steel industry.

International competitiveness has many aspects for the six cities. Exporting is one aspect. The mining industries (e.g. gold and coal) and other industries such as steel making and steel-related products are continuing to export, although steel-related exports have declined considerably since the global financial downturn (2008) and the economic recession in South Africa (2009). A factor pushing up the overall cost of exporting is the cost of transporting coal and steel to the coast, which has been worsened by unreliable rail transport that has forced steel exporters to transport steel by road from Gauteng to eThekwini (Durban). As a result, although some products are exported, steel products are generally uncompetitive on the international market.

Another aspect is the presence of large multinational corporations in the secondary cities. The current relationships between these corporations and the cities of uMhlathuze, Emfuleni, Matlosana and eMalahleni can at best be described as ad hoc. These multinational corporations change ownership more often than local corporations, making it difficult to build trust and local partnerships. Many of them are important external links for improving local knowledge and innovation, but their presence also carries certain risks. Compared to their total international operations, the output of their South African factories is minuscule. For example, ArcelorMittal's South African production represents only 1 per cent of the company's worldwide production. Furthermore, many of these multinational companies allow their various plants around the world to compete against one another for international tenders. The possibility that South African operations could be shut down is therefore not inconceivable.

In summary, whereas larger metros usually have a range of economic sectors with international links, secondary cities typically have only one or two important international market sectors (such as steel, gold, coal, aluminium or tourism). This makes them vulnerable to external shocks and internal problems related to these specific sectors. They thus face increasing pressure to respond in appropriate (and differentiated) ways related to both institutional support and available finance.

High levels of vulnerability

As their economies are generally smaller than those of metros, secondary cities are more dependent on one or two main sectors, such as mining or large-scale manufacturing. This narrow economic base makes many of these cities particularly vulnerable to economic shocks, poor municipal management, poor business–government relations and the impact of sector-specific national government decisions. For example, 45 per cent of eMalahleni's GVA comes from coal mining and 32 per cent of Emfuleni's from steel production. Historically, 53 per cent of the City of Matlosana's GVA (1996 figures) came from gold mining.

Figure 9.2 shows that, interestingly, the six case study cities are more dependent than the metros on mining and utilities, and that it is really only in financial services and trade that the metros are making a proportionally much larger contribution to the economy. Noteworthy also is that the contribution of manufacturing to the economy is similar for metros and the six cities.

However, the structure of the manufacturing sector is different: in five of the six secondary cities one manufacturing subsector is responsible for more than a third of the city's manufacturing GVA output. In contrast, only one of the eight metros (Nelson Mandela Bay / Port Elizabeth) has a subsector (vehicle manufacturing) that dominates the manufacturing output. Metal manufacturing dominates

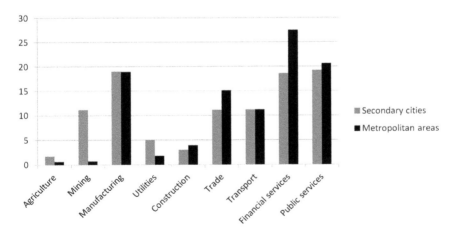

Figure 9.2 Economic structure of the six secondary cities and metropolitan areas (2011)

Source: SACN, 2014

in three of the secondary cities (Emfuleni, eMalahleni and uMhlathuze), while food production contributes more than one third of manufacturing GVA output in Polokwane and the City of Matlosana. In short, the six secondary cities are (1) more dependent on mining, (2) responsible for large-scale energy generation and (3) dominated by one manufacturing subsector.

Even those secondary cities that are less dependent on mining and energy generation face the risks of a narrow economic base. Although George and Polokwane have more diverse economies than the other four case study cities, their recent growth relies on high-risk economic sectors. Over the past 20 years, growth in Polokwane has centred largely on its status as the provincial capital and its role as a trading mecca, especially for Zimbabweans. The dependence on administrative jobs linked to being a provincial capital holds risks for the city's future economic diversification and ability to find new pathways. George has historically been a rural service centre, but tourism and the retirement-related sector are becoming increasingly important. Tourism, especially long-distance tourism, and second homes are heavily dependent on international economic trends, and the retirement sector is largely based on the decreasing ability of the affluent (in this case white) population to afford retirement.

The risks associated with the decline of mining are widely discussed in the literature. However, less prominent is the notion that mining areas should plan for the eventuality of mine downscaling and closure. It should be accepted that most mining areas are locked into a mining-dependent existence, in terms of both their growth and their inevitable decline. Table 9.3 compares the economic growth and decline of secondary cities with that of the metros.

Table 9.3 Annual economic growth and decline in the metropolitan municipalities and the six secondary cities (1996–2011)

Economic sector	Metros			Secondary cities		
	1996–2001 (%)	2001–2011 (%)	1996–2011 (%)	1996–2001 (%)	2001–2011 (%)	1996–2011 (%)
Agriculture	0.5	1.8	1.3	1.2	2.9	2.3
Mining	(1.2)	2.1	1.0	(1.7)	(4.3)	(3.4)
Manufacturing	3.5	2.4	2.7	(0.9)	2.3	1.3
Utilities	(0.3)	2.2	1.3	(1.0)	2.2	1.1
Construction	2.1	8.2	6.1	(1.6)	7.1	4.1
Trade	4.7	3.8	4.1	2.5	3.6	3.3
Transport	7.2	4.8	5.6	6.6	4.9	5.4
Financial services	6.0	5.5	5.7	2.6	5.0	4.2
Public services	0.0	3.3	2.2	1.8	3.0	2.6
Total	3.5	4.0	3.9	0.7	2.3	1.8

Source: SACN (2014).

The overall economic growth rate of the metros (3.9 per cent per annum between 1996 and 2011) is more than double that of the six case study cities (1.8 per cent per annum between 1996 and 2011). Growth rates in the metros are consistently higher than in the secondary cities for all sectors except agriculture and public services. For example, between 1996 and 2011 public services grew by 2.6 per cent per annum in the secondary cities compared to 2.2 per cent in the metros. In general, the broader economic basis of the metros makes them less dependent on decline in specific sectors.

LED strategies and spatial planning

All six cities suffer from rather mediocre strategic planning that seldom considers international competitiveness and its implications. Many of them are struggling to get even the *basic* governance and management requirements right, as evidenced by the rapid turnover of municipal and finance managers and the severe governance problems, such as fierce infighting in city councils, lack of council audit committees, and inability to obtain clean local government audits. The worst is probably eMalahleni, which was under administration in terms of Section 139 of the Constitution at the time of the study. In these circumstances, the cities struggle to carry out basic functions effectively and find it almost impossible to implement the more strategic LED functions.

The overemphasis on five-year IDPs means that not much long-term planning is being done. Unlike many of the metros, none of the six case study cities has developed strategies looking 20 to 30 years into the future. This short-term perspective is even more problematic when there is a regime change in local government, even if the change is within the same ruling party. New leaders often call for new five-year programmes and plans, with little concern for continuity in meeting or building upon prior goals, and little focus on maintenance or sustainability. The IDPs are also narrowly focused on service delivery and may even promote micro-development projects in specific ward localities (as is the case in eMalahleni and Emfuleni). Such an approach is not without merit but can mean that the big picture gets lost.

The problem with weak strategic planning is that the plans either ignore the basic economic trends or show a limited understanding of the importance of main industries. Some cities have ambitious plans that would be very difficult or impossible to achieve, such as locating airports and logistic hubs in Emfuleni and the City of Matlosana or positioning George as a knowledge-based city. Sometimes the obvious development route is ignored, such as the retirement industry in George or international competitiveness in Emfuleni, neither of which is mentioned in the city's IDP. Another example is uMhlathuze's failure to include the Richards Bay port in its IDP, which perhaps indicates that the port is poorly integrated or controlled independently by Transnet (i.e. without any relation to the city).

According to recent European research, secondary cities that make deliberate attempts to build international networks have the best chance of finding new growth paths (Rodríguez-Pose and Dahl Fitjar, 2013). However, South African secondary cities with international connections may require intensive institutional and strategic support to minimise their vulnerability to global economic shocks and to help them recognise and develop international links.

Secondary cities, because of their economic vulnerability, narrow economic base and smaller economic size, are more likely than the metros to be plagued by bad relations between local government and business. Ongoing racial divisions and lack of coordinated planning between municipalities and the private sector are hampering the future growth of these cities. Polokwane and George have the best municipal–business relationships of the six case studies. In Polokwane, top municipal officials have been assigned to help the 100 biggest businesses deal with those businesses' potential problems and concerns. In the other four cities, municipal–business relationships can be described as ad hoc at best, with very little structured engagement taking place. In the two cities in the mining areas (City of Matlosana and eMalahleni), the mining companies' social and labour plans (SLP) and the municipalities' IDPs are not aligned with each other, which may be due largely to the racial divide. Whatever the reason, the lack of a coordinated approach will hurt these cities in the long run.

The six case studies reveal high levels of path dependency in their LED planning; in other words, they are locked into their historical development paths. This is partly due to their smallish size and the old technologies used in their industries, neither of which are helpful factors in changing the existing pathways. The international literature suggests that it is very difficult to change a city's historical pathway, even with concerted effort at local level.

We used the five basic principles set out in the National Development Plan on spatial integration to assess the six case studies: spatial justice, spatial sustainability, spatial resilience, spatial quality and spatial efficiency. Overall, the spatial planning outcomes for these cities were disappointing, with one or two exceptions. All six still display apartheid segregation patterns. In Polokwane and uMhlathuze, the previous regime had forced the black townships behind 'homeland' boundaries (R293 towns), a process commonly known as 'displaced urbanisation' or 'hidden urbanities' (Bernstein, 1991). Spatial planning has in general not led to improved spatial justice in these cities, despite considerable residential desegregation in parts of some of them. In the City of Matlosana, more than 50 per cent of the previously white suburbs, in particular Orkney and Stilfontein, are now occupied by black residents. In Emfuleni, Vanderbijlpark is now 59 per cent black and Vereeniging 48 per cent black, according to the 2011 census data. Polokwane is considered to be one of South Africa's fastest desegregating cities. To a lesser degree, uMhlathuze and eMalahleni also show signs of desegregation. Among the factors contributing to desegregation are lower house prices, particularly in areas with mine downscaling or shrinking industries (Orkney and Stilfontein in the City of Matlosana and Vanderbijlpark in Emfuleni), the growth of the black middle class (Polokwane), and the mining companies' shift from single-sex hostels to family housing (eMalahleni).

Environmental sustainability is a major concern for all six cities. Acid mine water is a serious threat to river ecologies and has serious implications for farming in mining areas. The presence of acid mine water in the Vaal river (despite attempts to neutralise it) and the Olifants river makes it difficult to ensure the long-term spatial resilience of these two ecosystems. Heavy industry in eMalahleni, Emfuleni and uMhlathuze causes air pollution not only in these cities themselves but also in nearby settlements. However, there have been some success stories, such as the Mondi factory in uMhlathuze, which has decreased its water consumption per unit of production by 75 per cent over the past 20 years.

There is only limited and scattered evidence of good spatial planning aimed at achieving spatial efficiency or resilience in any of the secondary cities. UMhlathuze and Polokwane both experience spatial conflict between urban and communal land. These municipalities are legally unable to enforce land tax on communal land, and the Polokwane Municipality delivers water to communal areas without being able to recover its costs. Making the problem worse, the current development moratorium in Polokwane because of water restrictions might result in new developments on communal land that disregard the water shortage. Indeed, anecdotal evidence suggests that such developments are already taking place.

Strategic planning and the knowledge economy

Regional and urban development, particularly as regards innovation and communication technology, is increasingly being influenced by the knowledge economy. Globally, specialised activities such as innovation and experimentation are typically located in metro or secondary urban areas where highly skilled labour, good communications networks and high-quality living environments are available. In South Africa the current spread of innovation and experimentation happens primarily in the metros and in some secondary city or town areas that have universities and research institutions (Adendorff and Donaldson, 2012). Although some of South Africa's secondary cities have managed to adapt to new technologies (e.g. Metsimaholo and Stellenbosch), the six cities in this book are all dependent on older technologies and (to some degree) on old economies. Their industries are based on either extractive technologies (as opposed to beneficiation) or on primary metal production of steel and aluminium (as opposed to product development). This is partly because of the cities' smaller economies and existing economic structures. Unfortunately, cities that rely on extractive and primary metal production industries are likely to battle to find alternative development pathways. To some degree, these cities are in a catch-22 situation: their major industries do not find new pathways because of their old technology and not very creative human capital, and because they do not find new pathways they cannot afford new technology and their human capital does not improve.

Dependence on mining and primary production brings many risks. Areas linked to extractive industries face rapid decline once the minerals are depleted or those remaining are too deep to be mined profitably, and primary metal production industries face competition from other technologies such as plastics for packaging. Steel and aluminium production industries rely on simple and mostly old technologies, which are energy-intensive and affected by the dramatic increase in energy prices over the past five years. The factories in Emfuleni, dependent on old technologies involving energy intensive blast furnaces, may be contrasted with the more cost-effective new technologies that have been introduced in Saldanha.

Despite having economies that are fundamentally different from the other four case study cities, Polokwane and George also depend largely on old technologies (with the exception of the tourism industry in George). Polokwane is largely reliant on government services and trade, which are unlikely to produce the human capital needed to create new economies, and a large proportion of the economy of George is geared to the retirement industry.

Environmental confrontations

The ecological footprints of cities usually extend beyond their immediate boundaries, and so secondary cities need to deal with both short-term geographically close and long-term far-ranging environmental concerns. Factors contributing to the cities' environmental problems include old technology, heavy dependence on energy, the dominance of the mining sector and outdated infrastructure.

In some cases, environmental limitations can affect development. For George, for example, biodiversity is a competitive advantage but at the same time a potential hindrance to long-term development and growth in industries not related to conservation. Similar limitations are faced by uMhlathuze because of the protected wetlands. If current environmental legislation had been in place during the initial development of uMhlathuze and its Richards Bay port in the 1970s, which involved draining part of the wetlands, the city probably would not have developed at all.

Because South Africa is a water-scarce country, water is an vital environmental issue. Polokwane has placed a moratorium on new development because of water shortage. EMalahleni's municipality is struggling to maintain an adequate water supply. George's water supply came under pressure following the severe drought of 2009–2010, and the water-sensitive urban design strategies that were introduced had only limited success (Lottering et al., 2015). Emfuleni, dependent on the limited resources of the Vaal River and the Lesotho Highlands Water Scheme, is facing possible water shortages, like the rest of Gauteng. The exception is the City of Matlosana, where the decline in mining has reduced the demand for water. Yet this city also has to deal with the long-term effect of mining on its water supply, because acid mine water could affect agricultural production and pollute nearby rivers. This is also a serious concern for eMalahleni and Emfuleni. In eMalahleni, the acid mine water is expected to damage the ecology of the Olifants river in the near future. In Emfuleni, inadequate infrastructure maintenance by the municipality led to sewage spills that polluted the Vaal river. Community-based organisations took the matter to court. The court ordered the municipality to clear the Vaal river of dead fish. A general warning by the municipality not to use the river then had negative repercussions for the area's tourism.

Another serious environmental concern for the cities of Emfuleni, eMalahleni and uMhlathuze is air pollution caused by heavy industry and coal combustion. Although industry seems to be mostly compliant with environmental regulations, international pressure is likely to result in higher air-quality standards in the future. Innovations in non-renewable energies (at present lacking) will in all likelihood become a policy feature in the near future.

Environmental legislation has certainly had positive effects, but its extremely narrow view of environmental concerns has drawbacks. For example, in considering possible upgrades to the Ermelo (Mpumalanga)–Richards Bay (uMhlathuze) and Johannesburg–Durban railway lines, the environmental debate has failed to take into account the energy efficiency of the two lines. The former is shorter and less energy dependent (because of its more gentle gradient), which gives Richards Bay a clear advantage over Durban's port – despite the fact that Transnet views Richards Bay as a coal-exporting terminal and Durban as a container terminal. Another example, from the steel industry in Emfuleni, shows how legislation can cause costly delays. In 2012 one of ArcelorMittal's steelmaking blast furnaces had mechanical problems. To continue producing, the firm needed to revert to an older, more polluting technology. This required municipal permission. Luckily, the problem had been fixed long before the municipality finally got round to making a decision.

How important are secondary cities for development in South Africa?

In the preceding sections we have discussed characteristics or trends in the six secondary cities that are echoed to various degrees in the international literature on secondary cities. We now list some reasons why secondary cities are important for development in South Africa specifically.

The first reason is *connectedness*, although in the six case study cities it is limited to one or two specific subsectors of the economy. We have noted that gold, coal and small amounts of steel are exported from the City of Matlosana, eMalahleni, uMhlathuze and Emfuleni. International connectedness in the form of tourism makes George and Polokwane important – both have hosted major international sport events, such as the Rugby World Sevens and the FIFA World Cup, respectively. These international links provide substantial jobs for South Africans.

The second reason is the contribution secondary cities in South Africa make to *the economy* – amounting to about 15 per cent to 18 per cent of the country's economic output. Of their country-wide economic capabilities, steelmaking in Emfuleni is probably the most notable in terms of meeting local industrial needs. Other mining-related capabilities, such as aluminium smelting in uMhlathuze, are also significant. A 20-year review of South Africa's spatial development divides the country into five distinct categories: inner urban core, outer urban core, semi-periphery, periphery and deep periphery (Harrison, 2013). All six case study cities fall within the first category. They are also considered to be areas with economies of scale in the National Spatial Development Perspective (NSDP), although the economic growth picture within the inner urban core is uneven. These national assessments reveal very little of the history, economic trends, structure or vulnerability of the country's cities, whereas in this book we have assumed that our six secondary cities are more vulnerable than metros. National planning decisions and spatial targeting have a direct impact on the economy of these cities. For instance, uMhlathuze's ability to diversify its economy is directly related to Transnet's decisions regarding rail upgrades and the expansion of the Richards Bay port functions. And the expansion of these functions is hampered by the lack of appropriate cranes and by the government's decision to invest instead in the Coega port in the Eastern Cape. Further long-term damage could be done to uMhlathuze's economy if the upgrade of the Gauteng–Durban railway is prioritised above the Mpumalanga–uMhlathuze line.

The third reason is the secondary cities' role in helping to spread *development opportunities*. Development in South Africa has been spatially uneven, and secondary cities are helping to reduce this unevenness, in a natural, unforced way. At a political and policy level, however, in the face of rapidly growing city regions, it appears that emphasis will be on these city regions at the expense of secondary cities and other smaller settlements (Etherington and Jones, 2011).

The fourth reason is the secondary cities' value as *regional service centres*. Our six case studies all offer public and private schools, public and private hospitals and higher order financial services. George, Polokwane and the City of Matlosana have historically been important for regional services and eMalahleni, uMhlathuze and Emfuleni have developed this role more recently as they have expanded. All six are important for the development of their surrounding rural populations. Both Polokwane and uMhlathuze provide rural populations with direct access to urban functions. Although less prominent in this regard, the other four cities are also valuable to their rural surrounds. It is unfortunate that rural development efforts in South Africa seldom consider the potential role of secondary cities in their strategies.

And the final reason is the role these cities play in *managing urbanisation*. A recent study shows it to be similar to the role of the South African metros (Marais and Cloete, 2015). The main difference is the dependence on commodities – the secondary cities are far more vulnerable to commodity price shocks and this makes long-term planning more difficult.

In sum, although our secondary cities may not be as important as the main metros they nevertheless play a vital role in national development. They are linked to international, national and regional economies and are important nodes for achieving national development goals.

What are the policy issues for secondary cities?

We have described characteristics and trends in South African secondary cities that are similar to those of their counterparts worldwide, and we have suggested some reasons why our six case study cities are particularly important to South

Africa's development. We conclude this book by listing nine policy issues that are relevant to secondary cities in South Africa, many of which are not being paid sufficient attention.

The first issue is *municipal infrastructure and maintenance*. This is a critical factor that helps or hinders secondary cities in their regional, national and international roles. EMalahleni and Emfuleni have serious infrastructure problems, and most of the six cities struggle with antiquated infrastructure, such as old water pipes that tend to leak. They all urgently need to upgrade existing and build new infrastructure, and maintain it properly. New developments should go hand-in-hand with the expansion of infrastructure, but Emfuleni's sewerage works run at 150 per cent capacity because new developments have not considered the long-term need for an expanded municipal sanitation system. Emfuleni, the City of Matlosana and eMalahleni underspend on the repair and maintenance of infrastructure (less than 3 per cent, which compares badly with the national norm of about 5 per cent and the average of 5.2 per cent for metros) (SACN, 2014). In two of the six cities, infrastructure breakdowns have forced businesses to take over municipal functions: in eMalahleni Anglo American have built their own water purification plant and now sell water to the municipality and to individual users, and in Emfuleni some of the companies keep spare parts for municipal electrical transformers, to reduce delays in the event of breakdowns. While business–municipal partnerships may be desirable, they should be carefully set up, strategic and transparent, rather than ad hoc and short-sighted, as in these two cases.

Second, consideration needs to be given to the implications of *sectoral policies* for secondary cities. Current policies are largely spatially neutral, yet many have spatial implications. For example, if a decision was made to stop exporting coal (because of its strategic importance to South Africa's energy production), or demand for coal declined (and was replaced by alternative sources of energy), the mining areas (eMalahleni and uMhlathuze) would be affected. The steel industry is another example. The South African government and ArcelorMittal are currently involved in a dispute over ArcelorMittal's pricing policies, with the government threatening to establish a new steel mill if ArcelorMittal does not change these policies. If this happens, it could have far-reaching implications for Emfuleni.

The third issue is *logistics and freight infrastructure*, on which our six secondary are heavily dependent and which are overdue for maintenance and improvement. Road infrastructure has historically been very important for George and Polokwane, and uMhlathuze's development has been largely due to rail access, particularly for the Richards Bay port. The airports at George and Polokwane have been similarly important for those cities' development. Besides the historical importance of freight and logistics infrastructure, more recent developments are affecting some of the secondary cities. The unreliability of the rail network between Gauteng and Durban has obliged ArcelorMittal to transport steel exports by road, increasing the cost of these exports and making them uncompetitive, and adding to the wear and tear on the roads. In uMhlathuze, growth will depend on both the establishment of cranes in the harbour and the expansion of the existing rail network.

Fourthly, consideration should be given to the impact and implications of the *municipal border demarcation processes*. The decision in the late 1990s to create wall-to-wall municipalities was based largely on the idea of functional links. Yet functionality has been overlooked in four of the cities, Emfuleni, eMalahleni, Polokwane and uMhlathuze. The area historically known as the Vaal Triangle today includes Emfuleni in Gauteng and Metsimaholo in the Free State. Here two municipalities essentially have one interconnected economy but the provincial boundaries hamper the area's functionality. EMalahleni (formerly Witbank) and Steve Tshwete (formerly Middelburg) are similarly hampered: they are separate municipalities despite being only 30 km apart and having functional links. And uMhlathuze's fringe informal settlements fall within a different municipality despite being functionally connected to uMhlathuze.

The fifth issue is the *interface between urban and rural areas*. This needs to be considered and planned for as it is a problem for Polokwane and uMhlathuze, where more than half the population live in the rural areas. (This may be compared to the proportion from some metros, such as 17.5 per cent rural population in eThekwini and 5 per cent in Tshwane.) In Polokwane, 60 per cent of the population live in the rural areas, but many of these people are functionally linked to the urban core, and anecdotal evidence suggests that the moratorium on land development in Polokwane (because of water shortage) has pushed development onto rural land. The links with urban uMhlathuze are less clear for the just over 50 per cent rural population. However, the inability of uMhlathuze municipality to understand the importance of the Richards Bay port may also be related to the municipal governance structure's strong rural bias, which is certainly not the case in the metros.

Sixthly, secondary cities require specific *institutional support* to provide adequate strategic planning to deal with their vulnerabilities. Many secondary cities have a narrow economic base. They rely on one or two economic sectors and have only minor international links, also mainly within one or two sectors. This makes them vulnerable to international market trends and to national policies, programmes and decisions regarding trade policy and infrastructure investment. New policy proposals should therefore be evaluated for their possible effect on secondary cities. Secondary cities also have a more direct link with the natural environment than metros, yet environmental factors may limit their future growth. As environmental legislation may have a strong effect on secondary cities, they may require more direct support from the national Department of Environmental Affairs. This support should consider not just the short-term compliance issues; it should take an integrated approach to helping the cities overcome the long-term threats to their development. The ecological consequences of mining and heavy industry will be felt for years to come and secondary cities may lack the capacity to respond appropriately on their own. Many of the six case study cities have relatively poor strategic planning. They fail to recognise opportunities and to anticipate issues of international competitiveness and vulnerability.

The municipal boundary demarcation anomalies described above add to the problem. Having a large rural population, as in the case of Polokwane and uMhlathuze, may make it difficult for a secondary city to position itself within the global context. This can already be seen in uMhlathuze, which struggles to balance local needs with the need to think about the future of the city in relation to the port and international links. Secondary cities should create appropriate partnerships with business and develop strategic plans that adequately address the risks and opportunities. The five-year timeframe for strategic planning may be inadequate – longer-term planning frameworks should be added. These frameworks should consider city vulnerabilities associated with increasing dependence on international markets and a narrow economic base, and should encourage appropriate partnerships for economic development. Stakeholders at a national level, such as the Department of Cooperative Governance and Traditional Affairs and the National Treasury, should differentiate their support according to the vulnerabilities and opportunities associated with these cities.

The very important seventh issue is *governance and financial management.* Although the quality varied across the six case studies (George had good financial management while eMalahleni was under administration), governance and financial management were generally found to be weak and urgently in need of improvement. The inability of municipal institutions to get the fundamentals right could have a disproportionately larger negative impact on secondary cities than on larger cities with a more diverse economic structure. Cities with internationally competitive economic sectors are even more dependent on good governance and sound municipal management.

The eighth issue is *new trends.* Despite facing risks and vulnerabilities, the case study cities also exhibit promising new trends that could help them grow and increase their importance for national development. One of these trends is the way they are providing social and economic services and infrastructure to impoverished regions – rural development policies should take this into account. The secondary cities could play an important role in poverty reduction strategies, given that their percentage of poverty is higher than that of the metros. For example, the extended public works programmes (Chapter 11 of the National Development Plan) are currently run by metros but could be more effective if secondary cities had a more direct relationship with the Department of Public Works. Another promising trend is that some of these cities are far more racially integrated than most metros. Although a new non-racial middle class has yet to emerge in full, secondary cities might help lay the foundation for a new socially integrated South Africa.

The final policy issue is the *pressure to declare more metros in South Africa.* With the possible exception of Emfuleni (which was declared a metro at the start of the research that led to this book), the development trajectories of the case study cities do not suggest that they should become metros – rather the reverse. Most are resource-dependent centres at the mercy of boom-bust cycles and resource availability. Population and economic growth projections for these cities generally do not suggest rapid increases. Depending as they do on single economic sectors, their lack of economic diversity makes them unsuited to becoming metros.

References

Adendorff, A. and Donaldson, R., 2012. Knowledge-based service industry in a South African university town: the case of Stellenbosch, *Development Southern Africa*, 29(3), pp. 418–433.

Bernstein, A., 1991. Challenge of the cities. In: M. Swilling, R. Humphries and K. Shubane, eds. *Apartheid City in Transition*. Cape Town: Oxford University Press, pp. 322–333.

Donaldson, R. and Marais, L. (eds.), 2012. *Small Town Geographies in Africa. Experiences from South Africa and Elsewhere*. Nova Science Publishers: New York.

Etherington, D. and Jones, M., 2011. City-regions: new geographies of uneven development and inequality. In: M. Neuman and A. Hull, eds. *The Futures of the City Region*. London: Routledge, pp. 57–76.

Harrison P. 2013. Twenty-year review of South Africa's spatial development. Unpublished report, University of the Witwatersrand.

Lottering, N., Du Plessis, D. and Donaldson, R., 2015. Coping with drought: the experience of water sensitive urban design (WSUD) in the George Municipality. *Water SA*, 41(1), pp. 1–7.

Marais and Cloete, 2015. The role of secondary cities in managing urbanisation in South Africa. Paper presented at the European Network for Researchers on Urbanisation in the South, 19–21 November 2015, Dortmund, Germany.

Rodríguez-Pose, A. and Fitjar, R., 2013. Buzz, archipelago economics and the future of intermediate and peripheral areas in a spiky world. *European Planning Studies*, 21(3), pp. 355–372.

SACN (South African Cities Network), 2014. *Outside the Core: Towards Understanding of Intermediate Cities in South Africa*. Johannesburg: SACN.

Stats SA (Statistics South Africa), 2013. Census data for 1996, 2001 and 2011, Pretoria: Statistics South Africa.

Van der Merwe, I., 1992. In search of an urbanization policy for SA: towards a secondary city strategy. *Geographical Research Forum*, 12, pp. 102–127.

Visser, G., 2013. Looking beyond the urban poor in South Africa: the new terra incognita for urban geography? *Canadian Journal of African Studies*, 47, pp. 75–93.

Index

Africa 38–39

Afrikaner nationalism 17, 85–86, 88

agglomeration 30, 40, 101, 163

agriculture 101, 163, 168; eMalahleni 68, 69; Emfuleni 87, 98; George 106, 110, 112, 113, 118, 160; Matlosana 54, 59, 160; Polokwane 129, 164; uMhlathuze 143

air pollution: eMalahleni 10, 64, 70, 71, 75, 171, 173; Emfuleni 96, 97, 98, 171, 173; uMhlathuze 146–147, 149, 171, 173

air transport 32, 92, 164; George 106, 109, 112, 175; Polokwane 129, 130, 175

Algeria 39

aluminium 144–145, 147, 150, 152, 154, 166, 171–172, 173

AngloGold Ashanti 58

apartheid 6–7; eMalahleni 65, 70, 74; Emfuleni 88; George 103, 105, 107; Matlosana 53; Polokwane 126–127; steel industry 86; uMhlathuze 143, 144

Arboretum 141

ArcelorMittal 16, 85, 88, 91, 93, 95–98, 166, 175

Bashibisi 141

Bell, D. 27

Bell Industries 151

BHP Billiton 68, 70, 145, 147, 150, 154, 156

biodiversity 12, 17, 113–114, 119, 164, 172

Bloemfontein 7, 8, 160

Bolay, J. 27, 31, 32–33, 35, 39, 101

border demarcation processes 176

Borsdorf, A. 36

Botha, P. W. 16–17, 107

Botswana 166

Brazil 37

Brenner, N. 28–29

Brits (Madibeng) 6

Buffalo City 3, 5, 160; CSIR classification 6; employment 113; Google Scholar hits 8; gross value added 111

business: eMalahleni 63; Emfuleni 95; Matlosana 9, 57, 58–59; Polokwane 11, 128–129, 131–132, 134–135, 170; uMhlathuze 12, 151–152

Campbell, Malène 63–82

Canada 41

capacity building 37

Cape Town 2, 3; employment 112, 113; Garden Route region 117; Google Scholar hits 8; gross value added 110, 111; port 147; urbanisation 162

Caravaca, I. 32

Carlso, C. 41

central business districts (CBDs) 74, 116–117

Cetshwayo, King 143

Chakrabarti, P. 41

Chen, X. 27

China 39, 149

Cisco 85

Cities Alliance 28

City of Matlosana see Matlosana

climate change 11, 35, 42, 104

Cloete, Jan 83–100

clusters 29, 40, 101, 118

coal industry: electricity generation 76–77; eMalahleni 63, 64–71, 74–75, 77–78,

164, 165, 166, 167; Emfuleni 16, 88, 164; Maputo port 149; policies 175; uMhlathuze 17, 147, 152, 155–156, 160, 164, 166
Coega 18, 147, 149, 154, 155, 174
colonisation 30, 34, 104–105, 142–143
connectedness 173
construction 168; eMalahleni 69; Emfuleni 87; George 103, 105–106, 109, 112, 118; Matlosana 54
corruption 71–72, 77, 153
Council for Scientific and Industrial Research (CSIR) 6, 144, 154
crime 34, 77, 104

DAV Steel 85
De Boeck, F. 27, 35
debt: Emfuleni 94; Matlosana 56, 57; Polokwane 130, 133; uMhlathuze 153
decentralisation 7, 28, 36–37, 42; George 117, 119; industrial 37; institutional capacity 13, 43
desegregation 170; Emfuleni 83, 90–91; Polokwane 126, 127, 129, 136
Dewar, D. 7
Dikkop 107
disasters 9, 10–11, 104, 106–107
district municipalities 3
diversification: George 110; import substitution 75; Matlosana 53–54, 56; Polokwane 168; uMhlathuze 152, 154, 155, 156, 174
Donaldson, Ronnie 1–26, 27–47, 101–123, 159–178
Drakenstein (Paarl) 6, 7
Duranton, I. 36
Durban (eThekwini) 2, 143, 156, 166; employment 113; Gauteng-Durban railway 174; Google Scholar hits 8; gross value added 111; harbour 18, 97, 147

East London 7, 8, 160
economic development 6–7, 27, 42, 169–171, 177; eMalahleni 66–67; Emfuleni 92; George 115–116, 118; National Spatial Development Perspective 5; *see also* integrated development plans; local economic development

economic growth 1, 32, 101, 168–169, 174, 177; China 39, 149; eMalahleni 63, 67, 70, 73, 77, 78; Emfuleni 87, 89; export-oriented 27; George 108, 109–111, 116; historical and functional reasons for 30; lack of data 35; Matlosana 56; Polokwane 126, 129, 137, 168; primary cities 38; uMhlathuze 150; urbanisation 34
economic trade corridors 29, 101
economy 167–169; eMalahleni 68–70, 74, 75, 77; Emfuleni 87, 89; George 109–113, 118; Matlosana 53–54; Polokwane 128–129; uMhlathuze 146–151
education: eMalahleni 70, 74; Emfuleni 83; George 104, 112, 114; Matlosana 9, 54; Polokwane 128; privatised 162; *see also* universities
Egypt 39
Ekurhuleni 3; CSIR classification 6; employment 113; Google Scholar hits 8; gross value added 111; steel industry 89
electricity 159–160, 165; eMalahleni 63, 64–65, 76–77; Emfuleni 89, 92, 93, 94, 95, 98; Polokwane 133; uMhlathuze 145, 150, 153
elites 38
Ellisras (Lephalale) 6
eMalahleni (Witbank) 2, 7, 10, 15–16, 63–82; border demarcation processes 176; connectedness 173; CSIR classification 6; demographic and population change 67–68; economy and employment 68–70, 113; future challenges 74–75; gross value added 111, 167; historical development 64–67; infrastructure problems 175; innovation and skills 74; international connections 166; key attributes 13; location attributes 164; manufacturing 167–168; mono-functionality 160; multinational corporations 166; municipal governance 71–72, 165, 169; National Treasury classification 6; natural resources and the environment 70–71, 171, 172–173; regional services 174; size indicators 161; social concerns 70; spatial planning 72–74; universities 9

Emfuleni 2, 7, 10, 15, 16, 83–100;
border demarcation processes 176;
connectedness 173; CSIR classification
6; employment 113; environmental
threats 96–97, 171, 172–173; finances
93–95; Google Scholar hits 8, 9;
gross value added 111, 167; historical
development 85–88; infrastructure
problems 165, 175; integrated
development plan 91–92; internal trends
and pressures 88–91; key attributes 13;
location attributes 164; manufacturing
167–168; metro status 3, 177; mono-
functionality 160; multinational
corporations 166; municipal governance
165; national planning 97; National
Treasury classification 6; old
technologies 99, 172; planning 169, 170;
regional services 174; size indicators
160, 161; universities 9; utilities 92–93
Empangeni 17, 141, 146, 160; colonisation
143; demographic and population
changes 145; regional services 157; *see
also* uMhlathuze
employment: eMalahleni 10, 65, 68–69,
73, 74, 76; Emfuleni 89, 99; George
110, 112–113; Matlosana 52, 53, 54;
mining 50; Polokwane 128, 136
energy: eMalahleni 63, 64–65, 68, 69,
74–75, 76–77, 164; Emfuleni 98, 164;
see also coal industry; electricity
entrepreneurship 103
environmental issues 13, 41–42, 43, 164,
170–171, 172–173; climate change 35;
eMalahleni 10, 16, 64, 67, 68, 70–71,
73, 75, 77, 78; Emfuleni 83, 93, 96–97,
98; George 11, 17, 104, 113–114, 119,
172; Matlosana 59, 60; policy 176;
uMhlathuze 11–12, 146–147, 148, 149,
154–155, 172
Ermelo 7
eSikhawini 141, 144, 146
Eskom 65, 66, 68, 77, 93, 133, 150
eThekwini (Durban) 2, 3, 143, 156, 166;
employment 113; Gauteng-Durban
railway 174; Google Scholar hits 8;
gross value added 111; harbour 18, 97,
147
Europe 41

Evraz Highveld Steel and Vanadium 76,
85
exports 27, 30, 67, 75, 166, 173

Fahmi, F. 36
Felixton 141, 143, 145, 151
Ferro Metals 76
finance 162, 165, 168, 177; eMalahleni 67,
68, 69; Emfuleni 87, 89, 93–95; George
109, 112, 114, 115, 118; Matlosana 53,
54, 57; Polokwane 128, 129, 130, 131,
134
Fitjar, R. 40, 118
flooding 104, 107, 118
foreign investment 68
France 41
Fraser, Simon 51
functions of secondary cities 3, 13, 29,
31–35, 43, 101, 160–162

gated developments 117, 119
George 2, 7, 10–11, 15, 16–17, 101–123;
connectedness 173; CSIR classification
6; demographic and social conditions
108–109; disasters 106–107; distant
markets 106; economic structure and
growth 109–111; Google Scholar hits
8; historical development 104–105;
holidaying and retirement 105–106,
168; international connections 166; key
attributes 13; leadership and politics
107; location attributes 164; mono-
functionality 160; municipal governance
114–115, 165; National Treasury
classification 6; natural resources and
the environment 113–114, 172; old
technologies 172; planning 115–117,
169; regional services 114, 174; size
indicators 161; transport infrastructure
175; universities 9
Gini coefficient 70, 89–90
globalisation 2, 27, 39–40, 101, 142, 154
gold mining 49, 50, 51–52, 59–60, 65,
164, 167
Google Scholar 8
Govan Mbeki (Secunda) 6, 7
governance 165, 169, 177; eMalahleni 64,
67, 71–72, 77; Emfuleni 98; George 11,
104, 114–115; Matlosana 9; Polokwane

11, 131–132; uMhlathuze 153; *see also* local government; planning
Grahamstown 7
Grobler, Wynand 83–100
gross value added (GVA) 12, 14, 161, 168; eMalahleni 76, 77, 167; George 110–111, 112; Richards Bay 146
growth 30, 101, 169–170; eMalahleni 64; George 107, 108, 118, 119; Polokwane 126, 127–128; *see also* economic growth
growth points 7, 38, 107
growth poles 29, 37

Hardoy, J. 30, 36, 37, 38
health 9, 54, 58, 71, 104, 162
higher education 41, 103–104; *see also* universities
Hohmann, R. 29–30, 35, 101
'homeland' development 6–7
hospitality: eMalahleni 68, 69; George 105, 112, 116; *see also* tourism
housing: eMalahleni 64, 65, 67, 70, 74, 75; Emfuleni 90–91; George 109, 115, 117, 119; Polokwane 136–137
Human Development Index (HDI): eMalahleni 70; Emfuleni 89; Matlosana 55

import substitution 75
Indonesia 31
inequality: eMalahleni 70; Emfuleni 89–90; Matlosana 55
informal settlements: eMalahleni 16, 67, 70, 71, 74; Emfuleni 90; George 109, 115; uMhlathuze 146, 176; urbanisation 34
infrastructure 159, 175; eMalahleni 66, 75, 77, 175; Emfuleni 83, 92, 93, 94–95, 98, 175; George 108, 114; Matlosana 60, 175; National Spatial Development Perspective 5; Polokwane 130, 131, 132–134, 136–137; transport 164, 175; uMhlathuze 141, 143, 153; underspending on 165
innovation 40, 74, 118, 171
institutional capacity 13, 43, 163–165
institutional support 176
integrated development plans (IDPs) 5, 169; eMalahleni 73, 170; Emfuleni 83,

91–92, 95; George 108, 115; Matlosana 55, 57, 58, 60, 170; Polokwane 131, 132, 135; uMhlathuze 152–153
internationalisation 16, 88, 89, 165–166
investment: attracting 41, 103; eMalahleni 75; foreign 68; globalisation 39, 101; industrial decentralisation 37; National Spatial Development Perspective 5; Polokwane 131, 137; South Korea 36; uMhlathuze 143, 150, 156–157
iron industry 83, 84, 88
Iscor 16, 84, 85–88, 90–91
Israel 37

Jayne, M. 27
Jegou, L. 41
Johannesburg 2, 3, 7, 83; CSIR classification 6; employment 113; Google Scholar hits 8; gross value added 110, 111; steel industry 89
Joubert, Petrus 126

Kanna, A. 27
Khoikhoi 104, 106–107
Kimberley (Sol Plaatjie) 6, 7, 111, 113, 129
King Williamstown 7
Klerksdorp *see* Matlosana
knowledge economy 33, 40–41, 42, 171–172; George 103–104, 118; strategy development 13, 43
Kroonstad 7
Kruger, Paul 51
Krugersdorp (Mogale City) 6, 111, 113
Kumba Iron Ore 84, 88

labour *see* employment
Ladysmith 7
land-use management 72
leadership: George 107, 120; traditional 135–136
lead-secondary cities 29
Lebowa 126–127
legislation 3–5; eMalahleni 65; environmental 59, 96, 173, 176; Mineral and Petroleum Resources Development Act 50; *see also* policy
Lenka, Molefi 49–62, 83–100
Lephalae (Ellisras) 6

Lesotho 65
Levy, R. 41
Linn, J. 37
LNV Holdings 88
local economic development (LED) 13, 43, 169–171; Emfuleni 10, 92, 95; George 103, 109, 114, 115–116, 118; Matlosana 55–59; Polokwane 11, 132; social and labour plans 50–51; uMhlathuze 12, 151; *see also* economic development
local government 36–37, 101; eMalahleni 75, 77; Emfuleni 95; institutional capacity 163–165; Polokwane 134–135; *see also* governance
local municipalities 3
location 3, 13, 29, 35–36, 43, 66, 163
logistics infrastructure 175

Madibeng (Brits) 6
Mafikeng 6
Malema, Julius 131
Mangaung 3, 5, 160; CSIR classification 6; economic growth 129; employment 113; Google Scholar hits 8; gross value added 111
Mankweng 126–127, 128, 130, 132, 133, 136
manufacturing 85, 167–168; eMalahleni 68, 69, 78; Emfuleni 87, 89, 95; George 118; global 2, 28; Matlosana 54; Polokwane 127, 129; uMhlathuze 142; *see also* steel industry
Maputo Development Corridor 66–67, 68, 78
Maputo port 18, 67, 148–149
Marais, Lochner 1–26, 27–47, 83–100, 159–178
markets 33, 39, 42, 101, 106, 118
Marks, Sammy 86
Matjhabeng (Welkom) 6, 7, 83
Matlosana (Klerksdorp) 2, 7, 9, 15, 49–62; connectedness 173; CSIR classification 6; demographic and economic trends 53–54; employment 113; environmental issues 172; external pressures 59; Google Scholar hits 8; gross value added 111, 167, 168; historical development 51–53; infrastructure problems 165, 175; international connections 166; key

attributes 13; location attributes 164; mono-functionality 160; multinational corporations 166; municipal governance 165; National Treasury classification 6; planning 55–59, 169, 170; poverty and development 54–55; regional services 174; size indicators 161
Mbeki, Thabo 90
Mbombela (Nelspruit) 6, 7, 111, 113, 129
metropolisation 14
metropolitan municipalities 3, 5
Middelburg (Steve Tshwete) 6, 7, 72, 78n2, 176
middle class: George 102; Polokwane 17, 126, 129, 136–137, 170; social integration 177
migrants 31, 88; eMalahleni 10, 65, 68; George 105, 108; Polokwane 130, 136–137
migration: eMalahleni 67–68; Emfuleni 160; George 105, 108; Matlosana 60; Polokwane 127, 128; urbanisation 33
Mineral and Petroleum Resources Development Act (2002) 50
mining 14–15, 31–32, 101, 163, 168, 173; dependence on 171; ecological consequences of 42, 176; eMalahleni 15–16, 63–65, 67–71, 74–78, 160, 165, 167, 170; Emfuleni 16, 87; exports 166; Matlosana 15, 49–60, 160, 165, 170; uMhlathuze 142, 151, 155–156; *see also* coal industry; gold mining
Mmabatho 7
Mogale City (Krugersdorp) 6, 111, 113
Mohan, R. 37
Molefe, Brian 156
Mondi 151, 171
mono-functionality 160
Montagu, John 107
Mozambique 10, 64, 65, 66, 128
Mphambukeli, Thulisile 63–82
Msunduzi (Pietermaritzburg) 6, 7, 111, 113
Mtata 7
multi-functionality 31, 101
multinational corporations 16, 68, 151, 166
municipal legislation 3–5
municipalities 3

N4 Maputo Development Corridor 66–67, 68, 78
national development 34, 38, 177
National Environmental Management Act (1998) 59
National Spatial Development Perspective (NSDP) 5, 68, 117, 173–174
National Treasury 6
natural resources 31, 64, 163; eMalahleni 70–71; George 113–114; uMhlathuze 154–155; *see also* mining; water
Nel, Etienne 1–26, 27–47, 159–178
Nel, Verna 63–82
Nelson Mandela Bay 3, 8, 111, 113, 117, 167
Nelspruit (Mbombela) 6, 7, 111, 113, 129
neoliberalism 72
networks 36, 42, 169–170
Newcastle 6, 7, 111, 113
Ntema, John 125–139

Obeng-Odoom, F. 31
Oppenheimer, Harry 66
Otiso, K. 33, 35, 36, 38
Outeniqualand *see* George

Paarl (Drakenstein) 6, 7
Pacalt, Charles 107
participatory appraisal of competitive advantage (PACA) 115–116
partnerships 177
Pietermaritzburg (Msunduzi) 6, 7, 111, 113
Pietersburg *see* Polokwane
'pipeline' approach 40
planning 169–172, 174, 177; apartheid 6–7; eMalahleni 72–74, 75; Emfuleni 97, 98; George 115–117, 119; Matlosana 9, 55–59, 60; policy failures 36; Polokwane 11, 17, 132, 137; pressures of globalisation 39, 40; regional 32; social and labour plans 51; uMhlathuze 152–153, 157, 174; *see also* integrated development plans; local economic development
policy 14, 36–39, 174–177; eMalahleni 68; experimentation 32; George 116; mining 50; uMhlathuze 156–157; urbanisation 34–35; *see also* governance; legislation

politics: Emfuleni 91; George 107, 114, 116, 118; political will 36; Polokwane 131, 137; uMhlathuze 153, 154; *see also* governance
pollution 170–171, 172–173; eMalahleni 10, 64, 70–71, 75, 171, 172–173; Emfuleni 96–97, 98, 171, 172–173; George 113; uMhlathuze 146–147, 149, 171, 173; *see also* environmental issues
Polokwane (Pietersburg) 2, 7, 11, 15, 17, 125–139; border demarcation processes 176; businesses and local government 134–135, 170; connectedness 173; CSIR classification 6; demographic trends 127–128; desegregation 83; economic trends 128–129, 168; employment 113; environmental issues 172; external pressures 130; Google Scholar hits 8, 9; gross value added 111, 168; historical development 126–127; infrastructure problems 130, 132–134; international connections 166; key attributes 13; location attributes 164; mono-functionality 160; municipal finance 134; municipal governance 131–132, 165; National Treasury classification 6; old technologies 172; planning 132, 170, 171; regional services 174; rural areas 176–177; size indicators 160, 161; spatial integration 129; traditional leaders 135–136; transport infrastructure 175; universities 9
population 3, 12, 160, 161; definition of secondary cities 29, 30; density 161; eMalahleni 16, 67–68, 73, 77; Emfuleni 16, 88–89; George 17, 102, 108, 110; Matlosana 15, 53; Polokwane 17, 126, 127–128; smaller cities 28; types of settlement 4; uMhlathuze 17, 145–146
Port Elizabeth 8, 167
ports 17–18, 146–149, 152, 154, 156
Potchefstroom (Tlokwe) 6, 7
poverty 29–30, 33, 177; eMalahleni 70; Emfuleni 89–90, 91; George 114; Matlosana 54–55; urbanisation 34
Pretoria 3, 6, 8, 83, 86
'primate cities' 33, 36, 37
Prinsloo, D. 55
privatisation 16, 87, 88, 90–91, 165

protests 90
public services 5, 68, 69, 168, 169; *see also* services

Rabinovich, A. 27, 31, 32–33, 35, 39, 101
race 170; eMalahleni 65, 170; Emfuleni 83, 95; George 105, 108, 109, 112, 118; integration 177; Matlosana 60, 170; Polokwane 17, 126; uMhlathuze 145; *see also* apartheid; desegregation
rail transport: eMalahleni 66, 67; Emfuleni 97; Europe 32; George 106; uMhlathuze 143, 144, 145, 148, 155–156, 173, 174, 175
Rani, Kholisa 141–158
real estate: eMalahleni 68, 69; George 109–110, 112
regional services 6, 160–162, 174; Emfuleni 83; George 15, 106, 114, 160; Matlosana 15, 49, 53, 56, 58, 59–60, 160; Polokwane 126, 127, 130; uMhlathuze 143, 157
research methods 15
'resource curse' thesis 31, 64; *see also* natural resources
retail: George 109, 112, 114, 117, 118; National Spatial Development Perspective 5; Polokwane 128, 130
retirement 17, 105–106, 110, 118, 119, 168
Richards Bay 7, 11–12, 17–18, 141, 160; CSIR classification 6; demographic and population changes 145; economic trends 146–150; environmental issues 154–155, 173; globalisation 142; Google Scholar hits 8; historical developments 143–144; industrial development 145; international connections 146, 151, 166; National Treasury classification 6; planning 169, 174; politics 154; port consultative committee 152; regional services 157; spatial development framework 152; transport infrastructure 67, 175; *see also* uMhlathuze
Richards Bay Industrial Development Zone (RBIDZ) 145, 149–150
road transport 164; eMalahleni 66–67; George 106, 175; Polokwane 127, 175

Roberts, B. 29–30, 35, 101
Rodríguez-Pose, A. 40, 118
Rondinelli, D. 1, 27, 31, 32, 36
rural development 1, 32–33, 176, 177
Rustenburg 6, 7, 111, 113

sanitation: Emfuleni 92–93, 96, 98; Polokwane 133–134
Sasol 86–87
Satterthwaite, D. 30, 36, 37, 38
Scaw Metals 85
Schmid, C. 28–29
Scott, Jack 51
secondary city, definition of 29–30
sectoral policies 175
Secunda (Govan Mbeki) 6, 7
services: eMalahleni 67, 69, 72, 75, 77; Emfuleni 87, 89; George 114, 115; global 2, 28; Matlosana 53, 54; National Spatial Development Perspective 5; Polokwane 129, 130, 134; secondary and tertiary 32; *see also* regional services
Seshego 7, 126–127, 128, 129, 130, 132, 133, 136
settlement hierarchy 37, 38
settlements, classification of 3, 4, 6, 14
sewage 172, 175; Emfuleni 92–93, 96, 98; Polokwane 133–134
size 3, 13, 30, 43, 159–160; definition of secondary cities 29; functional complexity 31, 101; location and 163
skills 5, 74, 137
social and labour plans (SLPs) 50–51, 58, 60, 170
social issues: eMalahleni 70; George 11, 104; uMhlathuze 12
socio-economic needs 108
sociospatial transformation 28–29, 103
Sol Plaatjie (Kimberley) 6, 7, 111, 113, 129
South African Cities Network (SACN) 5, 7, 12, 14
South Korea 36, 37
spatial development frameworks (SDFs) 73, 117, 152
spatial planning *see* planning
Steel, G. 31–32

steel industry: eMalahleni 66, 68, 74, 76, 78, 166; Emfuleni 16, 83, 86–89, 91, 93, 95–99, 160, 164, 167, 173; policies 175; South African 84–85; technologies 171–172; uMhlathuze 145, 150
Stellenbosch 6, 7
Steve Tshwete (Middelburg) 6, 7, 72, 78n2, 176
strategies 13, 36–39, 43, 169–171; George 115; Matlosana 55; Polokwane 132; *see also* planning
sub-national cities 29
sustainability 42, 170–171
Swilling, M. 28

Tata Steel 145, 147, 150, 156
taxes 37, 159–160; Emfuleni 94, 98; Matlosana 57; Polokwane 130, 134
technology 28, 41, 171–172; George 115; steel industry 99; transport 13, 32, 35, 43, 106
Tlokwe (Potchfstroom) 6, 7
Toerian, Daan 101–123
tourism 5, 101; Emfuleni 83, 89, 92, 98, 172; George 10, 16–17, 103, 105, 108, 110, 115–116, 118–119, 160, 168, 173; Matlosana 59; Polokwane 173; uMhlathuze 12
townships: eMalahleni 73; Emfuleni 88; Matlosana 52, 53, 59; Polokwane 126–127, 128, 130, 136, 170; uMhlathuze 17, 144, 146, 153, 157n1, 170
trade 33, 168; eMalahleni 68, 69; Emfuleni 87, 89; George 106, 109; Matlosana 53, 54, 58–59; Polokwane 127, 129; trade corridors 29, 101
traditional leaders 135–136
Transnet 145, 147, 148–149, 154, 155–156, 173, 174
transport 160, 163, 168; eMalahleni 69, 78; Emfuleni 87; George 10, 103, 106, 119; infrastructure 164, 175; Matlosana 53, 54; Polokwane 17, 129; technology 13, 32, 35, 43, 106; *see also* air transport; rail transport; road transport
Tshwane 8, 111, 113
Tunisia 39

uMhlathuze 2, 7, 11–12, 15, 17–18, 141–158; border demarcation processes 176; business/government relationship 151–152; connectedness 173; CSIR classification 6; demographic and population changes 145–146; economic trends 146–151; employment 113; Google Scholar hits 8; gross value added 111; historical development 142–144; infrastructure expenditure 165; international connections 166; key attributes 13; location attributes 164; manufacturing 167–168; mono-functionality 160; multinational corporations 166; municipal governance 153, 165; National Treasury classification 6; natural resources and the environment 154–155, 171, 172–173; planning 152–153, 169, 170, 171, 174; political pressures 154; regional services 174; rural areas 176–177; size indicators 161; transport infrastructure 175; *see also* Richards Bay
Umtata 7
unemployment: eMalahleni 68, 70, 77; Emfuleni 96; ex-mining areas 75; George 105, 112, 119; Matlosana 54–55, 56; Polokwane 136
United Nations Centre for Human Settlements (UNCHS) 38
United States 41
universities 9, 30, 103–104, 171; eMalahleni 74; Emfuleni 10, 83, 89, 90; George 11, 104, 109; Polokwane 129; uMhlathuze 12
Urban Development Framework 3
Urban Foundation 7
urbanisation 13, 33–35, 43, 162, 174; apartheid 6, 88; definition of secondary cities 29–30; Polokwane 126, 127; uMhlathuze 146, 157; UNCHS Report 38
utilities 54, 87, 92–93, 159–160, 168; *see also* electricity; water

Van der Merwe, Izak 7, 34, 38, 163
Van Kervel, A. G. 107
Van Rooyen, Deidre 49–62
Van Vuuren, Theo 67, 72, 73

Vanderbijlpark 8, 16, 85, 86–88, 89, 90, 170; *see also* Emfuleni
Venter, Anita 125–139
venture capital 41
Vereeniging 8, 16, 85, 86–87, 90, 170; *see also* Emfuleni
violence 154
vulnerability 167–169, 170, 176, 177

water 159–160, 170–171; eMalahleni 16, 67, 71, 75; Emfuleni 89, 92, 96, 98; George 107, 109, 113, 114; Matlosana 59, 172; Polokwane 130, 132–133, 137, 164, 171, 172; uMhlathuze 153; *see also* sanitation

Welkom (Matjhabeng) 6, 7, 83
Wessels, Johannes 141–158
White, Henry Fancourt 107
White Paper of Local Government 3
Witbank *see* eMalahleni
women 12
wood 151, 164
Wood, W. 31
Worcester 7
World Bank 33–35, 36, 37, 42, 73
Wright, Horace 86

Zimbabwe 126, 127, 128, 130, 137, 166
Zulu Kingdom 142–143

Taylor & Francis eBooks

Helping you to choose the right eBooks for your Library

Add Routledge titles to your library's digital collection today. Taylor and Francis ebooks contains over 50,000 titles in the Humanities, Social Sciences, Behavioural Sciences, Built Environment and Law.

Choose from a range of subject packages or create your own!

Benefits for you

>> Free MARC records
>> COUNTER-compliant usage statistics
>> Flexible purchase and pricing options
>> All titles DRM-free.

Benefits for your user

>> Off-site, anytime access via Athens or referring URL
>> Print or copy pages or chapters
>> Full content search
>> Bookmark, highlight and annotate text
>> Access to thousands of pages of quality research at the click of a button.

REQUEST YOUR FREE INSTITUTIONAL TRIAL TODAY

Free Trials Available
We offer free trials to qualifying academic, corporate and government customers.

eCollections – Choose from over 30 subject eCollections, including:

Archaeology	Language Learning
Architecture	Law
Asian Studies	Literature
Business & Management	Media & Communication
Classical Studies	Middle East Studies
Construction	Music
Creative & Media Arts	Philosophy
Criminology & Criminal Justice	Planning
Economics	Politics
Education	Psychology & Mental Health
Energy	Religion
Engineering	Security
English Language & Linguistics	Social Work
Environment & Sustainability	Sociology
Geography	Sport
Health Studies	Theatre & Performance
History	Tourism, Hospitality & Events

For more information, pricing enquiries or to order a free trial, please contact your local sales team:
www.tandfebooks.com/page/sales

Routledge
Taylor & Francis Group

The home of
Routledge books

www.tandfebooks.com

For Product Safety Concerns and Information please contact our EU
representative GPSR@taylorandfrancis.com
Taylor & Francis Verlag GmbH, Kaufingerstraße 24, 80331 München, Germany

* 9 7 8 0 3 6 7 8 7 4 9 6 4 *